FRYE · TONY GUZOWSKI · JOHN TEDORE · JACK DITT... · JEI

GILLIAM · KEN PLOEN · JIM GIBBO... · J

BILL RINGER · WILBURN HOLLIS · M... MCKINI

LAZAR · CHUCK LONG · MIKE HAIGHT · LARRY STATION · QUI

ERMAN · JARED DEVRIES · MATT HUGHES · MATT BOWEN · LEV

BRAD BANKS · WARREN HOLLOWAY · CHAD GREENWAY · BRI

EDDS · BRYAN BULAGA · RICKY STANZI · JERRY BURNS · GEOI

· ERWIN "ERV" PRASSE · HENRY "HANK" VOLLENWEIDER · GEOI

HILGENBERG · WARREN "BUD" LAWSON · JERRY REICHOW · FRA

TON · RAY JAUCH · CHARLIE LEE · AL MILLER · MARK MANDEI

MESKIMEN · BILL WINDAUER · DAN DICKEL · JIM JENSEN · J

RLY · CHUCK HARTLIEB · BRAD QUAST · DANAN HUGHES · MA

OODS · ANTHONY HERRON · NATE KAEDING · SEAN CONSIDI

NTZ · ED HINKEL · DREW TATE · MITCH KING · MATT KROUL ·

· JOHN STREIF · BILL BRASHIER · CHRIS DOYLE · NORM PARKI

FRYE · TONY GUZOWSKI · JOHN TEDORE · JACK DITTMER · JEI

GILLIAM · KEN PLOEN · JIM GIBBONS · RANDY DUNCAN · J

BILL RINGER · WILBURN HOLLIS · MIKE REILLY · SILAS MCKINI

LAZAR · CHUCK LONG · MIKE HAIGHT · LARRY STATION · QUI

WHAT IT MEANS TO BE A HAWKEYE

WHAT IT MEANS TO BE A HAWKEYE

KIRK FERENTZ

AND IOWA'S GREATEST PLAYERS

LYLE HAMMES, MICHAEL MAXWELL,
AND NEAL ROZENDAAL

TRIUMPH BOOKS

Library of Congress Cataloging-in-Publication Data

Rozendaal, Neal.
What it means to be a Hawkeye : Kirk Ferentz and Iowa's greatest players / Neal Rozendaal, Lyle Hammes, and Michael Maxwell.
p. cm.
ISBN 978-1-60078-564-1 (alk. paper)
1. University of Iowa—Football—History. 2. Iowa Hawkeyes (Football team)—History. 3. Football players—United States—Biography. 4. Ferentz, Kirk. I. Hammes, Lyle. II. Maxwell, Michael, 1971- III. Title.

GV958.U526R69 2011
796.332'6309777—dc23

2011017789

This book is available in quantity at special discounts for your group or organization. For further information, contact:

Triumph Books
542 South Dearborn Street
Suite 750
Chicago, Illinois 60605
(312) 939-3330
Fax (312) 663-3557
www.triumphbooks.com

Printed in U.S.A.
ISBN: 978-1-60078-564-1
Design by Nick Panos
Editorial production and layout by Prologue Publishing Services, LLC
All photos courtesy of Iowa Photo Service unless otherwise specified

To Hawkeye fans everywhere

CONTENTS

FOREWORD

What It Means to Be a Hawkeye

First of all, it was pretty much by luck that I got here in the first place. Truth be known, I really wanted to stay at Pitt for another year. I was a grad assistant there in 1980, and I had a two-year agreement with my wife that when I went there, she was going to support me for two years. Grad assistants don't make any money, so, really, the master plan for us was to stay there for the fall of '81 and then go look for a job. The main reason I wanted to come to Iowa was to get some experience at interviewing so I'd know what to do. But once I got here, I was completely overwhelmed with not only the place but also Coach [Hayden] Fry and all the people I met when I was here.

I think what separates this Iowa program from many others is the people. That's what jumped out at me when I first arrived here in 1981. I came in with very low expectations. I knew nothing about the state, the university, or the program. I really didn't expect much. I was surprised at just how beautiful this town is. Above everything else, the one thing that really jumped out at me on the very first day was the quality of people here, not only the people I met that day professionally—Coach Fry, Bill Snyder, Barry Alvarez, the guys on campus I interviewed with—but also everybody I met around town. I still hear similar comments from recruits and parents all the time.

Probably the most influential person overall in my career was my high school coach, Joe Moore. I later worked for Joe at the University of Pittsburgh in 1980. He's probably the guy who was as influential as anybody in terms of convincing Coach Fry to hire me. I learned as much about coaching football, people, and everything from Joe as anybody. He not only influenced me like that as a coach, but outside of my parents, Joe Moore invested more in me than anybody I'd been with.

I give a lot of credit to Coach Fry, too. There probably wasn't another head coach in the country in Division I at that time who would have hired me—probably most D-I-AA schools wouldn't have, either. I really was inexperienced; I did not have the résumé suitable to the job. As much as anybody, Coach Fry helped shape my thoughts about how college football should be, the approach it should take. A lot of my thoughts about what we've done here the last 12 years go right back to my experience here in the '80s. And certainly, when I was here in the '80s, I watched what was being done and tried to analyze it. That was one of the most enjoyable periods of my life. Ultimately, it just came down to the people I was associated with on a day-to-day basis.

I've been really lucky in my career. I have not worked for many people, but the people I have worked with have been top-shelf individuals. When I was in the NFL, I worked with Bill Belichick my first three years and with Ted Marchibroda the second three years. They were very different but both excellent people and excellent football coaches. I've always worked for and with good people. The assistant coaches I've worked with have been great as well, so I've been really lucky.

I guess if I hadn't gotten the offer to come back to Iowa as the head coach in 1999, I'd probably still be coaching in the National Football League. I enjoyed my job there, and at that time, it was never a goal of mine to go back to college coaching. It wasn't necessarily a goal of mine to be a head coach, either. This is probably the only college job I would have been interested in, just because my wife and I had a great comfort level with Iowa City in our nine years here. I didn't grow up here, but it just felt like home to us.

I know Bob Stoops was also a candidate for the job in 1999, but my dad once made the observation that it probably worked out the best for both parties, and I would agree. Bob's done a wonderful job at Oklahoma. While you almost get the feeling people sometimes portray it like Bob and I were divided over this, that was never the case. Bob's always been a good friend of mine. I've had a great respect for him ever since I met him in 1981. He's a tremendous coach. He's obviously done a fantastic job there, and the nice thing is that it worked out very well for both parties.

When I came back in 1999, the major difference from 1981 was due to Coach Fry and the work he and the players had done. In 1999 there was a strong sense of tradition, and our facilities had come a long way. In 1981 there really was no recent tradition at that point, and while the facilities were in the process of being improved, they still needed attention. Also, there was no documented evidence of the ability to compete for championships when I came here in '81. Now it's been proven teams can be very successful here. Players can play at the highest level and graduate from our program. And most important, it's been proven they can be successful for life by getting an education that's going to serve them well and by being around people who are going to help serve them well for their future. Those things are very, very important.

I had three priorities when I took over in 1999. I was hoping we could put a staff together like we had in the '80s, because I enjoyed being a part of that staff so much. I wanted to put together a coaching staff of people who would be great teachers, good mentors, and just good people. The second phase was recruiting, because that's such a nonstop thing now in college football. And obviously the third thing was working with the players on our roster, trying to recruit them and guide them through the transition, because transitions are never easy.

Assistant coaches are everything, in my opinion. Looking through the staff in '81, there was nobody on that staff who had a knockout résumé, necessarily, before they came to the University of Iowa—or maybe you could say there were reasons why these guys shouldn't or couldn't have been hired by Coach Fry, yet they were. I think Coach Fry had a real gift of seeing things—unique things—in people. I always thought that was interesting, his ability to pick people who ended up working pretty well as a team. That was a tremendous staff, and we had good continuity. Seven years later, there was not one change on that staff. There were no egos or jockeying for position on the staff. Everyone's focus was on what's best for the team and carrying out the plan for that given day, that week, or that month. It was just a really good environment for everybody involved.

That was something I was hoping to re-create, and that's why I took so much time putting my staff together. It was the thing I was probably the most meticulous with. A lot of people had opinions about the pace I worked at, and there were a lot of people questioning the background of some of the people we hired. One that comes to mind was our offensive line coach, Joe Philbin, who we brought here from Harvard. He ended up doing a tremendous job with our line and went on to be the tight ends coach, line coach,

Kirk Ferentz won Big Ten Coach of the Year honors in 2002, 2004, and 2009, becoming one of only four people to ever win the award three times. *Photo courtesy of Bob Rasmus*

and now serves as offensive coordinator of the Green Bay Packers. I think the most important thing was getting the right kind of people on board. If you're doing a good job there, then you're not getting coaches who only end up being here for two years before leaving for something different. That's important, because, in my mind, continuity really makes it a better environment for our players. Everything we do should be geared toward providing a place where our players can really have an opportunity to learn and develop in all regards, not just as football players. That's why stability on a staff is so important. Fortunately, I think we've put together a great staff. We've had a couple guys come and go, but not many, and most of the guys who have left are currently head coaches in college or NFL assistants. I'm just thrilled with how it turned out.

I can give you the exact count—if you read the papers, they did a nice job of keeping score—we were actually 2–18 our first 20 games. That was obviously a trying period. Behind the scenes, one thing coaches get to do is see the players and have a pulse on their attitudes. We also get to watch them practice, and we had seen improvement that wasn't showing up on the scoreboard. So, for the most part, we felt like things were moving in the right direction. But at some point players have to experience some success or you run the risk of losing them.

More specifically, probably the only time I ever let the thought in my mind that we might not get this program turned around was the Tuesday just before the Ohio State game in 2000. We'd had a run of injuries on our offensive linemen, and on that day of practice, one of our backs ran into the back of one of our starters, and the guy went down like he got shot. Needless to say, we lost him for that game. I allowed myself to think for a little bit, *Geez, you know, maybe this isn't meant to be.* But I got up the next day and just went right back to work. That was probably the only little window where maybe I had to wonder if this just wasn't meant to be.

I'm not always big on turning points, but the 2001 Alamo Bowl was certainly a huge step in the progression of things for us. It was huge for us to get to a bowl, first of all, but it was every bit as important for us to win. I think it really gave us a lot of momentum to carry into the next year. It was a little bit like winning the Freedom Bowl in 1984. That year wasn't a signature year—we had some injuries and what have you—but that momentum we came out of the Freedom Bowl with really helped propel the next year's team to a great season. I think you could probably draw a parallel to 2001–2002. Winning a bowl game can give you a little bit of extra energy going into the next season.

If you look at my total time here, you always start with the Big Ten championship teams. I was fortunate to be around four of them—the 1981, 1985, 2002, and 2004 teams. Those were all great seasons and all great stories, and they were all different stories, too, which I think is kind of neat. There are probably some direct parallels, from my vantage point at least, between the '85 and 2002 teams, and probably some direct parallels between the '81 and 2004 teams. But other seasons were maybe equally as enjoyable. For instance, in the '82 season, we started out just terribly and ended up winning eight out of 10. The 2001 season was one of my favorites because we got the corner turned a little bit. But then, it's kind of like picking one kid over another, and I've always believed everything's important. I think a lot of things that happened in 1999 and 2000 were very important in our success that showed up in 2002. I'd have to mention the 2003 team, as well. We probably weren't as talented in 2003 as we were in 2002 or 2004, yet that 2003 team ended up being ranked in the top 10 and just found a way to have success that maybe people on the outside wouldn't typically expect or predict. And of course, the 2008 and 2009 teams have been very memorable, too.

I've been asked about the 2010 Orange Bowl because some thought it was the pinnacle of my head-coaching career. I just have a hard time separating the win in Miami from our first Big Ten win against Michigan State in 2000 or the Alamo Bowl in 2001, which was pretty special at that point. If you put it in terms of wins and games, there have been a lot of them, fortunately, both as an assistant and as a head coach the last 12 years, and there have been an awful lot of things that have been really important and gratifying.

Football is just so different from every other sport. There aren't many sports out there where you have more than 100 guys on a roster or a staff of nine assistants, so it takes great teamwork. I have to give a lot of credit for our success to the staff who I've been very fortunate to work with. Then you've got all the support staff who are so important. We've been very lucky—everybody on every level has just been committed to the welfare of the team. We've had great support administratively. We've had tremendous stability—we've had three athletics directors now since 1970 and two head football coaches since 1979. I've been fortunate that I've worked with great athletics directors and outstanding presidents, and those things are important. Most important, we've had tremendous players through the years. That doesn't mean they were only tremendous football players, but they were tremendous team members, as well.

If I were going to describe what we hope our team is, I'd say we hope they're hardworking, determined, and play like a team. In the '80s that's what Iowa football was about, and those are some of the traits we hope our kids possess today. We've recently had a lot of success with players in the NFL, and

I think those aspects are a big part of that. NFL teams want to acquire players who have those traits. Obviously, there's always a requisite ability level that has to be met, but those other characteristics are very important, too. Every NFL team wants a guy who's hardworking, who's going to be determined, and who's going to be a good team member and teammate. If there was a company coming to hire a business grad, I think it'd be looking for the same things. The guys who have excelled, in our program at least, understand those things are important.

We also try to educate our guys that, unlike getting a job in teaching or sales, the NFL's a pretty temporary profession. The average career of an NFL player is under four years, so we just try to let them know that it's kind of a luxury item. We want guys to try to achieve at the highest level, but we also let them know that they're just young people when they're done playing football. There's a whole life that's going to be waiting for them, so don't put all your eggs in that basket. You have to work like it matters, but at the end of the day, you're not going to be playing football really long. Even if you are fortunate enough to play 10 years in the NFL, that's only a fraction of your adult life.

Overall, the best part of coaching is watching players develop, grow, and feel good about themselves, both from a sports standpoint but also beyond that. When they walk out of here and you know they're going to be just fine once they leave campus, that's a good feeling. You hope when they leave college that they're on the right path to a nice adult life and that they're going to be able to achieve some things professionally and, more important, personally. You hope they're going to feel good about what they're doing and be able to raise families and just have a good grip on things. That's the best part about coaching, actually.

Having everyone in the program participating in the community is very important to me. I just think if you work with athletes on any level, that's an obligation you should have as a coach. It's so easy for a sense of entitlement to creep in, not just in athletics but anywhere where you're singled out a little bit—entertainers, politicians, whatever. Being a coach is just like being a parent, and we have to remind the young people we work with that while football is very important, certainly—it's the main reason that brings us all together—there's a lot more to life than that. What kind of citizen and community member are you going to be? We always try to engage our players and get them involved in public-service projects. There's a reason why we steer them in that direction—we want them to learn the lesson that you get a lot more by giving than taking.

When I came here in 1981, there was a real sense of community and family within this program. That's something we've certainly promoted consciously, but I think it's also just one of the byproducts of the way we do things. What impacted me was how players of all generations really had a great love for the university and a great feeling about their experience here. It didn't really matter if they were from the '70s, '60s, '50s, or '40s—it just seemed like everybody really had a strong bond to the place. Obviously, we've got a couple more generations and decades covered now, but things haven't changed. I've met more and more players from past years since I've been back. We have what's called the honorary captain program, where we invite somebody back for every home game. It's been really educational, not only for myself but for everybody involved with our program, to hear guys from as far back as the '40s right up to somewhat recent players talk about their experiences here. It's been an awful lot of fun just to get to meet a lot of people who I really hadn't known, and it's been really neat to hear their stories and their perspectives on their Iowa experiences.

I remember our last ballgame against Minnesota in my first year as head coach at Iowa. We were a 1–9 football team at that point, and we had more than 55,000 people in the stands. I remember people saying in the papers the next day that we played "only" in front of 55,000 fans, and I was thinking to myself, *How many places in America would have over 55,000 fans show up to watch a team that was 1–9?* The most prominent showing of our fan support is when we go to bowl games, and nobody travels better to bowl games than Hawkeye fans. When we travel on the road, our fans are always there supporting us. We're very encouraged by that. I think Iowa fans are much more positive in their approach than they are at a lot of places. When I came here in 1981, Iowa had had 19 straight non-winning seasons at that point, and every game that year was a sellout. I don't think that would take place anywhere else in America. I just think that's very unusual, and certainly we're very proud and very fortunate to have such great fan support.

Kinnick Stadium is a great stadium. There are more than 70,000 seats now, and there's not a bad seat in the place. Another great feature is the name on the stadium and what it stands for. The thing that jumps out at me when I think of Nile Kinnick is that he was a great player but an even more impressive person. Just listening to his Heisman Trophy acceptance speech gives you a real glimpse of the uncommon maturity level, vision, and leadership capabilities he had. After you talk to different people about Nile Kinnick—the people who actually knew him or were his teammates, and I've had a chance to visit with a few of them—you realize he's the kind of person who might have gone on to be a governor, a senator, possibly even president. That wouldn't have shocked me based on the comments I've heard.

On top of all that, our fans are very knowledgeable, enthusiastic, and vocal, and the way the stadium's structured makes it one of the loudest stadiums you can find anywhere. It's a huge edge for us. When I was working in the National Football League, if any player came from the Big Ten—he wouldn't know who I was or anything like that—I would ask him, "Where was the toughest place to play in the Big Ten?" They'd always name two or three schools, and every guy mentioned Iowa as one of the toughest. It sounds like the people right behind the visitors' bench know what to do, too!

Coming down that tunnel is great. What's even better is once the team walks out into that corner and you can actually see the stadium and the fans. I enjoy that every time. It's such an unusual experience. I remember vividly coming out of the tunnel in 1981 for my first game here as an assistant. It was unlike anything I had ever experienced. It was the opening game of the '81 season against Nebraska—it was just an absolutely amazing moment, and then the game ended up being a great upset victory. From that day on, every time I've come out of the tunnel, it's been special, it's been unique, and it doesn't get old at all. It's every bit as special now as it was 30 years ago.

Being down there on the field is also very special. My wife discovered that on Senior Day in 2005 for our son's last game. She's been to Kinnick as much as I have, but that's the first time she had been down on the field. She couldn't believe how different it was, and being down there and looking up is just really a special thing. I feel very fortunate to have had the opportunity to coach two of my sons at Iowa. It's just been great. When our boys were in junior high and high school, I missed out on a lot of chances to watch them compete on Friday nights. Without a doubt, this makes up for some of that time I did miss. It's a very special opportunity I've been afforded, and it really has been a great pleasure.

I always tell recruits—in the grand scheme of things, I don't know any recruit nearly as well as their parents and high school coaches know them—

that it would really be presumptuous for me or any other college coach to think any of us know, at the end of the day, what's best for them. In the same way, I always get a kick out of people who think they know what I am looking for or should be looking for. Really, it's pretty simple. It's just basically about the quality of life, both on a personal level and also on a professional level. The two things I've always looked at would be, first, "How's it going to be for our family?" Second, I always wanted to be somewhere where you had a realistic chance to compete for championships and also where you like and respect the people you work with and for. Fortunately, we've been able to enjoy both of those things at Iowa.

This has been a tremendous place for our family. We've lived 21 of our adult years here now. It's been great for me, my wife, and our kids. Iowa's afforded our kids an opportunity to know where home is, and that's hard to do in coaching. On the professional level, I've enjoyed it. I love college football, and this is a great college football town. It's a tremendous university that has outstanding academics and supports college football. Finally, the people I work with on a daily basis are people I have a whole lot of admiration and respect for. From our players to our coaching staff to our support staff, I'm around quality people every day, and I appreciate that.

What it means to be a Hawkeye—that's a tough one to put into words. It's just a very special thing. I think it's a unique experience, and I think everybody who's been associated with this program as a player or a coach would tell you the same thing. It's hard to describe to people who didn't grow up here, and I'm not sure people from Iowa always appreciate how different we may be than people from other places. But you visit different places as a coach, and you realize this is a pretty unique situation. The culture here, the sense of family, the sense of belonging to something that's a lot bigger than yourself—I think those are all prominent traits of this experience.

If you had told my wife and me in 1981 that we were going to live in the state of Iowa for 20 years as adults, we would have said you were crazy. But we're going on our 22nd year here right now and are thrilled about it. The University of Iowa has been very good for our family. Four of our five kids have been students at the University of Iowa, and we just feel like the University of Iowa has afforded us to have the kind of life we enjoy. I'm doing the thing I love to do, which is coach football, and we're doing it in a fabulous place, so we feel very fortunate.

—Kirk Ferentz

INTRODUCTION

When Lyle Hammes, Michael Maxwell, and I agreed to write *What It Means to Be a Hawkeye* for Triumph Books, we were understandably excited. All three of us had already written a book on the Hawkeyes—Michael wrote *The 50 Greatest Plays in Iowa Hawkeyes Football History*, while Lyle and I had coauthored *Hawkeye Greats, by the Numbers*. In those books, we told the stories of some of the greatest players in Iowa history, as we understood them.

We quickly learned that this book would be truly unique. Instead of writing about the great players in Hawkeye history, we presented the players with an opportunity to tell their own stories. While we would provide the canvas, it would be the athletes themselves painting the picture for us, and for you, of what it was like to represent the University of Iowa on the football field. This is what it means to be a Hawkeye, as told by those who can tell it best.

The accounts of these men tell the history of Iowa football from a first-person perspective. It begins in the 1930s and '40s with athletes hardened by the prospect of war. While they sacrificed to deliver victory to Iowa on the gridiron, they sacrificed far more to deliver victory to our country in World War II. They formed the foundation for the modern Hawkeye program, yet remarkably, in the end, we discover this was not even their most extraordinary achievement.

The men of the 1950s played for Iowa at a time of unparalleled success. In a five-year span, the Hawkeyes had four one-loss seasons, three Big Ten titles, and two Rose Bowl victories. It is not a stretch to claim that the Iowa program under Coach Forest Evashevski was as great as any in the nation, and the athletes featured in this book were a big reason why.

The players of the 1960s and '70s, conversely, witnessed the program at its nadir. I have a particular admiration for these men—they put just as much effort and passion into the program as the players of any other era, but they did not receive the rewards of winning seasons or bowl games. For these Hawkeyes, the stories of their college careers are inevitably bittersweet. Still, the football program would not be what it is today without the work of those men, and they can take pride in Iowa's current success, knowing they will forever have a place in Iowa tradition.

As all Hawkeye fans know, success—and lots of it—did return to Iowa with the arrival of Coach Hayden Fry. Fry's protégé, Kirk Ferentz, has built upon Fry's impressive legacy and carried it into the 21st century. The 1980s, '90s, and 2000s have been decades filled with remarkable accomplishments. Fry's and Ferentz's players provide perspective into the modern prosperity of the Hawkeye program and take us to the present day. Future generations of Hawkeyes will continue to add new chapters to the story of Iowa football, carrying forward the legacies of those mentioned here.

One of the most difficult aspects of pulling this book together was deciding which players to include. Nearly 2,000 men have earned letters for playing football at the University of Iowa, and every single one has a unique and interesting story to tell. Almost every former player we contacted was more than willing to share his experiences with us, and for that, they each have our sincere thanks. By design, however, this book can only include a small fraction of the stories that make Iowa football great.

With that in mind, we would like to dedicate this book to those Hawkeye football players whose stories do not appear here. Many former Hawkeye players are deceased, and one can only imagine what Aubrey Devine, Nile Kinnick, Calvin Jones, and Reggie Roby would have prepared for us here if given the opportunity. We would like to recognize former players like Bob Stoops and Dan McCarney, who we felt it would not be appropriate to contact at the current time but who still maintain an abiding love for the university where their college football journeys began. Finally, we want to pay tribute to the hundreds of former Hawkeye athletes who were willing to participate but could not be included, unless this book were allowed to be 10,000 pages long.

This book is the latest installment in the *What It Means* series of books that focus on a part of a particular college or professional sports club. Being just one part of such a series raises the question of what makes the Iowa Hawkeyes unique. You could always fall back on standard clichés or talk about how Iowa has won conference championships and major bowl games, spawned numerous All-America players, been led by Hall of Fame coaches, and been supported by passionate, loyal fans. But dozens of other college and professional sports franchises can make similar statements. So what makes Iowa so special?

Maybe it's the fact that our home games are played in a terrific stadium named after a Heisman Trophy winner, who was so much more than a mere football player. Maybe it's the feeling of being in the presence of 70,000 fellow Hawkeye fans who are organized enough to alternate the sections of Kinnick Stadium in black and gold. Maybe it's the sound of "In Heaven There Is No Beer" or Meredith Willson's "Iowa Fight Song" playing after a hard-fought victory. Maybe it's the sight of the I-O-W-A flags and chant, or Hayden's pink visitors' locker room, or "the swarm" coming onto the field.

Personally, I think a big part of what makes Iowa football special is the fact that, prior to the addition of our new rivals from Nebraska, the University of Iowa had always been the smallest public institution in the Big Ten and located in the smallest state in the conference. As a result, Iowa has always fought an uphill battle against larger, wealthier, and more strategically located foes. Considering this opposition, it is outstanding that the Hawkeyes have overcome those hurdles to develop into a very competitive Big Ten program. I think those challenges serve as a constant reminder to Iowa fans that success is never guaranteed or something to which a particular school is entitled, and Hawkeye fans accordingly take particular delight in our school's successes. Iowa fans cherish and savor every victory and every achievement by our program, and we remain steadfast in our support, win or lose.

Our relatively small state has forced us to band together, making the Hawkeyes an exclusive club of people who treat each other as family. All are welcome to join the Iowa family by embracing our unique traditions and proud history, and once you're a Hawkeye, you're always a Hawkeye. When you've adopted the Hawkeyes as your team, you can expect to see the Tigerhawk anywhere and everywhere you go, and you will learn that you can strike up an easy conversation with anyone you meet who is wearing the familiar black and gold. This camaraderie and sense of winning against larger odds is a big part of what binds us together as fans and an indisputable part of what it means to be a Hawkeye.

It is a peculiar combination of many factors that makes our university unique. Iowa City, the former state capital, is a City of Literature, a charming college town that defies outsiders' expectations of cornfields and nondescript flat plains. The University of Iowa, while quick to remind us that America needs farmers, has made a name for itself by training the next generation's supply of doctors, nurses, lawyers, pharmacists, and writers. In addition, no other Iowa school has the tradition of major bowl games and conference championships on college football's biggest stage that its flagship university possesses. With no teams in the four major professional sports leagues, the fan support of the Iowa Hawkeyes is unmatched within the state's borders. Make no mistake—despite the objections of the widely outnumbered fans of other in-state schools, Iowa remains the Hawkeye State, as it has always been.

Ultimately, what makes Iowa football special, unique, and the pride of the state are the stories contained here. This book features both native Iowans and players from all over the country. Their stories chronicle wins and losses, highs and lows, championships and disappointments; yet despite all the differences in the individual stories, they share one common theme. Every story describes the narrator's deep, abiding love of Iowa—its city, its state, and its preeminent university.

In closing, I think the significance of this book is captured perfectly in a quote provided by former Hawkeye halfback Jim Jensen:

> The wins and losses, game statistics, and newspaper clippings are all a matter of public record and can be found and read by everyone. Not so are the personal recollections and behind-the-scenes stories known by the players. These are the memories never before written about or publicized. These are the experiences behind the numbers on the uniforms and the realities of the young men who wore the Iowa Hawkeye gold and black. It is my hope that today's generation learns from the experiences of those who have created the Iowa Hawkeye legacy and that they can appreciate the victories and glory of wearing the black and gold more than ever before.

On behalf of my coauthors, I hope you enjoy reading what these estimable men have to say about what it means to be a Hawkeye. Go Hawks.

—Neal Rozendaal

The THIRTIES

IN MEMORIAM

ERWIN "ERV" PRASSE

OFFENSIVE END

1937–1939

Editor's note: Erwin "Erv" Prasse was the captain of the 1939 Ironmen, the most acclaimed team in school history. Although he passed away in 2005, his wife of 63 years, Norma Prasse, was gracious enough to share her memories of Erv.

• • •

UNFORTUNATELY, I DID NOT GET TO SEE ERWIN PLAY. I can watch a few CDs that I've gotten. But I was just a girl back home, I guess, and he was so busy with his three sports—they went one right into the other—he really didn't have a lot of social time. The three sports that he played were so consecutive, he'd get himself into trouble with the football coach. He played baseball, and they wanted him out for spring training. I remember him telling me he told [coach Eddie] Anderson he wasn't coming out for spring practice, and Anderson said, "You're not gonna what?" And Erv said, "No, I can't. My baseball team is doing good, and I gotta be there for 'em." So he did not get in too good with the coach on that score. Plus, he needed a few extra credits—that's why he went a few extra semesters, to finish up and get his degree.

We got married in February 1942, right after he graduated from the university. Erv was 6′2″ when we got married. He weighed about 185. If he got over 200, he didn't like that; he felt he was too heavy because he was always active. Even at 87 years old, he was still very thin. His friends would say, "How do you keep so fit?" He'd say, "I just keep movin'."

Erv actually was not Catholic when we got married. At that time, you were not allowed to be married in church if you married a non-Catholic. So he always used to tell everybody, "Oh, we got married in the latrine over at the rectory. We could hardly fit in there," because my family was very large, you know. But he always kidded about that. And then after we were married about 20 years, he said, "I may as well be what you are. I like it." So he did turn Catholic. He was a good person; he didn't need to do that, because that was never a problem for us. I think he was Lutheran, but he made his confirmation, and that was the end of it.

He signed with the St. Louis Cardinals, and he went right from college with another young man from the university to talk to Branch Rickey for a tryout. Well, the friend who went with him got sick to his stomach he got so nervous. And I guess Branch Rickey didn't care for people who couldn't keep their heads and their stomachs together. Erv said his friend never got a contract from them.

Erv was offered a bonus of $2,000, I think. He was given $1,000 and then he was also nominated to play on the College Football All-Star Team. But Branch Rickey told him that he was under contract to him now, and he couldn't do that. Rickey said if he played, he'd lose the other thousand. $1,000 was a lot of money back then, so he opted not to play. He didn't play in that All-Star Game; he wasn't allowed to. He did play with the basketball All-Stars, though.

Branch Rickey told him, "You're not a second baseman. You belong out on the field." I think because of his speed and his size, Rickey thought he would be a good outfielder. He was tall, and when they ran laps in college, he'd beat [Nile] Kinnick. And he did catch a quite a few passes from him, so he was good on his feet.

Erv played minor league baseball with the St. Louis Cardinals. He was in Triple A with the Cardinals. And he loved it; he loved baseball the best. He said, "It takes more brains to play baseball than any other sport." But he never did get to the majors. When he came back from the war, he was too old, and his arm was not perfect anymore.

Erwin Prasse was the captain of Iowa's 1939 Ironmen team and was just the fifth Hawkeye to earn nine athletic letters at the University of Iowa, lettering three times in football, basketball, and baseball.

After he came out of the service, he played one season with the Oshkosh All-Stars, the basketball team, which was in the NBL at that time. After he saw how poorly he played, that was the end of that, but he did play one season with them. Actually, he played two years of basketball before the war and one season after the war, so they counted six years of professional basketball. As a consequence, he got an NBA pension, because he played before the war and after the war, and they were nice enough to pay for that. They allowed him to get a pension for that for six years because he was gone to war for three years.

He did not really want to go to war. I was pregnant, and we had just gotten married, and he said, "I'm going, but I'm not going until they tell me I have to." We were married in February of 1942, and he left in July.

He went in as a buck private, but he soon went to officer training school once they saw his qualifications. And because he could play basketball and do all of the things that he could do, they made use of that, too. He would be the manager of the team wherever he was. There was always a colonel who liked to watch sports, so that way he got noticed a little more than maybe someone else. He put out; he was always willing to do what he had to do.

He was on a mission in a little town of Julich, up in northern Germany. They had to cross the river and find out how deep it was and how fast it was. They were pretty close to the German lines. As a matter of fact, he took a boat over one night. He climbed up the hill on the other side and heard the Germans talking. He understood German, so he got the heck out of there. He had learned German at home from his parents. When you went to school, you talked English, but up until that point, they talked German at home. Years ago, that's just the way it was when you were an immigrant. He found out he couldn't speak it as well as he thought he could, but he did understand the phrase, "What was that?" So he got out of there, but when he went back to the other side of the river—like I say, they weren't too far from the Germans—he was hit by shrapnel. He was on the other side behind a house, and the shrapnel hit his right arm. Had it not been where it was, it would have killed him, because his arm protected his heart. It hit his arm bone high above his elbow.

He was taken back to England, and he recovered and then went back to Germany again. They kept him over there managing baseball teams, anything to keep the soldiers busy, because there were so many over there. They were desperate to get all those boys home, but in the meantime, they had to be entertained while they were there. Pro sports was the best thing the officers above him could think of, and so that's what he did. He managed whatever they figured up—baseball teams, basketball teams, anything to keep these guys busy so they wouldn't get into trouble. You know, when they finally did come home, they came back by boat. They weren't flown home at all. He came back on a banana boat. He said he thought they were going to lose each other in the middle of the Atlantic Ocean.

After he came home from service, it took us about eight or nine years to save the money to buy a house, because, you know, the Army doesn't pay well. He went in in July, and I think it wasn't until November before I got the first paycheck. I was without husband and money all that time, and I never thought of complaining or doing anything. I lived with my parents. I went back to my own home until he came back from the service. At that time my father had died, so he took over helping my mom for a while until we got some money together, and then we moved out here to Naperville, Illinois. That was 53 years ago.

We had 10 kids. I'm one of 10 myself, so I wouldn't trade what I've got in my life for anything, and he said the same thing. You learn a lot from each other. We had 10 children—boy, girl, boy, girl, boy, girl, boy, girl, girl, boy. Five and five. None of my children played college sports. It's hard to compete with a prominent parent. They all tried it, but none of them were as good as he was.

He would fix everything around the house. That's why I miss him so much—when something breaks, I never had to call anybody in to fix it. He would look at it and maybe consult a few people, but if it was wood, he would fix it. He fixed a lot of antique furniture that my kids had broke, and other people would call him to see if he could put something back together, which he loved doing. He was kind of a craftsman who learned just doing it by himself for the love of it.

He donated his football suit to the University of Iowa Hall of Fame. He put it out there along with a stained-glass lamp shade that he made for Bump Elliott. Bump Elliott donated it to the Hall of Fame. Erv also donated a football from the Notre Dame–Iowa game, so that's out there, too.

He always kept in touch with the Ironmen. They had a 20-year and a 25-year reunion. They were a very great bunch of guys, nice people. They had nice wives, in most cases. The key is that there was only about 27 of them, and not all of them played as much as the others. So many of them played the whole game. And then there were some on the fringe who were very nice, and they'd come, and we'd always have a good time.

Dick Evans and Erv were very close. They were both from Illinois and the Chicago area. They knew each other in high school, and they went to college together. Dick later went into the coaching field, which Erv did not want. They used to play basketball against each other at different times. Oh, they had so many leagues. Back then, sports were tough, and it was what you did with your time.

Dick always was a very nice person. He had very blond hair, so he was kind of known as "Whitey." And when blacks became more integrated in the sports field, Erv would always yell at him if he ever saw him anywhere, "Hey, Whitey!" Dick would get so mad and say, "Don't call me that anymore! That's not proper!" So they'd laugh about that. Erv would always tease him by continuing to call him Whitey. He said, "I don't care what anybody says. You're Whitey to me."

It's not a heck of a lot of fun growing old, but I have lots of very good memories, and that's what it's all about. We did everything we wanted to do, and I think that's quite a nice thing to be able to say about your life—that you did things the way you wanted to and things worked out good.

Erwin Prasse was the captain of Iowa's 1939 Ironmen team and was named a second-team All-American that year. He caught three touchdown passes from Nile Kinnick against Indiana in 1939, which set an Iowa Stadium record that lasted for 66 years. Prasse was just the fifth Hawkeye to earn nine athletic letters at the University of Iowa, lettering three times in football, basketball, and baseball. He helped lead Iowa to two Big Ten baseball titles in 1938 and 1939 and was the baseball team's MVP in 1938. Erwin Prasse was one of 10 football players inducted into the University of Iowa's Hall of Fame in their inaugural class in 1989.

The FORTIES

HENRY "HANK" VOLLENWEIDER

FULLBACK/LINEBACKER

1939–1941

I WAS BORN AND RAISED IN DUBUQUE, IOWA. When I was young, my friends and I would go out swimming by the river in the summertime. We used to go tramping in the woods, trying to catch groundhogs. One time we saw a trap, pulled it out, and guess what? We got sprayed. We'd caught a skunk! That was my childhood.

I went to Dubuque Senior High School and graduated from there in '38. I played football, basketball, and track. When I graduated, I was an all-state football player, and I had won two events in state track hurdles. I won the state championship in the high hurdles in 1937 and in the low hurdles in 1938. Believe it or not, I had visions of getting into the 1944 Olympics. Whether I would have made it or not, I don't know. Anyway, I had fun dreaming about it.

One reason I went to Iowa was because George Bresnahan was the hurdles coach, and I ran hurdles. He was a coach in the '32 Olympics, and George Saling from Iowa had won a gold medal in hurdles in the Olympics. As a freshman,

I felt Coach Bresnahan would help me quite a bit. Of course, they didn't have a very good football team at that time. The old motto was, "Minnesota 50, Iowa Fights." I don't know what the meaning was, but that's what they used to say. Anyway, I went out to Iowa mostly because of Coach Bresnahan.

There were no scholarships. If there were, I never heard of them. If you wanted to go to school, you either paid or worked. I worked like all the other boys for 35¢ an hour to pay off my tuition, because all of us at that time were pretty poor. Tuition cost $65 a semester. We cut grass, dug holes, laid pipe, watered the grass, killed weeds, you name it. We'd do just about anything for 35¢ an hour. I worked in a restaurant, too. I washed the dishes, pots, and pans, and then I waited on tables later, for three hours or for three meals. It wasn't bad. Shucks, we were kids; we all enjoyed it. It was fun.

We lived up in the Field House. That's where we slept in the summertime, on the third floor. We used to call it the Boar's Nest. We had all the athletes together—football, baseball, track—and the coach made us work out in the gym all the time there. It didn't cost us a cent. With the university closed [for the night], they dished out for the athletes. Every day we'd get a change in towels so we could take showers. Yessir, we didn't have to send our clothes back to Mom to wash. We used the athletic department's shorts and T-shirts and socks. We were as rich as we were poor. We didn't have money, but we didn't need it. We had our own fun, our own enjoyment.

In the fall of '38, I did not go out for freshman football. I wanted to compete in indoor track, and I felt I could do better by focusing on track. In those days, the football freshmen were meatballs. They never played a game. They were just practice players on defense for the varsity, and I didn't want that. I wanted to have my chance, too, so I stayed with track in the fall.

Then '39 came, and I went out for football. In Dubuque, there's a college called Loras that used to be called Columbia College. Eddie Anderson was a coach at Columbia College when I was growing up. When I was six, seven, eight years old, I lived about three or four blocks from Columbia College. While he was coaching, we used to go down there and play on the grass; we'd steal a football so we could play on the sideline. Back then, Anderson didn't know who I was, and I didn't know what he was. He was a good friend of Don Ameche. Ameche married a girl from Dubuque, and whenever he could, Don Ameche used to come and sit on our bench when we were playing. Bob Feller used to come, too, and sit on our bench. They were awfully, awfully nice people.

As I say, I started football in the fall of '39. I played halfback and fullback. James Murphy, Bill Green, and myself were considered the fullbacks. We were quite loaded, so I didn't expect to play. But I enjoyed playing football. Plus, we got the training table and got something to eat!

My great call to fame, I guess you might say, would be in the game against South Dakota. South Dakota was the first game that we had in '39. Anderson started me in the second half, and they kicked the football to me! And guess what? I was scared and I ran. That was the start of the second half, and that was the first time I touched the football. I caught the ball on the 8-yard line, and gosh, I was scared. I ran 92 yards for a touchdown and set the stadium record. That put us up 34–0. That stadium record lasted for 10 years. Anyway, I enjoyed it; I used to water that grass in the summertime.

That is my only claim to fame for the 1939 team. However, I did play a number of games that year. Of course, I was a substitute. The fellas ahead of me were one year ahead of me in playing time because they were either upperclassmen or they had played during their freshman year. I was just a lowly sophomore, but I had fun. I played in just about all the games in 1939.

I played linebacker on defense. You played both ways back then. People asked me, "How'd you like your leather helmets?" I said, "They were good for one thing—to keep cotton." At that time, you didn't have face masks or guards. At the top of the helmet, there was some elastic stuff, and behind it we used to put cotton. If your nose bled, you took the cotton out, put it up your nose, and kept on going. Those were the days. You played with your nose runnin' or not. If you came out of the football game, you couldn't go back in for the rest of the quarter. So there were very few substitutions. You played until you cracked your arm or something. But it was fun.

It was an altogether different game than they have today. At that particular time, they had benches, and the ones who weren't playing sat on the benches. Everybody sat down. It's not like today where everybody on the sideline stands along the field. And you couldn't use your hands or pile on like they do today. You couldn't take a safety coming up and jumping on the pile and the guy's down. You had to keep your arms and hands in. It could be called a pleasant game.

My greatest memory at Iowa was probably beating Notre Dame. We had three coaches—Anderson, Frank Carideo, and Jim Harris, the line coach—who were all from Notre Dame. Carideo, the backfield coach, was an All-American at Notre Dame. He and Nile Kinnick used to have contests

In Iowa's first game of the 1939 season, Henry Vollenweider set an Iowa Stadium record with a 92-yard kickoff return for a touchdown. Vollenweider's kick return is still the sixth-longest kickoff return in what is now Kinnick Stadium history.

between them, kicking the football and putting it in certain spots and so forth. One time, there was a fella working down the line a ways. Frank Carideo said, "Now watch this." He kicked it and hit the guy in the back. It was a punt. It was just luck, but he did it.

Anyway, Anderson said at the beginning of the year, "The worst beating you can give a team is 7–6, so let's do that to Notre Dame." He said that at the beginning of the season! So that's what we did. As I recall, they came out in dark jerseys, and then in the second half they came out with green jerseys. They changed their jerseys at halftime!

Everything went like clockwork. We were lucky. We had a very close team, and we looked out after each other. We were all poor as church mice, you might say, but we were quite a bunch. We had a lot of fun.

There were only 27 of us on the traveling team in '39. Oops Gilleard was one of my best friends on the team. His real name was Burdell. He had a voice problem, and he would talk in a high-pitched squeaking voice. Everything he did, he'd go, "Oops!" That was why he had the nickname "Oops." We used to work together cutting grass on the campus, but he was later killed in the invasion of the Philippines.

Mike Enich was from Boone. His parents were Polish immigrants, I believe. During the Indiana game, I don't know what the temperature was, but it was awfully hot. Mike came out of the game a few minutes before the end of the game, and he was just pooped. He said, "I'm not in shape. I'm not in shape." But he was a man who was loved by everybody. He later went to law school and became a judge. He and I and Oops Gilleard all worked together in the summertime.

I raced against Bill Green in high school, at the state meet, I think. He won the dash, and I won the hurdles. He was probably the fastest guy on the team. We never had any races or anything like that, but I know he was fast. He played against Mike Enich in high school because they were in the same conference or something like that.

Erwin Prasse won nine letters—three each in football, basketball, and baseball. He was the leader of the team, and everybody looked up to him. He was the captain and played end. His good friend, Henry Luebcke, happened to be one of the biggest men on the team at 300 pounds. Prasse was also friends with Dick Evans. Evans played on the other end, and he and Prasse were two good ends.

Of course, I knew Nile Kinnick. Nile was a wonderful man and a very good football player, as you know. I never really associated with him at all; Nile Kinnick was a fella who more or less stayed by himself. He was a fraternity boy, and I was a Boar's Nest boy, and there was a difference there. But he was very, very nice fella. He was older than I was, and he had his own friends. I played with him—not very often, however. I had just started football when I was a sophomore and he was a senior, but playing with Nile was really, really great. I enjoyed it, but as far as being with him, I was only really around him on the football field. As far as playing football, he knew just about everybody's position and everybody's assignment. He was a halfback. He did all the passing and did all the punting. He was a very, very likeable gentleman—a gentleman all the way through.

I had many great teammates. Al Couppee was a tough quarterback. Although he had been an all-state player like me, I never knew him until we both met at Iowa. Ray Murphy played fullback. When he would run, his knees would knock like a piston, and he was very hard to tackle. Bill Diehl went to Temple one year before he came to Iowa. He was an awfully nice fella. Everybody liked him. In fact, the whole team got along with each other.

They were all good kids from all over. We had one fella—he was a junior, a Native American—he was small and he asked Anderson if he could come out for football. Anderson asked if he was very fast. He said, "I'm faster than a hiccup!" So he came out for football and scrimmaged with us. He never played or anything, but he was always faster than a hiccup.

I played football in my junior and senior years. In the spring, I ran track. I started a couple of games in my career, but I don't remember which ones they were anymore. I really didn't play that much. I won a letter, and that's about it. As I say, my big ambition was track. I was captain of the track team my senior year.

I remember playing Michigan in 1940 with Tom Harmon. He was an All-American, and they had a big team. I also remember when we played at Wisconsin in 1941. They had a man by the name of Pat Harder, and I can still hear the crowd saying, "Hit 'em again, Harder, hit 'em again, Harder." That was one of the moments I really remember. Then there was an Illinois game where I sort of rolled into somebody's knee or somebody's shin and got my nose splattered. But they took care of it when we got back to Iowa City at the hospital. They couldn't find enough novocaine, but they put rags or cloth up my nose. Still, let's say that I had a very pleasant four years.

As I said, I loved the hurdles, and my ambition was to try out for the 1944 Olympics. I graduated in '42, and I had done all of my work to graduate and go to commencement. Eight days later, I was in the service. They mailed me my diploma. I wound up in the service, and the Olympics were canceled on account of the war.

Vic Siegel, Wilbur Nead, George Poulos, and I all joined the Coast Guard together. They had a program where they had a lot of athletes as instructors at the bases. That blew up, and it ended up that they sent us I don't know where. Vic Siegel and I went to sea and wound up in the North Atlantic someplace. It was quite a shock—we lost everything, including contacts with a lot of people.

I missed Nile before he went on his last voyage. We happened to be in the States; we came in for repairs and stuff. I forget where he was, but I tried to get ahold of him, but his ship had left. And on that cruise was when he went down. I missed him on that. He was quite a boy.

I wasn't able to see the Iowa teams very much while spending 15 years in Salt Lake City. Though I used to go to games when I was living in Davenport, St. Louis is quite a distance to go to a game. But I'm getting along okay, and it is a privilege to say that. I've joined with the Hawkeye I-Club here. We're quite active, and we had one meeting the other night with one of the football coaches.

Iowa is a great state, and to me it is quite an honor and a privilege to be a Hawkeye. It's just too bad that people today can't have the fun that we had, living together in what we called the Boar's Nest. We couldn't afford anything, but we had fun. We were a bunch of nothings. We had nothing to start with, and we left with nothing! But I have a lot of memories, and all I can say is that I had a wonderful time at the university. Red Frye and I are the only ones left out of that team. Good luck to you, and keep rooting for the Hawkeyes!

Henry Vollenweider was a reserve sophomore fullback for the 1939 Ironmen. In Iowa's first game that season against South Dakota, Vollenweider set an Iowa Stadium record with a 92-yard kickoff return for a touchdown. The record stood for 10 years, until it was broken by Bill Reichardt's 99-yard return against Oregon. He later earned his degree from Iowa in economics and worked for decades for Lenox Industries.

GEORGE "RED" FRYE

CENTER/LINEBACKER

1939–1941

I GREW UP IN ALBIA, and I think we had some Albia connections to Iowa. Glenn Devine was the assistant athletics director at Iowa at the time, and he contacted me. He came down and talked to the Albia High School class. He pretty much recruited me to come up to Iowa City for an interview. That's when I went to Iowa and accepted a scholarship, so to speak.

We had a football dormitory in the Field House. That's where we hung out most of the AMs. Regular guys who weren't involved with fraternities or in other locations lived at the Field House dormitory. It was up on the third floor of the Field House, and we called it the Boar's Nest. Hank Vollenweider was there. Ken Pettit and his brother, Roger Pettit, were both up there, too.

In the summer, I worked at the stadium. I painted all the numbers on the west side of the stadium one summer, the summer of '39. They're still there—of course, I think they've been painted over since then or had plastic put over them or something. They were just plain wooden seats with numbers on them.

Freshman couldn't play at that time, so my sophomore year in 1939, I played both center and linebacker. Everyone played both ways back then. We

As a reserve sophomore center/linebacker in 1939, George Frye played all 60 minutes in the last game of the season. He was one of 13 Hawkeyes to play a full 60-minute game for Iowa's 1939 Ironmen.

used a no-huddle offense. Without using that huddle, we'd just line up and go and line up and go, and we'd get those guys on their heels when we ran it like that.

Eddie Anderson was very intelligent and psychological. He used psychology on everybody. There were three Notre Dame men—Eddie Anderson was an All-American at Notre Dame, Jim Harris was an honorable mention All-American at Notre Dame, and Frank Carideo was also an honorable mention All-American. Carideo was the quarterback at Notre Dame, and he was our backfield coach.

I didn't start all of the games, of course, but I did start one game at center. My sophomore year, I started and played the whole game at Northwestern. That was one of my career trophies—playing in that game. Northwestern was a great team. All of the rest of them were great games. Of course, we played and beat Notre Dame 7–6. We won just about every game we played.

I remember the game against Purdue, where Mike Enich blocked two punts, and we won the game 4–0. Eddie Anderson said in a speech, "Enich blocked the punt and got the safety, and then he blocked the second one just to make it convincing."

Mike Enich was known as "the Iron Horse." I think he played more 60-minute games than anyone, and he was elected captain in 1940. He was from Boone, Iowa, and he had been a fullback in high school. When he came down to Iowa, Eddie Anderson made him a tackle. He was a leader as far as conditioning was concerned. Mike Enich would take over on his own—at his request, he didn't make us—he said, "Let's go and get some training." And we'd go over to the stadium and run up and down the steps of the stadium just to get into shape in the summertime. He was a natural leader.

Nile Kinnick was a quiet leader. He was very, very intelligent and very determined. He was a quiet guy. He was a great student, and he knew football, baseball, and basketball, too. He played all three sports. But he was very sharp and very conservative. He never said a whole lot, but when he said it, he meant it.

Nile Kinnick was the star halfback, but he wasn't the big shot of the team. Al Couppee was the coach on the field. Couppee was the quarterback and knew football backward and forward. He knew every player and how they could perform and all that stuff. Al Couppee ran the football team, there's no doubt about that. He was intelligent. In those days, freshmen had to take an entrance examination when they arrived at the university. He got the highest grade on that test of all freshmen at the university. He was out of Council Bluffs, Iowa. As the quarterback, he called everything out loud; we almost never went to a huddle. He'd say, "Get on the line." We'd line up, and he'd call out a series of numbers. You'd have to pick out the numbers to know the play. You could hear him all over the stadium—he had a real loud voice. He knew what everybody was supposed to do, and he even told Captain Prasse on a couple of occasions what to do and where to go. We called him "the little dictator." He left Iowa and became a sports announcer and part owner of the San Diego Chargers.

Erwin Prasse was our captain. He was a nine-letter man. He played football, basketball, and baseball. He knew the game real well, and he knew all the guys. He was a leader.

We were mostly a group of in-state guys. Prasse and Dick Evans were from Chicago. Evans played football and basketball. He was a very good receiver. We threw to him quite a bit, too. He was tall, lanky, and very good both offensively and defensively. Prasse and Evans both started in both football and basketball at Iowa.

We had a lot of great guys on that team, including Bill Diehl, Chuck Tollefson, and Oops Gilleard. Oops was a sophomore that year, and he played quite a bit. He was real fast. I think he was all-state from New London, a small town in southeastern Iowa. He was an orphan and was killed during World War II.

We had two fullbacks, Bill Green and Ray Murphy. Green was from Newton, and he was probably the fastest man on the squad. Ray Murphy was a senior that year. He played fullback. We'd start the game out with Ray Murphy, because he'd go through and soften 'em up. And then we'd put Bill Green in there, and with his speed, he'd just outrun 'em.

We played football, and we won most of those games. When I finished college after my senior year, I signed with the Cleveland Rams. But I never got to play with them, because I had to go to the service. I didn't get to play pro ball; I went to the service, and I played with the Navy.

In the Navy I played football under Minnesota coach Bernie Bierman with the Iowa Seahawks. They were a military team, and they played a lot of Big Ten schools. Bernie Bierman was a reserve colonel in the Marine Corps, so they just transferred him down there and put him in charge of the Navy Preflight school football team. The Marine Corps and the Navy were sort of big brothers back then. We played several Big Ten schools, and we beat Notre Dame again.

When I was commissioned as a pilot, I was commissioned in the Marine Corps as a torpedo bomber. I went up through the ranks and lived in the South Pacific. I had an injury, but that didn't amount to anything. I was shot at, and my plane was hit; that was the main thing. I got several rounds of ammunition from ground fire. I served on a carrier and then went to ground base. That's when I was with the artillery. I carried an artillery spotter with me, and he would direct artillery fire on these locations. I was discharged as a major.

The University of Iowa was my school. I got an athletic scholarship, and I'm glad that that's where I went to school. It was an honor in the first place, and it was a recognized honor nationally because of the winning and the football teams we had. We had the All-American and the Heisman Trophy winner, Nile Kinnick. Al Couppee was a sports announcer, and he was pretty well-known as an Iowa quarterback. The University of Iowa is pretty well recognized as a football team. Coach Ferentz has had a good program, and I've been quite pleased with his coaching. I still go to the first game every year, and I still follow the Hawkeyes and look forward to every game.

George Frye was a reserve sophomore center/linebacker in 1939. He played behind Bill Diehl and Bruno Andruska for most of that season. When Diehl and Andruska were unable to play in the season's final game against Northwestern due to injuries, Frye played all 60 minutes at the center/linebacker position in Iowa's 7–7 tie against the Wildcats. Frye was one of 13 Hawkeyes to play a full 60-minute game for Iowa's 1939 Ironmen. He later got his degree in physical education and occupational therapy at Iowa and worked for 30 years as a hospital administrator for the Veterans Administration. Frye passed away in March 2011.

TONY GUZOWSKI

Right End/Defensive End

1946–1948

I grew up in Iron River in northern Michigan, and we lived more or less on the other side of the tracks. It was a lively community. There was a mixture of Italians, Finlanders, and Poles—a real melting pot. I remember Forest Evashevski would call Iron River "Little Finland" because there are a lot of Finnish people up there.

I went to Iron River High School and played football and basketball. Right after I got out of high school, I went in the Marines. I went into the Marines in August of '41, and I was in there for four years, 30 days, and two hours. I was the first to get in and the first to get out.

I came back here in '44. I ended up in Chicago, and I played Marine Corps basketball. It was one of the coaches there who recommended me to Iowa. I got discharged from the Marine Corps and left Great Lakes in September of '45. I arrived at Iowa shortly after that. Clem Crowe was the football coach that year. He graduated from Notre Dame, but that was about all I remember about him.

I actually didn't want to go out for football in college. It was too cold! But Eddie Anderson persuaded me, so I went out. Of course, Anderson was well-known for having coached the Ironmen, and I used to know quite a few of them. I met just about every one of the Ironmen.

Frank Carideo was Anderson's backfield coach. He knew all that stuff backward and forward. Even though he wasn't my positions coach, I got quite an education from him. I later applied a lot of the teaching that he did to my coaching career, and it was successful. Frank had been an All-American at Notre Dame, and he had a hell of a knowledge of football. I think Frank Carideo was one of the outstanding coaches of his time. Frank went on to broadcast Iowa games in Cedar Rapids with Tait Cummins, and he did those games at Iowa for a number of years. He was very, very good. I thought he was a hell of a coach.

I remember Jack Dittmer really well. As a matter of fact, Jack Dittmer was briefly my roommate when he first got to campus. I was a few years older than he was, and he was a young kid just out of high school. One day I was smoking a cigar, so they pulled him out and put him with the younger guys! I don't know what happened. I guess he didn't like that I was smoking a cigar!

John Tedore recently sent me a picture I haven't seen in about 60 years of us beating Ohio State 14–7 in 1948. I do remember that game, because late in the game, the Buckeyes were threatening to tie the game with a touchdown. I was crashing, and I think the linebacker happened to hit Joe Whisler, and I just fell on the ball! I don't know who the hell caused the fumble, but I got the credit for recovering it. The other thing was, I lost more than 15 pounds in that game. We played both ways then. We had these big old woolen jerseys, and they'd soak up all the water. I remember that Eddie Anderson had that whole Ironman thing. Well, when I coached football, I did away with that real quick! I got the fastest and the freshest guys out there, instead of playing Ironman football. That passed on with the ages.

For my last football game, we went to Boston and played Boston University at the end of the season. It rained like hell. I called John Tedore a mudder, because he'd go tackle somebody and get up soaking wet with mud all over him. He was a hell of an athlete at East High from what I understand and he was a great football and baseball player at the University of Iowa. He was the cocaptain of the baseball team, I know.

I laughed like hell about that Boston game. The only thing was, you couldn't scalp your tickets there! The best place to scalp tickets was at Ohio State. See, they allowed you so many tickets for so many letters. I got to the

Tony Guzowski never intended to play college football because it was too cold, but he changed his mind and lettered three years in both football and basketball.

hotel with my four tickets, and bam! They snapped 'em up for $25 a lick. That was good money in those days.

We had to work our way through school back then. I worked for the Amana colonies, and I worked for Dr. Scanlon. It was pretty interesting. I started out working on the railroad for 99¢ an hour. I was wasting more in shoes than it was worth, so I turned around and became a bartender. That was a lot easier, and I got paid better. You got $1.25 an hour. You washed dishes for your food at one of those restaurants, and then you picked up an odd job like working in a bar or a waiter or something like that.

I lettered three years in basketball, as well. I played against Bud Grant. We used to play in basketball and football and laugh like hell. He was from Minnesota, and he was quite an athlete back then. As for my teammates, I knew the Wilkinson brothers [Herb and Clayton] and Dave Danner pretty well. Murray Wier was just a sophomore when I got there, but later he was the athletics director at Waterloo East High when I was coaching there. He had quite a sense of humor; he was really comical. And he was an All-American when he was playing.

Hayden Fry and Kirk Ferentz have done a great job at Iowa, but in my opinion, they'll never match Evashevski's record. He could recruit 'em from everywhere. He was a really good coach. Jerry Burns was the coach later on up there. He was the most humorous coach I ever met. He always had a great sense of humor.

As far as what it means to be a Hawkeye, well, that's pretty hard to answer. I've been a loyal Hawkeye fan for most of my life since I was at Iowa, and I belonged to the I-Club for many years. Iowa City's a really beautiful town. I enjoyed it, and I'll always remember that I had a good experience there.

Tony Guzowski earned three letters in football and basketball at Iowa and was the third-leading scorer on Iowa's 1949 basketball team. He later enjoyed a long high school coaching career at Waterloo East and Algona. Guzowski was inducted into Michigan's Upper Peninsula Sports Hall of Fame in 2003.

JOHN TEDORE

FULLBACK/HALFBACK

1946–1948

I READ AN ARTICLE WHERE THIS HISTORIAN said that I caught a pass for the last play of the last game in the history of Creighton football. I graduated high school in 1942, and I got a scholarship to Creighton University, which at that time really had pretty good football. We were playing teams like Tulsa, Oklahoma State, Texas Tech, and some other pretty good schools. I really had a good experience there in terms of playing football. I was a backfield man, and on account of the war, freshmen were eligible. I had a good year there, and I really, really enjoyed it.

At Creighton, we were aware that people were going to be drafted. I went out and took the examinations to get into the Air Corps, but they said they had more enlistments than they could handle and that they would get back to me when there was an opening. Well, in the meantime, I got drafted! We got sent over to Italy, and we could see the guns going off far and near. That's when I volunteered for the Special Service Force. It was made up of Canadians and Americans. It was really a special attack force, and those were the types of things—raids and patrols and all that kind of stuff—that we were performing. We say that we are the grandfathers of the Special Forces, which we really are. It was really a unique outfit. They made a movie of it called *The Devil's Brigade*. There's a certain amount of embellishment in that movie, but basically it was true.

I had no problems adjusting back to regular life. I was anxious to get back and return to school. Honestly, I probably would have gone back to Creighton after the war if they would have continued football, but after 1942 they discontinued the program. I still wanted to play football, so when I got out of the Army, I enrolled at Iowa. My high school coach at East Waterloo was very adamant about that. His name was Leonard Raffensperger, and he became the head coach at the University of Iowa in 1950.

Eddie Anderson was not one of those hard-knuckle guys who some coaches are. I knew that Eddie was the coach of the Ironmen, but I always had the feeling that his assistant, Frank Carideo, was the basis of the teaching, where Eddie was more like the chief executive. It was probably because I had to work with Carideo more than Anderson, but that was my opinion when I went there. There were a lot of techniques that I remember Carideo for. For example, he was a prime punter, and he taught punting the way it should have been taught. As far as playing defense, I felt that Carideo was mostly the one who I had to listen to. But no doubt there was conversation between those two, and Anderson had to have a say on things, too. I just felt that Eddie was the executive type and Frank was the nuts-and-bolts type. But that's just one guy's opinion. All the guys loved Anderson, but my contact was more with Carideo.

When we played Notre Dame, I always remembered those games. They always had some guys like Leon Hart who were getting a lot of publicity. As a fullback on offense, I usually had to do a lot of blocking on the end, and those big ends like Leon Hart were big moose, I'll tell you that. We played UCLA out in California once, too, and I really enjoyed that one. We played them all—Minnesota, Purdue, and all of those schools. Minnesota had a couple of tackles who were big and tough. Back then, players weren't that big. When we played somebody that had these big people on them, we really thought that was something.

Ohio State had a pretty good team in 1948. Woody Hayes wasn't the coach, but they did have some good players at that time. I remember that big stadium they have there and everything, but the thing I remember most now is that when we played them, Iowa hadn't beaten them in Columbus in 20 years. But it was just another game as far as I was concerned—a game we wanted to win and felt we could.

At that time as compared with now, when you were on the squad, you could count on the first 11 guys. These 11 guys were also expected to play defense, because that's just the way it was back then. Now when you're planning for a game, you plan for 22 or more guys, including defense and special teams, but it wasn't that way then. It wasn't anything like it is now.

I was the fullback, and normally my defensive position would have been linebacker because of that. But we had some good halfbacks, and they played a lot of offense. I would substitute for them on defense. I wasn't that good in terms of doing a lot of running and stuff, but I did play defense and enjoyed it very much. We did everything, really. I would say that in my three years there, I played about half defense and half offense. It wasn't like it is now, where you send 10 new guys in on defense. It was maybe one to three guys who would go in on defense.

One of our great halfbacks was Emlen Tunnell. He was the greatest football player. He was very humble and just a really nice guy. I was sometimes his substitute. Other times, I played one halfback and he played the other halfback. I'll tell you, Emlen Tunnell was probably as good a guy as you could find. He was a terrific ball carrier, and he is in the Hall of Fame in terms of playing defensive back with the New York Giants. He was a great one.

I played a lot of baseball at Iowa, too. Our coach, Otto Vogel, had played with the Cubs, and he really knew his business. He was just a good baseball coach. He was all business and a good teacher. We had some good players, and he could coach us and not be afraid to knock us down if we needed it. Otto Vogel had been there a long time and had a good reputation. We did well.

I played both football and baseball alongside Jack Dittmer. Jack was a terrific second baseman. What can I say? He was just tops. He had to have been to get drafted into the major leagues. He was just a good, reliable baseball player. I don't remember him committing many errors. He always knew what to do. He was a good one and held that infield together.

After I graduated, I stayed for another year and got my master's degree at Iowa. Leonard Raffensperger had joined the coaching staff as the coach of the freshman team, so I spent a year on the staff there working with him and the freshmen. The following year, he was hired as Iowa's head football coach when Anderson left. Raffensperger was a very clean-cut, tall fella who was just wonderful. He wasn't one of those guys who yelled and all that, but he was just all business and very intellectual. He was really a fine coach. He had some tough luck when he got the Iowa job. He was there for two years, and

John Tedore lettered in football and also was part of the Hawkeyes' 1949 Big Ten champion baseball team.

they had some rough times winning games back then. But it was one of those times when the talent just wasn't there. He was only there for two years, and I always felt kind of bad about that. There were a lot of other guys who would have liked to have had that job, and I think some of them were kind of nasty about the whole deal. But Raffensperger was a great guy.

As far as coaches go, I think Coach Ferentz has to be tops. He's been there for 12 years, and he's not a braggart or a big mouth or anything like that. The information that comes out is that they do everything right, and he has good assistants. One of his and Fry's attributes is that they hired good people and gave them a lot of responsibility, and those assistants really responded. That's the way it is at Iowa right now. Iowa has done a good job—just compare that to when they had a lot of different coaches for about 20 years there. Fry came in and solidified that program, and ever since, Iowa's had some really good teams. I think they do very well, considering that other people are just closer to a lot of the talent in Ohio and some of those places. That has to be one of the big secrets to coaching, having good talent.

As far as I was concerned, I was always happy to be a part of a program like the one in Iowa City, because in the state of Iowa, you have really good people. There's not a lot of bickering and all that stuff going on that you read about in the papers at some other programs. I was very proud to be a member of the Iowa athletics program in football and baseball. I'm very happy and I have no hard feelings about anything. I enjoyed it and worked with nice people who were tops. I guess that's how I'd summarize it.

John Tedore finished third in the Big Nine in 1946 in average kickoff return yardage. He scored a touchdown and recovered a fumble in Iowa's 14–7 victory over Ohio State in 1948, and he earned four letters in baseball. Tedore was a member of Iowa's Big Ten champion baseball team in 1949. He later had a long career as a high school teacher and coach. John Tedore has six children, five of whom also went to the University of Iowa.

JACK DITTMER

Offensive End

1946–1949

I HAD FOLLOWED IOWA EVER SINCE I WAS A KID, to tell you the truth. I used to go to some of their games, and I got to know some of their players down there. They gave me a scholarship, so I took it. I didn't really go shopping around for any other schools, and there were some other ones that talked to me. But I told them I'd already made up my mind that I was going to go to the University of Iowa.

We had great fan support down there in those days. Everybody seemed like they got treated very well. I sure didn't have any problems going there in any way, shape, or form. I really liked the school, and it wasn't too far from home, either. That was another reason why I went that way. My folks and some of the other people around here could come and see me play if they wanted to—after I made the team, of course!

I played for Eddie Anderson in football and Otto Vogel in baseball. Coach Anderson was pretty well down to earth, and you did it his way or you didn't do it at all. I guess if he liked you, he treated you pretty good, and if he didn't like you, well, he made it twice as tough for you.

In 1946 we had some guys who were really good on defense, but we played some teams that were really good back then. I remember Buddy Young and his boys at Illinois beat us 7–0, but we gave them all they wanted that day. They went to the Rose Bowl that year and played UCLA and kicked the hell out of 'em.

I played halfback when I was in high school, and then I played end when I was in college. I also played defense once in a while, but not too often. Sometimes Anderson put me in at halfback on defense to try to intercept passes, off and on. I got spotty playing time on defense; I didn't ever play regularly there. In that Illinois game—this is the honest to God truth—Anderson said, "Dittmer, get in there at outside linebacker and intercept this lateral." Of course, I didn't know what the hell he was talking about, so I got out there. This back went in motion, so I broke toward the back. And I'll be damned if the quarterback didn't pitch him the ball, and he no sooner pitched it to him as I tackled him. But if I'd been two steps quicker, I probably could have intercepted that play. How he surmised that that play was going to happen, I have no idea. I still wonder about it. I threw him for a six- or seven-yard loss, but Anderson wanted me to intercept it and run for the touchdown!

Emlen Tunnell was a great friend of mine and a great ballplayer. He really had a lot of athletic ability. He always put out, too; he didn't mess around. He could play halfback on offense, and he played halfback on defense. He later played pro football. He was with the Green Bay Packers for quite a while after he played for the New York Giants. He was a real good baseball player, too. We played for George Foerstner's team. Foerstner was from Amana and was a big contributor down there at Iowa. Emlen pitched on that team, and I played second base on that team for 'em. He was a real good baseball player.

We played up in Minnesota in 1946. I don't know what the temperature was, but the wind was about 35 or 40 mph, and Emlen's hands froze up so bad at halftime he couldn't play the second half. Honest to God, that was a terrible day! It was probably the worst day I ever played in any sport, because that wind was so cold, it went right through you. In the first half, Tunnell was back to throw a pass, and I thought he was trapped. I got behind everybody, and I mean by like 15 to 20 yards, and I stopped. All of a sudden, there came the ball, and I started taking off after it. I got into the end zone, but I didn't catch it. I thought I broke my hand when I came down! It was that cold.

I caught two touchdown passes against Wisconsin in 1948. One was a wing pass, and they had the halfback in front of me in the end zone. I jumped up and I tipped the ball over his head—he was short, too—picked it out of the air and caught the ball as I fell down. I think we beat 'em 19–13. In fact, they

Jack Dittmer was inducted into the University of Iowa Hall of Fame in 1993 for his accomplishments across three sports—he lettered a total of nine times in football, baseball, and basketball. He was an honorable mention All-American in football in 1949 and a second-team All-American in baseball that same year.

marched down the field, but then our defense really took over, and I think they were stopped at about our 13- or 14-yard line.

Bill Reichardt was a sophomore my senior year. He was a well-built lad and could handle himself really well. He ran out of the fullback position, and he had good power. He knew where the line was and where the holes were, and he followed them the best he could. He had a lot of ability. He place-kicked for us, too.

I played special teams almost all the time. I remember I threw a block against Oregon in 1949 when Reichardt ran a kickoff 99 yards for a touchdown. People often forget that Bob Longley ran a punt back in that game, too, 94 yards for a touchdown. We were behind quite a ways but finally ended up beating them by three points.

Jerry Faske was our running back for a couple years. He was a good back, too. He could run, he was strong, and he was a left-handed passer. I know because he threw me one pass that I caught—I don't remember if it was for a first down or a touchdown—and he was running to his left when he threw that pass to me.

I played baseball at Iowa for Otto Vogel. He was at Iowa a really long time, and he knew everything there was about baseball. He was a very good coach. He told you just how to do it, and you did the best you could to try to do it. We won the Big Ten title in 1949, and we played great baseball. Jack Bruner was a great pitcher from Waterloo. We had some other really good ballplayers. A lot of those guys were seniors when I was a freshman, and we played a lot of great ball, that's for sure.

Playing two sports wasn't tough at all. I had played multiple sports at Elkader High School, and I got a pretty good start there that I could handle myself all right. A lot of the teams we played against had a lot of guys who were bigger than I was. I think probably about the heaviest I was about 160 pounds. I always ran scared, so I never got hurt too much, because they didn't catch me! Of course, I used to get racked up pretty good sometimes, but I was pretty fortunate. I had a few bruises, but that was about all. You could say I took good care of myself my whole life.

Actually, basketball was my favorite sport of all of them. But I went out for basketball when I was a freshman at Iowa, and I flunked a course that first year, so I decided I wasn't going to do that anymore. I had to go to summer school to make that course up, and so I just stuck with football and baseball until my senior year.

Oh, Pops Harrison [the Iowa basketball coach]—Popsie had some good ballplayers, and he handled them well. I think he was a good coach. My senior year, when I did finally go out for basketball, I think we had about three different coaches at one time or another. I can't remember exactly what happened all the way through now.

I knew all the basketball guys and knew them well. They were nice guys. Murray Wier was a little devil. He got in everybody's hair. He made some terrific shots that you'd think were impossible, but he made them get underneath the basket and he'd flip 'em up one way or another. He was a thorn in everybody's side, and he was a good hustler. He played good basketball, period. Iowa had a lot of good players then.

Herb Wilkinson played guard and did his job all the time. He always covered one of the best players on the other team. He could shoot from all sides, but there wasn't near as much shooting then as there is now. Herb's brother was a good ballplayer, too.

I don't think anybody else has won nine letters since I did, to the best of my knowledge. I'm sure it could be done, but this guy would have to be an awfully good student and have to take good care of himself. There's a lot of luck involved in it. I don't know—I sure haven't seen many guys who have been a three-sport man down there at all for some time now. But that's not saying there couldn't be a bunch of them coming up right now, too. You never know.

I played 10 seasons of pro baseball. I started in 1950 and quit after the 1959 season. My contract had been sold to Hawaii, and I checked to see how much time I had in for the pension plan. I had five years and three days of major league service; in other words, I'd made it. So we decided we weren't going to go to Hawaii. It's lucky I did, because my dad was still in the car business. That was 1960, and he died in '62. So I took that over, and that's what I've been doing ever since. It was lucky I was able to mine a little experience from him.

Being a Hawkeye has meant a good life for me. Of course, I got a scholarship. I had a couple of other offers, but I had decided long before if I was offered a scholarship, I was going to go there. I didn't care about who else offered me scholarships, I was just going to go to Iowa. I followed them all the time starting back with Kinnick, and they had those great games, and I always stuck up for Iowa. Being from Iowa and all, it just came natural is the only thing I can tell ya.

Jack Dittmer was the sixth and last Hawkeye to earn nine athletic letters at the University of Iowa, lettering four times in football and baseball and once in basketball. He was the football team's MVP as a senior in 1949, and he graduated with five school receiving records—career receptions, yards receiving in a season and career, and touchdown receptions in a season and career. Dittmer was an honorable mention All-American in football in 1949 and a second-team All-American in baseball that same year. He helped lead Iowa to the 1949 Big Ten baseball title before playing six seasons in the major leagues. Jack Dittmer was inducted into the University of Iowa Hall of Fame in 1993.

The FIFTIES

JERRY HILGENBERG

CENTER/LINEBACKER

1950–1953

MY FAMILY ORIGINATED IN COON RAPIDS, which is in western Iowa, and then moved to Wilton, Iowa, when I was in grade school. I graduated from Wilton High School in 1949. I had an older sister, Donna, and a younger brother, Wally. Both were very good athletes. We had a wonderful, close family. Our parents were Curly and LaVonne Hilgenberg.

I played basketball, baseball, and football in high school. Actually, Wilton did not have a football team until my senior year. We had a pretty good team that year, especially considering none of us had ever played football before, other than in each other's backyards. Archie Fry was our coach and did an excellent job with such an inexperienced group. I don't think some of our players had ever seen a football before, and none of us had ever played organized ball. I played spinback in the single wing offense. We had a great bunch of kids and a lot of fun. In a small town like Wilton, as kids, sometimes all there is to do is go with your friends and play sports. We would play until dark, then get up and meet our friends the next morning to start playing again. Wilton was a great place to live and raise a family.

We talked some about me playing football after high school, but I did not go to college thinking I would play sports. Once I was on campus my freshman year, I decided to give it a try in football. Freshmen, at that time, were not eligible to participate in varsity games. The freshmen had their own practices. I was a walk-on prospect and tried out for the quarterback position.

Iowa had recruited a number of good quarterbacks, so I was mostly standing around watching and didn't get much of an opportunity to play in many of the drills or scrimmages.

One need the team had was someone to snap the ball to the quarterbacks so they could practice their plays. The backfield would be practicing their plays at one end of the field, and the linemen were doing their own drills at the other end. Instead of just standing around, I jumped in a couple of times to snap the ball to the quarterbacks so they could run their plays. It sort of evolved into me snapping to the quarterbacks every day. Then, one time they needed a center to play in a scrimmage, and they told me to go in and play center. That's how it all started, and from then on I was a center. On defense I played linebacker.

Forest Evashevski became the head football coach at Iowa in the spring of 1952. He was a very intelligent man and extremely knowledgeable about the game of football. Evy's organization and preparations for practices and games were very detailed and well done. He was also a great motivator and psychologist. He was a psychology major at the University of Michigan. When Evy came to Iowa, he hired a great staff that included Bump Elliott, Bob Flora, Archie Kodros, Whitey Piro, and Wally Schwank. They were all wonderful people and great coaches.

Evy's first year at Iowa, 1952, was a tough year as far as wins and losses. However, the trend was set for the future with our 8-0 upset victory over Ohio State in Iowa City. That win knocked Ohio State out of the Big Ten championship and a trip to the Rose Bowl. We put in a different offense for that Ohio State game called the "digit offense." In the huddle, the quarterback would indicate a live digit—first, second, or third digit. At the line of scrimmage, the quarterback would look at the defensive alignment and call out three digits, the live digit called in the huddle would be the point of attack and the play we would run. The game was very tough that day, but the defense did a great job of shutting the Buckeyes out. It was very innovative and a great game plan by our coaching staff.

In the 1953 season Iowa made great progress as a football team. Although the team record that year was 5–3–1, a lot of good football was played against some top teams in the country. We lost a one-point heartbreaker at Michigan, as we failed to convert a field-goal attempt in the last few minutes of the game. Wisconsin beat us by a score of 10–6. Minnesota was always a big game, especially when their great halfback, Paul Giel, was having an outstanding year.

Jerry Hilgenberg became the first of six Hilgenbergs to letter for Iowa when he walked on to the team as a freshman. Together, the Hilgenbergs have earned a total of 19 football letters.

Iowa beat Minnesota at home 27–0 in 1953. The Iowa coaches spotted some tendencies displayed by Giel in previous games and added them to the scouting report. Whitey Piro discovered that when Giel would run and fake a pass, he would then continue on a running play. When he would fake the run, he would then pass the ball. This proved to be a very successful coaching point, and Giel gained only 55 yards that day.

Another game in 1953 that is prominent in my memory is when we tied Notre Dame 14–14. Notre Dame was ranked No. 1 in the country, and had been for the nine previous weeks, but after our game they were dubbed the "Fainting Irish." At the very end of the second and fourth quarters, Iowa was ahead by one touchdown. Notre Dame was out of timeouts and the clock was running, but there appeared to be Notre Dame players on the field feigning injuries to stop the clock. Unfortunately, in both cases it worked, and each time they managed to score on the next play after the injury time-outs to tie the game. Coach Evashevski was pretty hot about that one. Here we had a chance to beat the top team in the country and then that happens. People will never forget Coach Evashevski's words after that loss. Paraphrasing Grantland Rice, Evy said, "When the One Great Scorer comes to write against your name, he won't ask that we won or lost, but how we got gypped at Notre Dame." This tie did prevent Notre Dame from winning the national title that year. Iowa ended the 1953 season ranked ninth in the AP poll and 10th in the coaches' poll. All the games we played—the wins, losses, and tie—were special in representing the University of Iowa and the Iowa football team.

Being named All-American in 1953 by the Football Writers Association of America was a great honor. A lot of credit goes to the entire 1953 Iowa football team for the award. We had a 5–3–1 record our senior year, which was a big improvement, and Iowa's football program gained a lot of respect that year.

In the spring of 1954 I was drafted in the fourth round by the Cleveland Browns. I signed with Cleveland and expected to report to their training camp that spring. However, I had taken Air Force ROTC at the university, and that spring I received orders to report to the U.S. Air Force to fulfill my service commitment. After serving my two years in the Air Force, I was in contact with the Browns and received an offer to sign a new contract. Then an opportunity came from Coach Evashevski to join him and his staff at Iowa. We talked several times on the telephone and then met in person. Since I was married, and JoAnn and I had a young baby boy, I decided to take the coaching opportunity at the university with Evy and his staff in the spring of 1956. It was great to be back at Iowa as an assistant coach. I had only been away two years in the Air Force, so many of my former teammates were still on the team. I was an assistant coach for eight years, from 1956 through the 1963 season, and enjoyed coaching very much.

In the spring of 1956 our coaching staff installed the wing-T offensive system. It was so successful that Iowa won the Big Ten championship in 1956, and then won the Rose Bowl against Oregon State 35–19. In 1957 Iowa's record was 7–1–1, which earned second place in the Big Ten. In 1958 Iowa won the Big Ten championship with an 8–1–1 record and also won the 1959 Rose Bowl by beating California 38–12. In 1960 Iowa's record was 8–1, and they shared the Big Ten title with Minnesota. Iowa was not eligible to participate in the Rose Bowl game that year because of Big Ten Conference rules. Evy was inducted into the College Football Hall of Fame for his outstanding coaching career.

There is no question that Iowa Football has played a major role in our family's lives for many years. It has been that way from 1950 through the present day, and I am sure it will continue. Some of the most enjoyable benefits we have experienced from our participating in athletics, other than the games, are the many opportunities we have had for family gatherings at the games. The Hilgenberg family has had six University of Iowa football letter winners, which include: me; my sons, Jim, Jay, and Joel; my brother, Wally; and his son, Eric. Wally and two of my sons, Jay and Joel, also had long careers in the NFL. There have been many discussions about football and games with this group, and a couple of times I thought they may end in a live scrimmage. The opportunity, because of Iowa football, for me to have such a close relationship with my family has been really special.

We thank the University of Iowa for giving us these opportunities. Go Hawks!

Jerry Hilgenberg is the patriarch of the most decorated family in Iowa football history. He was the first of six Hilgenbergs to letter for Iowa. Jerry was a first-team All-America center in 1953. He served as an assistant coach under Forest Evashevski while his brother, Wally, played. Three of his sons played in the 1970s and 1980s, followed by his nephew in the 1990s.

WARREN "BUD" LAWSON

CENTER

1952–1954

I GREW UP IN FAIRFIELD, which is a small town in southeast Iowa, and at that time the home of Parsons College. In high school, I played football, basketball, and track. In football, I was one of the best players on the team.

Back then, the routine was that athletes with some ability went to Parsons College. My two older brothers were at Parsons, and I anticipated following in their footsteps. My senior year of high school, we got a new high school coach named Bob Liddy. He had been a Hawkeye and the MVP in 1943. He was a great coach and had a great impact on my future.

I was a center and linebacker on our high school team and a pretty good player, but I did not make first-team all-conference or any all-state mention. My biggest reward came immediately following our last game against Burlington. We had lost 43–42 to Burlington, but in the dressing room following the game, a guy [guard Max Hawkins] walked up to me and said, "Hey, partner, you played a great game." He shook hands with me and rolled his hand over so his University of Iowa ring showed and said, "How would you like to earn one of these?" I looked at that Iowa ring and thought, *My God, I'd do anything to get one of those.* And, as a matter of fact, after I got mine, I've worn it continuously to this day. That was the only recruiting visit I had from the Hawkeyes, but it was a memorable one since it was delivered in front of my teammates, which made it even more meaningful. It meant more than any all-state or all-conference honor I could have earned.

Since my brothers were at Parsons and since I could stay home, I had applied for a scholarship at Parsons. I was awarded that scholarship in the spring of 1951 and deferred acceptance until I got some word from Iowa about scholarship availability. Iowa offered me full tuition and a job at the Field House that paid $40 a month. That amount paid about half of the dormitory cost each month. They went on to say the scholarship would be enhanced to include room, board, and tuition if I made the team.

After the 1951 season, the athletics director fired Coach Raffensperger and hired Coach Evashevski. In spring practice, I was selected as the player who would "contribute the most to Iowa's future success." I was given a watch as an award and my scholarship went to a full ride.

The college football substitution rules changed in the seasons of 1952 and 1953. In 1952 we played offense and defense and substituted much like is done today. I was always competing with Jerry Hilgenberg, and he played the offense and I played defense. In 1953 the rules changed so that all players had to go both ways. And in that year Jerry Hilgenberg was on the first team and I was second team as a center. The first team was called "Binkey's Team" named for Binkey Broeder, who was a fullback on the first team. The second team was dubbed "Louis' Team" for Louis Matykiewicz, who was the second-team quarterback. Iowa still substituted full teams, but when you went into a game, you played both ways. In 1954 the rule remained the same, and I was the first-team center and linebacker.

In 1952 we opened the season at Pittsburgh and lost. We then played three more games and lost them, as well. Practices were tough after those three losses. We had to run lots of stadium steps and have extra scrimmages.

In the middle of the season, Coach Evy changed the entire signal system, and we went to the split-T formation with an unbalanced line. We had been running a lot of single wing prior to that. We had Ohio State in our stadium in 1952, and it was one of the first games I started at linebacker. We beat the Buckeyes 8–0. Almost 40 years later I had the occasion to meet Coach [Woody] Hayes at a conference in Columbus, Ohio. As the adjutant general of Iowa, I was introduced to Woody as the only adjutant general to play on a team that beat Ohio State. Woody said, "Where you from?" I answered, "Iowa." He said, "My God, 1952 in Iowa Stadium. You know that was the most painful loss I ever experienced in coaching? You guys beat us out of going to the Rose Bowl and winning the Big Ten Conference." Then he added, "But you never beat us again." I replied, "That is true, but we should have beaten you in 1954, because we had a touchdown called back on an Eddie Vincent scoring run that was called out of bounds." Eddie really never went out of bounds as the game films clearly showed. Following the game, Evy showed the film on television in Iowa and was criticized by the Big Ten Conference for doing it. I have a copy of that game film, and I clearly see the advantage current coaches have to challenge calls.

In 1953 we had Minnesota in Iowa City and we won that game 27–0. When we were about to take the field, Evy said, "Binkey, I want you to take them right out and across the center of the field. Those clowns from Minnesota last night put a big red 'M' in the middle of our stadium, and I want you guys to all look at it and rub their noses in it." After the fact, I believe we all figured out who had painted the field, but at the time we blamed Minnesota and did rub their noses in it.

A year earlier in Minneapolis, when we entered the dressing room, there was a sign on the wall that read, "Beat the Black Hawks from Iowa." Murray Warmath was the Minnesota coach, and since he was brought in from the South, it was believable that Minnesota did the sign. We had five starters at that time who were black. Evy called all the blacks together to counsel with them. And again, after the fact, I suspect the sign came from Iowa. Evy was clever at getting us emotionally built for the game.

The Notre Dame game in 1953 was a 14–14 tie. Notre Dame tied the game by players faking injuries in the final seconds of the first half and again with six seconds left in the game in the second half. It was our opinion that Sam Palumbo faked an injury in the first half and Frank Varrichione faked injury at the end of the game to give Notre Dame one last play to tie the score. Notre Dame passed for touchdowns in both cases, so the game was a 14–14 tie.

Now the interesting fact is after we played our senior season, Louis Matykiewicz and I played with Varrichione and Palumbo of Notre Dame in the North-South Game in Miami. Though the press made a big deal of us being on the same team, I will tell you they both emphatically denied faking an injury.

After graduation, I wanted to play professional football. I signed a contract with the San Francisco 49ers and thought I would first get my military obligation out of the way before I went to San Francisco to make the team. I was in the ROTC, and my senior year I was commander of the Corps of Cadets.

Warren "Bud" Lawson was a center on offense and was named the Hawkeyes' MVP in 1954.

Having a good scholastic record and success in athletics probably led to my selection to command the Corps of Cadets. As a result of ROTC, I would have a two-year active duty, a two-year reserve component, and a two-year standby reserve component for total military obligation of six years. The professor of military science called me in late in my senior year and said, "I've got a deal for you. If you will sign up for a regular Army commission, I will be able to get you and your wife orders to Europe for a three-year tour. If then you want to get out and play professional football, you can get out at the end of three years, and there will be no reserve obligation."

Since Korea was where most reserve officers were going at that time, I elected to go into the regular Army. After I got in the regular Army, had served my three great years in Germany, and returned to the United States, I decided to stay in the Army. I was a regular Army officer from 1955 to 1979. In 1979 I learned that Iowa's governor had fired the state's adjutant general and was soliciting applications to run the guard in Iowa. I was at that time in Virginia's Fort Houston and had orders to Turkey. I would have had to take my daughter out of her senior year of high school if I stayed in the active force, so I put in an application and was selected for the deputy position. Six years later I took over as adjutant general, a job I held for 14 years. In 1999 I retired as adjutant general of Iowa, completing a 44-year career in the military.

What does it mean to be a Hawkeye? I go back to my meeting with Max Hawkins in the Fairfield High School dressing room in 1951. That big "I" ring that Max showed on his hand inspired me then and it still does today. Every time I hear the Iowa fight song or picture the Iowa band coming on the field playing "On Iowa," I renew my love of this great university. I get a tear in my eye just listening to that song. I will have the "Iowa Fight Song" and "On Iowa" played as they move me out of the chapel at my funeral. To say I love the Hawkeyes is an understatement. I have a passion for them. I revel and celebrate their wins and pain for them in defeat. I will always be proud that I was and am a Hawkeye. I have a special place in my heart for all Hawkeyes and especially those whom I played with and those athletes who have followed us in the last 50-plus years.

Warren "Bud" Lawson grew up in Fairfield, Iowa, and lettered from 1952 to 1954. He was a center on offense and was named Iowa's MVP in 1954. In 1999 he retired as adjutant general of Iowa, which completed a 44-year career in the military. Lawson still resides in Iowa.

JERRY REICHOW

QUARTERBACK/ DEFENSIVE BACK

1953–1955

I've been an Iowa fan forever, I guess. Before television came along, I used to listen to the Iowa football and basketball games on the radio. When I got into high school, I started hitchhiking to the football games. We didn't have a car in those days, so it was up to me to bum a ride.

I'm from Decorah, Iowa, and I finished high school in the spring of 1952. I played basically everything in high school—football, basketball, and track—and did pretty well. I was a quarterback and defensive back in football.

I had offers to play football at other schools, and I almost did. This was the year that Coach Forest Evashevski came to Iowa, so there wasn't really much recruiting going on during the transition. Other schools followed me around, such as Drake, Indiana, and Iowa State. A local guy I worked for in a lumber yard was a big Iowa backer and wanted me to go to Iowa. I wanted to go to Iowa also, and eventually things fell into place despite the coaching transition.

I was in Evashevski's first freshman class. We couldn't play as freshmen back then, so I spent the year on the practice squad. When we got on the field to report for practice our freshman year, there were 128 of us the first day. I could hardly find a place to stand. I don't know where the guys kept coming from, but the next day a bunch of them would be gone, and another batch would arrive. I don't know where he was getting all these guys.

As freshmen we had to scrimmage the varsity, which was rough at first, but by the end of the year, we could hold our own. Then, as soon as football was over, Coach Evashevski enrolled us in a football class, so we kept football in our routine until spring practice. It was a tough, tough year. Coach Evashevski was trying to find out who wanted to play and who was tough enough to play.

The first game I started was at Michigan in 1953. I came from a town of 5,000, and there were 100,000 people in the stands. They really didn't like us very much, so that was an eye-opener.

The last game of the season was our 14–14 tie with Notre Dame, which I'm sure has been well documented. Notre Dame and Maryland were tied for first in the nation at that time. Since then, I've known some Maryland guys, and they always thank me for tying Notre Dame.

I had a memorable game our sophomore year at Wisconsin. The other Iowa quarterback was Louis Matykiewicz, who also played linebacker on defense. Things were different back then since you played both offense and defense. The coaches sent me in to throw the ball. Well, now I had to play linebacker on defense and had never played there in my life. Wisconsin handed the ball to Alan Ameche, who was a great player. A hole opened up, and I don't know if he tripped over me or what, but I somehow got him down. Nevertheless, I didn't want to be in that spot very long.

My junior year of 1954 kicked off with an exciting game against Michigan State. It came down to a fourth-down touchdown in the fourth quarter for us to win 14–10. It was a quarterback sneak, so there was nothing exceptional about it, but we scored to win, which was outstanding. It was one of the few games on television in those days. The big play of the game was actually Eldean Matheson's long run that set up the final score. He was a backup running back for us and returned punts. The funny thing was, television had taken a timeout during Eldean's run, and viewers didn't even get to see the play. Nevertheless, that was the big play of the game.

Nineteen fifty-five was a tough year. We lost a lot of guys early on to injuries, including Calvin Jones, Frankie Gilliam, and Earl Smith. We opened with a win against Kansas State, but then had to go to Wisconsin, which was the toughest team we played that year. We didn't do well there, and then we had UCLA, which was the national champ the year before, followed by Michigan. It was a frustrating year. We had offensive power, but for some reason we didn't do well on defense. The schedule was brutal. We only had four

Jerry Reichow was named Iowa's MVP in 1955. He was drafted by the Detroit Lions and played four years with Detroit, one with Philadelphia, and four with Minnesota.

home games. We had five on the road: at Wisconsin, UCLA, Michigan, Ohio State, and Notre Dame. It was like, *Who put this schedule together? This is murder.*

Our greatest player back then was Calvin Jones. He was supposed to go to Ohio State but switched to Iowa at the last minute to be with Frank Gilliam and Eddie Vincent. Woody Hayes went crazy. Boy, he was upset. The NCAA checked on the situation, but Calvin just wanted to be with his Steubenville, Ohio, friends. All three of them were starters as sophomores. Frankie told me that 11 kids who started for that Steubenville team got major-college scholarships. That was great football in Ohio back in those days, and it still is.

Coach Evashevski could attract that kind of talent. But make no mistake, once players got there, he was the boss. There was no question who was running the show. He was tough on the quarterbacks and wasn't my favorite person a lot of the time. But he just wanted tough, hard-nosed guys, and you had to respect him for his knowledge. Football was so different then. We didn't pass the ball but five times a game. It was just banging on people back and forth. The year after I left, they changed the offense to the wing-T, and it fit the new quarterback, Kenny Ploen, perfectly. They won the Rose Bowl that year.

After my senior year, I played in the East-West Shrine Game. I ended up winning the MVP honors for that game, so my draft status went up after that. They used to have a split draft in those days, because the Canadian Football League was a stronger opponent of the NFL then. In fact, it cost you money to stay in NFL rather than go to Canada. The NFL had three rounds during the year while we were still playing just so teams could contact these kids early and get them to come to the NFL rather than go to Canada. As soon as the all-star games were over, they had the remaining rounds, and I was the first player taken in that second draft. The Detroit Lions coaches coached in the all-star game, so they knew me and drafted me right away. I played nine years professionally, four with Detroit, one with Philadelphia, and the last four with Minnesota. I made the Pro Bowl in 1961.

After my playing career ended, I stayed with Minnesota as a scout. I worked in varying positions for the Vikings, such as personnel director, director of football operations, and assistant general manager for national scouting. A few years ago, I took the position of personnel consultant, so this is my 50th year with Minnesota right now.

Looking back, I'd been watching guys play at Iowa before I did, and I really wanted to be a part of that. I was a Hawkeye growing up, and I didn't know much else, to be honest with you. My brother, Bill, who was five years older, was on the football team also. He went to Iowa and broke his ankle. He then went in the service and came back, so I ended up finishing a year ahead of him. He was also a quarterback, and when he came back all of a sudden, oops, we were playing the same position. That was kind of uncomfortable. They eventually made a tackle out of him. We did get to start the Ohio State game together, but I'll be darned if he didn't break his shoulder there. He was bitten by the injury bug more than once.

I really enjoyed playing for Iowa and especially having the opportunity to play there with my brother. He was my hero growing up, and I tried to follow him all through high school and such. I also have a sister who had two boys play at the university, Tom and Mike Frantz. So we've all been close to the Iowa football program.

The 1950s were an exciting time to play sports at the University of Iowa. Though I didn't make it to the Rose Bowl like Kenny Ploen and Randy Duncan, I hope I helped establish the foundation for their success. I also played basketball for Iowa, which included one trip to the Final Four. My experience at Iowa was by all means a good one. I consider myself fortunate to have had the opportunity.

Jerry Reichow played quarterback for Iowa early in the Forest Evashevski era. Career highlights include a fourth-quarter, fourth-down plunge into the end zone to beat Michigan State in 1954. He was named Iowa's MVP in 1955. Reichow then played professionally for nine years and made the Pro Bowl in 1961. After his playing career, he joined the Minnesota Vikings organization as a scout, and has worked for the Vikings in various capacities for 50 years. Reichow currently resides in Santa Fe, New Mexico.

FRANK GILLIAM

End

1953–1956

I can't ever remember not knowing Eddie Vincent and Calvin Jones. We had grown up together since we were four years old in the same Steubenville, Ohio, neighborhood. Eddie, Calvin, and I played together all the time. We went to the same elementary, the same junior high school, and the same high school. So when it was time for Eddie and me to report to Iowa City for college, we stopped by Calvin's house to tell him good-bye.

Calvin Jones was the most outstanding lineman in the state of Ohio at that time, and he had committed to Ohio State. He was all set to go to Columbus and play for Woody Hayes. We told Calvin we were on our way, and we'd see him when we came home for the holidays. He looked at us and said, "I'm going with you." And the next thing I knew, he was running up the stairs and throwing his bags out the window to us. His mother was yelling at him, "You told Coach Hayes you were coming." Calvin replied, "Yes, I know, but I'm going to go to Iowa with Shags and Pumpkin." Calvin referred to me as "Shags," and Eddie was "Pumpkin."

We were driving west, and the first phone we came to we stopped and called Coach Forest Evashevski. We told him who we had in the car and asked if it was okay to bring Calvin. Evy said, "Get here as quick as you can and don't stop if you don't have to." I mean, this was the most outstanding player in the state of Ohio. This was a big recruit for the University of Iowa! That's the story of how all three of us came to play for the University of Iowa.

Coming to Iowa was like we had gone to another country. Steubenville was a small industrial town on the Ohio River about 39 miles west of Pittsburgh. It was a dirty town with lots of smoke stacks, steel mills, and foundries. The buildings were dirty from all the industrial activity, and there were very few environmental rules back then. Coming to Iowa was just a new stage and setting for us.

All three of us were starters our sophomore year, and we had a lot of other sophomores playing also. I started each year at both offensive and defensive end. The first game I ever played in was against Michigan State in 1953. The Spartans were a power in the league at that time. We were geared up, and the stadium was packed. We lost that game but went on to have a pretty good year. Iowa had been having a difficult time competing in the Big Ten, but Evy was getting things turned around.

Cal Jones was a great player. He would be a small guy now, but he was really physical. He made All-America because he played hard all the time. Football was made for him, so to speak, and it's a shame his life ended so early in that plane crash. [Cal Jones was killed in a December 1956 airplane accident. His Trans-Canada Airline flight left from Vancouver, Canada, where Jones had played in the Canadian Football League all-star game the previous day. One hour after the plane departed, it was caught in a violent windstorm and crashed into a mountain range.]

Before the second game of my senior year, we were practicing to play Wisconsin. Jerry Reichow threw me a high pass, which I caught. But my legs were spread, and the defensive back came down on my right leg and broke it. The kid who was playing defensive back was so sorry it happened, but it wasn't his fault. I tried to come back after missing about six games, but I couldn't do it. Evy said, "I'll tell you what we're going to do. We're going to keep you out and petition for another year. I don't know if they're going to give it to you or not, because you did play one game." It was a sad time for me. It wasn't the greatest year of my life, but I kept my spirits up. One of the happiest moments was that winter when they said they'd grant me another year. That was a great moment for me.

My final season was 1956. That spring, we installed the wing-T offense. Evy had consulted with Davey Nelson about this offense to better utilize our personnel. We learned the 100 series and went through those plays. Then we went through the 900 series, and then the counter series. They actually had blackboards out on the field, and we'd walk through the plays in this

Along with Eddie Vincent and Cal Jones, Frank Gilliam was an integral part of Iowa's famed "Steubenville Trio." His 1956 team was the first Iowa team to play in the Rose Bowl.

new system. It was made for a guy like our quarterback, Kenny Ploen. He was an outstanding athlete who could throw and run the ball. He was smart. Kenny was a good leader.

The offense was made for us collectively also, in that we weren't a large team. Our new blocking system used a lot of double-teams, especially at the point of attack, and a lot of misdirection and motion. We weren't big, but we were quick. It was a system seemingly designed for us. With all that motion, we had holes that sometimes you could drive a truck through. We caught guys off balance because they didn't know how to defend it.

We made it all the way to the Rose Bowl that year. Oregon State wasn't picked to win their conference either, but they came in with a good team. They ran the single wing offense, which is similar to the wing-T. I think they probably did the same thing on the West Coast as we did in the Midwest. Their team was athletic and relatively small like ours.

We were nip-and-tuck for a while in the Rose Bowl, but then we made some big plays. Mike Hagler made a real good run that kind of busted the game open for us. Ol' Mike ran what was called 138 criss-cross. I led the play, and when I got there, there wasn't anyone to block. I just turned inside and picked up a guy, and there went Mike. I looked up and saw Mike, and thought, *Aw, they're not gonna catch him now!* That kind of seemed to break the ice in that game, and we won 35–19.

I was drafted by the Green Bay Packers in 1957. I had some good days, and I had some bad days. They had a veteran team, but they weren't winning very much. It was the year before Lombardi came, and I think that's why he came in.

Then Bud Grant, who was coaching in the Canadian Football League, caught wind of me. They asked if I wanted to come to camp in Canada, and I agreed. I caught a plane and went up to Winnipeg. They had played a few games already, but I made the team and finished the season playing for them. We went to the Grey Cup, which is like our Super Bowl. I played a few more years in the CFL before I began coaching a junior college team from 1961 through the 1965 season.

That was before Ray Nagel, Iowa's new coach, called and asked if I wanted to be on his staff. I flew down to interview with Nagel in San Francisco, and he offered me the job. My first season was 1966, and I stayed there through 1970.

In December 1970 my former teammate, Jerry Reichow, called me. He was the director of player personnel for the Minnesota Vikings. They asked if I wanted to come up there and scout. At that time, Jerry was the only scout they had. Bud Grant was the head coach, and I had played for him in Canada. Jerry Burns was there also, so we all felt comfortable with each other. We knew and trusted each other, and I worked there for about 35 years.

To me, being a Hawkeye is all about the relationships. I met some really good people in my college experience who are friends I still talk to today. Man-for-man, we probably weren't as talented as Ohio State or Michigan, but as a team, we were in their class. We played together and were friends from day one.

I don't know how Evy managed to get that many guys to mesh together so quickly. There were guys like Jerry Reichow, who came from Decorah, Iowa. I came from Steubenville. We meshed like we'd known each other all our lives. Guys like Kenny Ploen and Bob Commings were there, as was John Burroughs. Earl Smith, Buck Stearnes, and Don Suchy—we all got along and played together. Jerry and I still talk regularly. And we're talking about relationships which started in 1952. I talk to Jeff Langston all the time. Eddie Vincent and I talk often, too. Orlando Pellegrino and I went to the Orange Bowl game together. Jim Gibbons and I are still close. I think the relationships we had as a team had a lot to do with the success we had on the field. Guys from the East meshed with guys from Iowa, Illinois, and Indiana. We had camaraderie, and all of those guys made me feel at home. That's what was special to me about my Iowa experience.

Frank Gilliam was one-third of Iowa's famed "Steubenville Trio" of the 1950s. Frank, along with Eddie Vincent and Cal Jones, was an integral part of Iowa's rise to prominence in the Big Ten under Forest Evashevski. Frank played both offensive and defensive end. He missed the 1955 season due to a leg injury, but was granted another year. His 1956 team was the first Iowa team to play in the Rose Bowl, where they handily defeated Oregon State for the second time that season. Gilliam was Iowa's leading receiver in both 1953 and 1954.

KEN PLOEN

Quarterback/ Defensive Back

1954–1956

My older brother, sister, and I grew up in Clinton, Iowa. I participated in all the major sports, as most everybody did, and I even had a chance to go to Kentucky on a basketball scholarship. But I happened to enjoy playing football, I guess, a little more than everything else. My older brother went to Iowa State, and he was out there when I was coming out of high school. They threw an offer at me to join him at Iowa State, but I had a chat with him. He knew what my dream was, and when I was awarded the Kinnick scholarship, there was no question in my mind that I wanted to go to the University of Iowa and try to make the Hawkeyes and play in the Big Ten. That was the decision that was made. It was not an easy one, but it was one where I look back and appreciate my brother's contribution on it because he backed me all the way. I couldn't have made a better choice.

We played both offense and defense. There were a lot of 60-minute ballplayers back then. Offense is the glory end of things, but I always liked playing defense. There's just something about playing defense. I was usually at a defensive halfback or defensive safety position. Particularly playing against teams like Purdue, where they had Lenny Dawson throwing the ball all over the field, was kind of fun back there, defending and going for interceptions and stuff.

I remember my senior year, we were picked—I don't know where the hell—the bottom half of the Big Ten, I know that. I know we had a lot of close games. We had a hell of a defensive team. Put that together with the new offense, and we won some pretty close games, most of them crucial. But we were always able to come out on top.

I was close to 6′2″ and maybe weighed 180 pounds. I was not a big, strapping, strong quarterback. We had been using the split-T stuff with the quarterback option going down the line of scrimmage and either running it or tossing it back. I think Evashevski recognized that I was not that type of quarterback. Not only that, but some of the linemen who we had were very mobile. We had pulling guards and tackles, and even some of our ends pulled on some of the plays. I think he looked at the personnel who were coming up my senior year, and Evashevski had a relationship with a guy by the name of Nelson from Delaware who came up with that wing-T offense. Evashevski brought it back from a coaches' convention and put it into our spring drills and actually built that offense around the talents not only of myself but the other seniors and juniors who were coming up. It fit to a tee, pardon the expression. They had never seen it in the Big Ten. I remember the opening game at Indiana—they couldn't figure out what the hell was going on.

You know, I always give credit to Evashevski. I thought he was one heck of a coach. Pro-wise it's a different story, but at the university level, I guess you have more influence. And he had great influence on us. He was a bit of a psychologist and could play with your head a little bit. He'd let us relax and have fun, and then he'd buckle down and say, "We're down to work." I thought he really handled us well over the season and was very instrumental in our success. He later proved that he was well worth it because he had a hell of a record when he was at Iowa.

It's hard to explain the atmosphere of Iowa City leading up to the Ohio State game. If you weren't there, I don't know how you put it into words. The whole student body—we were at a stage now where if we could win against Ohio State, we were probably going to go to the Rose Bowl. There were pep rallies. We got introduced here, there, and everywhere. It was a fun time, but it was a tough time, too, because there was a lot of pressure on us.

The touchdown pass to Jim Gibbons was a corner pattern. I came back and faked the ball to our halfback going to the right side and bootlegged out to the left. We had set that up with the running going down there. Jim Gibbons was just one hell of a receiver, not the fastest guy in the world but could really

Ken Ploen guided Iowa to its first ever Rose Bowl win in 1957 and was selected as the Rose Bowl MVP. He was inducted into the Canadian Football Hall of Fame in 1975 and was selected as the CFL's most outstanding player of the 1960s.

run a great pattern and turn defensive backs inside out. We had run the play successfully with Don Dobrino, running to the right off-tackle or around end on the sweep series. I kept noticing that defensively that end didn't pay a hell of a lot of attention to me when I faked the bootleg out there and the D-back was running over a bit, too. Gibbons went down and just took the guy in and ran him to the corner. Of course, I kept the ball, and he was so wide open that I was scared I'd miss him. It wasn't a long pass or anything. It was a play that was set up and executed well, and it turned out to be the main thing.

The interesting thing is [Bob] Prescott was our kicker, and he had made I don't know how many straight kicks, and he missed this one. It was the first miss I think he had that whole season. Now we were up 6–0 with a bit of a game to play yet. I thought, *Oh my God, if we end up losing this game 7–6, I'm gonna really be disappointed.* But the defense never let Ohio State even threaten. We had a great defensive unit, and they just shut 'em out. There was no way they could score. I don't know if they ever got across the 50-yard line in the latter part of that game because the defense really clamped down.

We had quite a history with Notre Dame. I know when I was a freshman, I wasn't even playing, but they tied us 14–14 when Notre Dame faked a couple of injuries. Well, my senior year, we had cinched the Big Ten. It was our last game in Iowa City, and we were relaxed. Evy said, "Just go out there and have fun," and we did. We just went out and kicked their butts 48–8. It was a very satisfying win, I can tell you.

That Rose Bowl was almost like a dream. We got ahead enough on 'em that almost everybody got to play. But there were a couple of plays in there that I really remember. I scored the first points of the game on a 49-yard run for a touchdown. That opening run was just a rollout pass to the right. The receivers were covered pretty well, and I had to take off. I got a couple of good blocks thrown for me, and the next thing I knew, I dodged a couple of guys and ended up in the end zone. How it happened and why it happened, who knows? It was just one of those plays. But we got off to a good start, and the defense was tough.

I missed a few plays in the second quarter because of a knee injury again, which still comes up occasionally. I got whomped on the side of it. But I got it taped up at halftime, and it held up, and I was able to play the second half. I know I threw a touchdown pass again to Gibbons on a similar play that we took against Ohio State. We had a great game out at the Rose Bowl, there's no question about that. It was a thrill of a lifetime because it was a dream of a lifetime to go out there and play in it, win, and then get the MVP. I couldn't ask for anything better.

I ended up being drafted after school by the Cleveland Browns, and I was actually drafted by them as a defensive back, not as a quarterback. That's one of the reasons I came to Canada. I had an opportunity with Bud Grant to come up here and play offense at quarterback immediately. Eagle Day, who was the starting quarterback here, had a kidney problem and had to sit out 1957, my first year in the pros, so the quarterback spot was wide open. I ended up playing quarterback and a lot of defense here in Canada.

You can run through the whole entire team; they're all important. That Rose Bowl team was a closely knit team. We went to classes together, we partied together, we played football together, we double-dated together—we did a lot of things together. I always enjoyed Don Dobrino, who was a big, strong, Polish boy and my roommate on trips. He played halfback and didn't have great breakaway speed or anything, but he was a powerful runner. When you needed a few yards, he was the guy to give the ball to, because he'd get the job done.

Jim Gibbons was a type of guy who could catch a ball in a crowd or go deep for you. He ran great patterns, and he was also a good blocker. I don't know if people realized or understood this, but back then when we ran that wing-T offense, the ends had to pull a number of times and come down the line behind it and open up a hole going on the other side of the line. Gibbons was certainly capable of doing that. You put those things all together, and it takes a special individual and a special athlete to do it.

Cal Jones played for Winnipeg and was an All-Star his first year in the CFL. He was at the All-Star Game and was supposed to come home. He decided he was going to stay over and come out the next day on a plane. He didn't go back with a good friend of mine who came up here from Minnesota, Bob McNamara. Bob went back, but Cal stayed over and got up the next morning and got on a plane. And that's the one that had to turn around for some reason and head back to Vancouver because of mechanical problems. Evidently this one mountain was high enough, and they didn't have radar or whatever the hell it was in that day. They flew right into the damn thing and killed the whole bunch—not only Cal, but [Gordon] Sturtridge and [Mario] DeMarco from the Saskatchewan Roughriders were on that flight, too. There were a few All-Star players who got killed in that crash.

I couldn't say enough about Cal Jones as a leader, as a football player, as a 60-minute man. He played offense, defense, didn't matter. He was rantin' and ravin' on that field. He was a great individual. Three great players came out to Iowa of that Steubenville Trio, and Cal stands out there pretty high.

There are personalities all over the place on a football team. Regardless of what you say about a guy, Alex Karras—he was a bit different and everything—but I'll tell you, on a football field, he was one heck of a ballplayer. For a big man, and he was, he was very quick on his feet and had a strong upper body. He was one great football player and went on to the pros and played very well with the Detroit Lions. In fact, I think he was one of their top draft choices.

Randy Duncan was a sophomore when I was a senior, and naturally he showed great potential right off the bat. He was not a great running quarterback but was a good thrower. I remember the first Oregon State game where he came back and actually won the game for us, and he participated in the Rose Bowl. He was an intelligent guy. He was a good ball handler and a great passer, and he could run—that just wasn't his strong point. If you look at the two of us, I was a better runner than I was a passer; he was a better passer than he was a runner. But it worked successfully for both of us.

In essence, we had no real, as I call it, superstars on our club. Although we had some damn good football players, nobody was out there to try to make himself look great. They just became part of the team and everybody did their job, and on certain games, one guy would stand out. The next game, another guy would stand out. As a quarterback calling plays, there wasn't just one go-to guy. You could almost depend on anybody at any time because the balance and talent were there.

The emphasis was always on the team aspect. I know that Karras stood out a bit, but Jim Gibbons did, too, and Don Dobrino at times. Even Duncan did when he got in. We had Bill Happel, John Nocera, Fred Harris, Don Suchy. I could go on. All these guys who played on that club were good ballplayers and good team players, and we just hit it off and came together and we weren't gonna get beat.

I've been able to return for a couple of Hawkeye games at different times through the years. I follow them whenever I can up here in newspapers, but they don't cover U.S. sports that much. I used to get the *Des Moines Register* up here all the time, just to keep myself informed. I follow Iowa and the Big Ten as much as I can. We get a lot of U.S. channels now, and we can cover the sports through it pretty well.

Being a Hawkeye means quite a bit to me. I can tell you I have a cottage on the lake. I go out fishing, and everybody always recognizes me because I've got an "I" on my cap that I wear. And I also have a shirt that's got a little Herky on it, so I'm easily recognized out on the lake. They all know where I'm from and where my roots are from and always will be.

As Iowa's starting quarterback in 1956, Ken Ploen helped lead Iowa to its first Big Ten championship in 34 years and won the *Chicago Tribune* Silver Football as the Big Ten's MVP. He finished ninth in the Heisman Trophy balloting and was named a first-team All-American. Ploen guided Iowa to its first ever Rose Bowl win in 1957 and was selected as the Rose Bowl MVP. He then played 11 seasons in the Canadian Football League for the Winnipeg Blue Bombers, leading his team to six Grey Cup appearances and four victories. Ken Ploen was inducted into the Canadian Football Hall of Fame in 1975 and was selected as the CFL's most outstanding player of the 1960s in 2009. Ploen lives in Winnipeg, Manitoba, Canada.

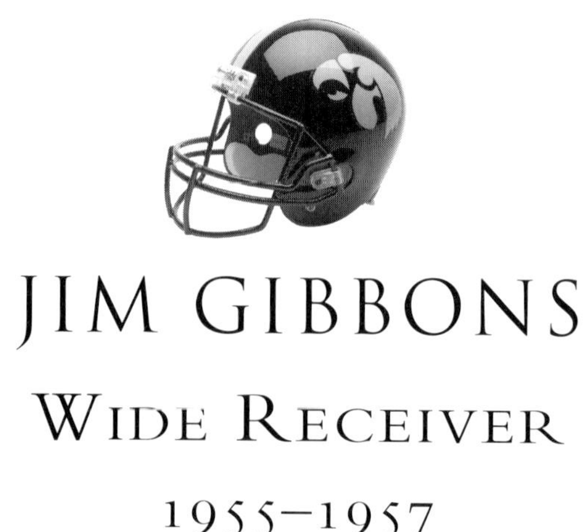

JIM GIBBONS

Wide Receiver

1955–1957

I grew up on the South Side of Chicago. As the oldest of five boys, I felt responsible for setting a good example for my brothers, such as being the first to graduate from a university. My dad was a typical Midwest working-class guy and a good family man. He worked in a General Motors factory his whole life. He had a great work ethic and was a good father. My mother was very supportive and loyal to her kids to the extreme. She was a loving mother who always spoke in a positive way about our team and my involvement.

I played football for Lindblom High School my junior and senior years. Unfortunately, our team never won a game. They actually won the city championship the year before I played and the year after I played, so I'm not sure what that says about my contribution. It was a very humbling experience, but I still loved playing the game, and I loved the coaches we had. The coach there was Dutch Von Bremer, and he played tackle for Wisconsin. I played offensive tackle and defensive end, but I always talked to him about playing offensive end and receiver. I felt I could contribute more for the team and to the game as an offensive end.

I also did some speed skating in high school with a longtime friend of mine named Bob Stifter. I was never very good at it, but it was great conditioning for the following season. Bob was actually very good. I loved the sport but wasn't quite fast enough. Other than football and speed skating, I played a lot of recreational baseball and basketball. Sports were pretty much my life, so I was always involved in something.

I was recruited to play football by quite a few teams. Looking back, I really don't know why, given that we didn't win a game. I think it was mostly because of my size. I was a big kid then. In the eighth grade, I was 6′2″ and 180 pounds. I had a lot of fun going to a variety of different campuses and meeting the coaches. Bob Stifter and I went to the campuses together, so that was fun for both of us, especially since these were our first trips away from home out on our own.

I received about 30 recruiting letters from different schools, and I visited about five of them. We went to Indiana and Northwestern to see what they were like, and also a couple of smaller schools. It was an eye-opener to visit the campuses and cities, comparing notes with other athletes, seeing the schools, meeting some of the students, and talking to the coaches. When we visited the University of Iowa, they took us to the Amana Colonies outside of Iowa City for family-style cooking. The friendliness of the people and the interest they showed toward us was memorable, and I pretty much fell in love with the Iowa people. I met people who were very supportive. Back home in Chicago, I didn't know people a block away from me. People were supportive, and it created just a great environment for me. Plus, their desire for us to play for Forest Evashevski was strong. I met with Coach Evashevski and his coaching staff, who had only been there for a few years.

I narrowed it down to two schools: Northwestern University and the University of Iowa. Northwestern was so close to home I figured I should visit there. But while there, a few derogatory things were said by a Northwestern coach toward Iowa about farmers and stuff like that. I remember that I was watching the Northwestern basketball game when he said that. Afterward, I was driving home thinking, *If he says that about Iowa people, what will he say about me after I walk out the door?* I got home and told my folks I was going to Iowa. That was where I wanted to be.

I had never played offensive end or caught a pass in a game when I asked the Iowa coaching staff if I could change my position. I wanted to go from tackle to receiver and defensive end, since at that time you had to play both ways. They said they would try me out and see what developed. I caught a touchdown pass in the spring game, and I guess it made an impression on them. I played offensive end and defensive end from then on.

At that time you had to play freshman football the first year and succeed with your grades before you had an opportunity to make the varsity squad. We had a good freshman team. Alex Karras was there; it was a whole different level from high school. We'd scrimmage the varsity and do very well against them, so we knew we had good potential going into our sophomore year.

The following year, a lot of us sophomores started. My good friend Frankie Gilliam broke his leg on the first play of the first game that year against Kansas State. It was a bad break for him but a good break for me—if you can call it that—because I was his backup. It gave me the opportunity to start the rest of 1955. I still talk to Frankie, and we laugh about what happened. Fortunately, he was able to redshirt that year. He played the next year and helped us go to the Rose Bowl.

We changed our offense before the 1956 season to the wing-T. It was an old-style offense led by our senior quarterback, Kenny Ploen. He was a great athlete. He could do it all; he could run, throw the ball, play defense.

We had a strong defensive team. That year we won games 7–0, 6–0, so you knew we had to play defense. We stopped a lot of teams. I played defensive end my whole life and loved it. I was there with Frankie Gilliam on the other side. Frankie was a great defensive end. He was probably as good a defensive end as anybody I've ever seen. He was only about 180 pounds, but he was so athletic. Frank was, and is, special to me.

I imagine the game most people remember me for is Kenny's pass to me against Ohio State during my junior year. In our offense we ran so much, but every once in a while we'd throw in a pass. We got down near the goal line, and they called my play. The pass was great. I caught it and scored. I probably get more credit than I deserve, but that's just the way it is. I was the guy who made the catch; it could have been Frankie or somebody else. I think it was that kind of a team we had. Everybody contributed, and whoever made the play at the right time, that's just the way it was. I was fortunate enough to be the guy who made that catch. It was the only score of the game, and the win sent us to the Rose Bowl to represent the Big Ten.

The Rose Bowl was great. It was our chance to go to the big stage. The media blew us way out of proportion, and Evashevski really jumped on that. He said, "All they're doing is building you up for a letdown." He probably worked us harder than he had the whole year. We got in the game, and it was just the way it was coached. Thank Evashevski for that. We were prepared, and we never thought about losing.

The Hawkeyes' receiver from 1955 to 1957, Jim Gibbons was voted All–Big Ten and All-America his senior year.

During my senior year of 1957, I was honored to be elected team captain. I played on a great college football team that only lost one game—to Ohio State. Back then the rules did not allow a team to go to the Rose Bowl two years in a row; otherwise we would have gone again. That rule was changed soon after.

I was voted All-America and All–Big Ten. I was selected to play in the Hula Bowl, the College All-Star Game where we beat the Detroit Lions, the Senior Bowl, plus the East-West Shrine Game. I played in so many postseason games that the department chair made me take an individual oral exam for anatomy/kinesiology. She said she'd never allow any player to take that class and compete in all of the extra games again (oh yes, I passed!).

Being a team player and playing on a team that was coached by Forest Evashevski and his staff was a great experience. It taught me the value of playing as a group, with each player focusing on doing his part to accomplish success. Coach Evashevski would always say, "Do your job, give 110 percent, and we will be successful." He has been a role model throughout my life, and I have tried to pass this philosophy on to my four kids. Like I've said, this has been my philosophy, so if this is wrong, my whole life has been wrong, but I don't think so.

I met my wife, Lila Morgan, in high school at the age of 16. She was a cheerleader, and it was love at first sight. Lila and I were married in college just a few weeks before our senior year in 1957, and two weeks before I reported back to the team for summer practice. Lila and I almost made it to our 50th wedding anniversary, but she unexpectedly passed away in her sleep from a heart attack in December 2004. On November 3, 2007, I married Gayle Van Voorhis, a wonderful California girl who moved to Colorado and is now my life partner and love of my life. She is great for me, and I think I am good for her. We make a great team. Evy would be proud.

My Christian church, my parents, and my brothers played a very important part in my formative years, and that continues today. Another lifetime important friendship (from kindergarten to today) is with my Hawkeye teammate Bob Stifter, who is like a brother to me. Bob is such a fine, honest person and a great athlete. I have continued to maintain contact with past teammates such as Jeff Langston, Frankie Gilliam, Fred Harris, my old quarterbacks Jerry Reichow and Randy Duncan, plus teammate and all-time great Alex Karras.

Alex was a very shy guy in college—he didn't say boo. I remember after his sophomore year, Evashevski told him if he didn't come back in shape, he wasn't going to have a scholarship. Alex came back at 235 pounds, and from his junior year on he was Alex Karras, the great football player. I went to Detroit with him in the pros. I was drafted by Cleveland and then traded to Detroit before the first league game. My wife and I stayed with Alex and his wife for two months and had a great time with them. I got to know him really well, and it's like somebody opened up a Pandora's Box. Alex went from a shy, quiet offensive and defensive lineman to a showman. But he was a great player and a great guy. I still have a lot of respect for him.

Jerry Reichow was my quarterback at both Iowa and Detroit. It was very comfortable for me coming into that offense. The Lions also had a great team and presented a wonderful opportunity for me to play and start my rookie year. The fans were great.

There are a lot of thanks to give for my time at Iowa. Evashevski was a big influence, so I owe a lot to him. Jerry Reichow, Kenny Ploen, and Randy Duncan were my quarterbacks. A receiver is nothing without his quarterback. I'm just a guy running out there hoping to get a ball. They threw the ball to me, it was my job to catch it, and I did. We built up a good trust during practice and before the season started. And that's important. The linemen are the backbone of the team, and you know how important they are.

My Iowa experience gave me a great example of how to live. Coach Evashevski, along with assistant coaches like Whitey Piro, Bob Flora, Bump Elliott, and Archie Kodros, set a wonderful example from which to learn. They taught us how to work as a team and how to win with humility and dignity. I attended a tremendous university. It was a great time in my life, and I am proud to be a Hawkeye.

Jim Gibbons is a Chicago native who played receiver at Iowa from 1955 to 1957. His most memorable moment to Hawkeye fans may be his 1956 touchdown reception from quarterback Ken Ploen to beat highly ranked Ohio State 6–0. During his senior year, he was voted All–Big Ten and All-America. He played 11 years for the Detroit Lions and made the Pro Bowl three times. Gibbons currently lives in Colorado.

RANDY DUNCAN

Quarterback

1956–1958

I was always very interested in sports and played them all. I spent most of my life growing up playing football, basketball, and baseball. Actually, two schools recruited me for college basketball: Iowa State and Wyoming, I think. At Iowa State, they told me I could play football and basketball, but I decided I wanted to play football instead and just concentrate on one sport. I had a lot of friends who went to the University of Colorado. My sister went there. I've always loved that school, but I'm glad I went to Iowa.

Bump Elliott was basically my recruiter, and Jerry Burns also helped recruit me. Bump was the backfield coach, and he was obviously a great football player himself. I met him during recruiting my senior year of high school. He was just a personable guy, a nice guy, and the kind of guy you want to play for. He was a hell of a recruiter, by the way. He could sell you about anything. Jerry was good, too. Jerry was only about 24 or 25, and he was still an assistant. Between those two guys, I really felt good. Jerry Hilgenberg was also one of my coaches and a good guy. He had just played in '53. I did meet Forest Evashevski a couple times and talked to him, but I basically was recruited by Bump.

Evashevski played a big role in my development. He was on my back so much all the time that I wanted to prove to him that I could be a player. That was his style. If you ran 70 yards for a touchdown, he would chew you out for not making it 80 yards. His philosophy was, "Keep driving. Keep driving. Don't praise anybody, get 'em pumped up, and always have somebody who's waiting to take your job." He wanted competition at every position. Evashevski was a great coach.

The biggest thing about Evashevski was that he was willing to change his whole offense or his whole defense for one game. He really didn't just stick to one thing. He pulled a lot of things on coaches that drove them nuts, because they'd prepare for one thing, and then all of a sudden here he'd come out in a single wing. I know he drove Woody Hayes nuts with his innovations. Now it's all about execution. Most people know where Kirk Ferentz is going. He can point to where he's going and say, "Now see if you can stop me."

I was a mid-year graduate, so I graduated in January 1955 and went right down to the University of Iowa. They hardly knew my name when I got there. I went there thinking I was going to be able to throw the football and be a quarterback, and they put me on defense all the time. I played with the scout squad for a year and a half, and it wasn't much fun because I didn't get to throw the ball much. We'd run the other teams' plays and get killed. Playing against Calvin Jones and those guys wasn't much fun. They had a good team in 1955. I thought about transferring to Iowa State my freshman year, but I think every player thinks about transferring. You just sit there your freshman year.

The first game I played as a sophomore I don't even remember because I hit my head—I don't remember anything about that game against Indiana. I had my ankle shot up before the second game of the year against Oregon State. I had a high ankle sprain the week before, and I could hardly walk. They shot me with novocaine, but I felt like I was on a stump. Bump saw me working out and said, "You're not going to play today." But Ken Ploen got hurt, and the other quarterback, Gene Veit, didn't get 'em moving. In the fourth quarter, Bump put me in, and we went for two touchdowns to beat Oregon State 14–13. I threw a touchdown pass to Jim Gibbons, and that was probably the best game I played that year. But I was on an ankle I couldn't even feel.

Ken Ploen was a great athlete—basketball player, track man, football player. But his greatest asset was the way he ran the football. Kenny was a runner. They had moved him from halfback to quarterback. Nobody ever really got a good piece of him. He was just one of those guys who was so hard to tackle because he was so elusive. He was a great guy and just a sensational athlete—he really was. We had a great relationship. I'd say we were different. He was a really good runner but didn't throw that well. I couldn't run and I'd get drilled. So we were entirely different types of quarterbacks. He was a sensational football player. It didn't bother me a bit playing behind him in 1956 because I should have been behind him.

Playing in the Rose Bowl was just great. My memory of that first Rose Bowl is coming out and seeing that blue sky and the green grass and all the people. It was just a beautiful setting and a great day to play a football game. And we blew Oregon State out.

In my first Big Ten game as a starter in 1957, we played Indiana. It hadn't rained in three weeks in Brown County, and we were in mud. We had our visiting whites on and were all muddy just in warm-ups! And Evashevski went crazy. He said, "I've never ever had a coach water a field on me before! This is an insult to the University of Iowa and our team." And then we went out and just killed 'em. I was sitting next to assistant coach Bob Flora on the way home, and we were talking about the game. He said, "It reminds me of the 1954 game when Notre Dame came into Iowa City and they had all those great backs. Evashevski got the whole staff up at midnight, and they went out and watered the field down." I said, "Oh, well, I thought he was so mad at Indiana!" Flora said, "Ah, that's just part of the game." That was his psychological gamesmanship.

I always had leg cramps. Against Michigan that year, I had to leave the game several times with those cramps. I got back in that game, and it was tied, and we had the momentum going. We had been down at halftime, and we all wanted to go in and try for a score. But Evashevski didn't want to; he wanted to keep that tie and not take a chance. We were called "The Team That Quit" by *Time* magazine the next week, which kind of hurt.

We went down to Columbus the second-to-last game of the year. They were No. 1 and we were No. 3, and we both were undefeated. We moved the ball all over the field on them; we really beat them. But we were inside their 20-yard line three times and fumbled the ball all three times, and they beat us by four points. Then they went on to win the Rose Bowl. They wound up being No. 1, and we wound up being No. 5.

That 1957 Hawkeye team wasn't better than the following year's team, but it was pretty good. The 1958 team had more speed by far, but the 1957 team had Karras and Dick Klein at the tackles. We had two great tackles, and two great tackles make a big difference on a team. So the '57 team was a better defensive team by a long ways.

I think Evashevski said that the tie against Air Force was what made our team what it was in 1958 because we were pretty fat and happy. We had beaten TCU the week before quite handily, and they were supposed to be

Randy Duncan finished second in the Heisman Trophy balloting in 1958 and was the first player in school history to earn unanimous first-team All-America honors that year.

the best team in their conference. They were preseason rated sixth. So we felt we were pretty good, and then Air Force brought us down to earth in a hurry. That really did help our season.

Bob Jeter, Willie Fleming, Ray Jauch, and Kevin Furlong—these are four great backs, and we had two good fullbacks—Johnny Nocera and Don Horn. There was just a lot of firepower on that team. Offensively, we could run and throw. That was quite a football team. We were undefeated until Ohio State came in there and beat us. We'd already clinched the Big Ten, but that didn't make any difference. Whoever had the ball last was going to win, and they happened to have it last, and they beat us. But it was quite a football game. We just moved the ball up and down the field both ways. We couldn't stop them, and they couldn't stop us.

After the second Rose Bowl, I think we came off of that field thinking, *Man, California would have been about middle of the pack in the Big Ten.* We just steamrolled them. We had a big lead, and then I think all the reserves got to play, which was great. It was a real kicking.

After I graduated, I had had a couple of calls about pro football, but I told the Green Bay general manager that I'm not going to go to any town that didn't have a law school in it. Green Bay didn't have a law school, but they went ahead and drafted me anyway. Then they didn't offer me as much money, so I went up to Canada. I was going to go to law school in Canada until I found out that the University of British Columbia law school had English common law, which wouldn't transfer back down to the States. Anyway, in those days, being a top NFL draft pick wasn't that big of a deal, and you didn't get paid much money, either—not like today.

I learned a lot from Evashevski, but the biggest lesson I learned from him was preparation. One thing Evashevski always said was, "It's not the will to win that counts. Everybody wants to win on Saturday. It's the will to prepare to win." That is so true and really true in the law. I'll tell you something—give me a guy who works hard over a guy who's got talent but doesn't work as hard. There was another great quote from Evashevski—he used to use it all the time—he said, "It is no sin to lose a football game, but it's the rankest kind of shame to be outfought in a football game."

I was a radio commentator with Jim Zabel for the Hawkeyes in the mid-1960s during all those years when Iowa couldn't win any games. Those were rough years, and I knew Jerry Burns and Ray Nagel, and I hated to see coaches getting fired. There was a lot of turmoil in Iowa City in those days, and a lot of it was conflict between Evashevski and Burns, Evashevski and Nagel. Then [Frank] Lauterbur and [Bob] Commings came in, and they didn't get it done. And then, finally, Bump hired Hayden Fry in 1979, and that was the start of this new era of Iowa football.

Hayden Fry resurrected that program. It had been two decades between winning seasons, and he came in and changed the whole mind-set. He sometimes put up a front like he didn't work hard and he was just this good ol' boy, but behind the scenes he was a hard worker and was in there outsmarting a lot of coaches. And Kirk Ferentz—you can't say enough about this guy. He's a class act and a guy you're proud of to represent the University of Iowa, plus he's recruiting pretty good athletes now. Take a look at the NFL and see how many Iowa guys are in there. There are a lot of his kids in there now. He's a great guy. He had me back as an honorary captain once. That's a great tradition he has going there. He's building a hell of an Iowa tradition, and I think that's great.

I'll always be an Iowan and a Hawkeye, and I just can't feel anything except great pride in being an Iowan and being able to represent the University of Iowa on a national level. That was a great time in my life. I'm proud that I still live in Iowa. I've got a lot of pride in Iowa, and I think one of the things that we lack in this state is sometimes we don't have enough pride in our own state and our own university. Having good football, although it's not the most important thing, helps give us pride in our state, and I feel proud that I was part of that tradition.

Randy Duncan led the nation in completion percentage and passing yardage as a senior in 1958 and was named the Big Ten's MVP. He led Iowa on touchdown drives in both the 1957 and 1959 Rose Bowl victories, and his lone touchdown pass in the 1959 Rose Bowl broke the school record for touchdown passes in a season, which had been set by Nile Kinnick in 1939. Duncan finished second in the Heisman Trophy balloting in 1958 and was the first player in school history to earn unanimous first-team All-America honors that year. He became the only Hawkeye ever drafted No. 1 overall in the NFL Draft when he was selected by the Green Bay Packers with the first overall pick in 1959. After graduating from Drake Law School in 1963, Duncan operated a successful law firm in Des Moines for several decades. Randy Duncan was inducted into the College Football Hall of Fame in 1997.

JEFF LANGSTON
OFFENSIVE END/ DEFENSIVE END
1956, 1958–1959

I've wanted to be a Hawkeye for as long as I can remember. I tell people I played with five All-America ends at Iowa. The first was Bill Fenton—he was my hero. He was at Iowa before me, but we used to work out in the summer together. We both went to Iowa City High School, and he was just like an older brother. Then came Frank Gilliam, who was All-America in 1956. We're great friends to this day. I played behind Jim Gibbons as a sophomore in 1956. He was from Chicago, and we were in a dog fight for playing time. He was All-America in 1957, and one of my best friends on that team. Then Curt Merz was All-America in 1958. Don Norton was All-America in 1959. We were also very close and spent a lot of time together. Norton was a real "burner;" he could really run. I was in great company with those five players.

I was all-state at Iowa City High and began drawing attention from Coach Evashevski's staff in 1954. We could get into all the practices and the games, so I grew up over there at Iowa football practice. I was always around the Hawks. I had a chance to go to other schools, such as Michigan, Wisconsin, and Missouri. My dad was a southerner and somewhat hoped I might go south. But Dad said he thought Evashevski was going to build a great program here at Iowa, and he liked him.

My recruiting process was a slam dunk—I didn't even take recruiting trips to other schools because all I'd ever wanted was to be a Hawkeye. When assistant coach Whitey Piro said he'd like me to come to Iowa, I just said, "Sure, where do I sign?"

I was an end on the 1955 freshman team and also ran quarterback; they moved me back and forth. We had so many high school All-Americans it was unbelievable. It was nerve-wracking because a lot of people didn't think I was going to make the team. They thought I wasn't big enough. I was 6′1″, but only weighed about 180 pounds. I was so anxious I often threw up before practice.

I lettered in 1956, and we had a great team. Bob Commings, a future coach of the Hawkeyes, was a friend and coach to me. Kenny Ploen was our quarterback. He was really the nucleus of that team. He was a good runner and passer and a tremendous defensive back. Kenny went to Clinton High School, and I had to try to guard him in high school basketball. He was a tremendous athlete. We didn't throw the ball much in our 1956 Rose Bowl season. Evy's genius to me was that he changed his offense for his personnel. That year we were more of a running team and defensive team.

It was a monumental step for Iowa to make the Rose Bowl in 1956. That's the first time Iowa had been to a bowl game. The Hawkeyes hadn't done much since 1939, and we had stars in our eyes just breathing that California air.

We worked hard during the day, and then they gave us cars at night to go out and explore. There were all kinds of Iowa alums having parties for us. One night we went down to Long Beach with probably 25 guys or more—it was a big alumni party. Everybody got in their cars and went back to Pasadena, and I was offered a ride with an alum. He ran into a culvert, and I dislocated my hip. Thank God there wasn't anyone else in the car and no one else got hurt. I woke up in the hospital, where I was told that I would never play football again and that I would need a series of surgeries to walk.

Several days after the accident, some of my teammates came to the hospital to visit and to tell me that I was no longer on the team. I was devastated. The accident happened before the game, so of course I didn't get to play in the Rose Bowl that year or the entire 1957 season. I was put in traction and kept in bed for six weeks, which was what they did in those days. Then I had crutches for six months. With the support of Dr. Webb Gelman at Mercy Hospital, I decided to refuse surgery, opting instead for physical therapy for a year—stretching, then swimming, then lifting and running. In early 1958 before spring practice, Evashevski, who hadn't spoken to me since

A late-December 1956 car accident just before Iowa's first Rose Bowl appearance took Jeff Langston out of the game. Doctors told him he would never play football again, but he returned to the field and lettered in both 1958 and 1959.

the accident, sent Whitey Piro to ask me if I wanted to come back out for football. I couldn't wait!

I came out again in the spring of 1958. Our trainer, Arnie Buntrock, told me to protect my right hip—to protect that side when I got tackled. I said,

"I'll try, Arnie, but I'm just gonna play." I was a step slower, and I had an atrophied right leg that never did fully come back from being laid up so long.

I had a great spring practice and a really good 1958 season. I had a super game at Wisconsin. We were getting beat 9–0 in Madison when Norton hit Dale Hackbart. I grabbed the ball in the air and ran it in for a touchdown. Then Bob Jeter scored later, and we won the game. That game was a turning point in 1958. I was voted "Unsung Hero" by the AP that week and got a lot of ribbing from my teammates for that. Randy Duncan, our quarterback, was a great passer and should have won the Heisman Trophy, for which he was voted runner-up. With Jeter, [Willie] Fleming, [Johnny] Nocera, [Ray] Jauch, and [Kevin] Furlong running, we had so many ways we could score. Our offense was second to none. We were a really balanced team.

As good as all those guys were, in my opinion Willie Fleming was the key to the 1958 team. He scored two touchdowns outside the 30-yard line in five or six games, and Evy didn't even play him the first three games. Jerry Burns told us 50 years later that Willie Fleming was the greatest running back he ever coached. Jerry said, "I've seen a lot of running backs, and Willie was the best. He was right up there with Gale Sayers."

We went to the Rose Bowl again in 1959. I started that game and caught the only touchdown pass. We just ran all over California. I had a great game. They called me "the Comeback Kid." The whole season was memorable because I considered myself the luckiest Hawkeye ever to be able to have a second chance at the Rose Bowl. To be able to go back and not only play in the Rose Bowl but start and be on that national championship team was wonderful. The 1958 team is the only Iowa team to be ranked No. 1 at the end of the year by the Football Writers of America. I was told by Coach Hayden Fry, who was the defensive coordinator for Baylor in 1958 and beat LSU, that in his opinion Iowa was a better team than LSU. I think we would have been voted No. 1 over LSU by both polls if they'd voted after the bowl games. The 1958 team was one of the greatest in the history of Hawkeye football. Our offense was virtually unstoppable. We had a great offensive line, backs who were fast, and receivers who dropped nothing. You couldn't have written a better ending had it ended right there. We didn't know it at the time, but 1959 was the second-to-last year Evy would coach Iowa.

In 1962 I was having dinner with Evashevski and Fritz Crisler in Washington, D.C., at an athletics directors' conference. It was just the three of us, and I was very nervous: there I was with my coach, and Evy with his—three generations. We spent the whole night together talking, and I was listening hard. In fact, Evy did a lot of listening, too, because Crisler was his old coach. I heard a lot of inside stories about Evashevski that night. I remember Crisler telling me, "You know, son, if you'd come to Michigan, I would have gotten a lot more out of you than he did." Evy didn't say a word! He was uncharacteristically quiet that night; I'd never been around Evashevski when he didn't dominate the room or whomever he was talking to. He just had that physical and mental presence that was beyond everybody. He was a psychologist. He was a powerful man physically, and was mentally very sharp. You could hardly get the best of him. The only time he lost was at the tail end of his athletic department skirmish. But he never lost as a coach, I'll tell you that. Not everybody on his teams liked him, but they all respected him.

Since I left Iowa I've been in some form of financial services or real estate the whole time. I still follow the Hawkeyes, and I love Coach Kirk Ferentz. I've been to some practices, and he treats you like you were there playing under him just five years ago. I have grandchildren who live in Iowa, and two daughters who live there. I have a lot of high school friends there also.

Being a Hawkeye was my whole life from 13 years of age through my early twenties. That's all I wanted to do. Then I got there, I lost it, and I got it back. I was lucky enough to have another shot at it. I always told my children that being on the team is its own reward. You don't have to be the star. We were a band of brothers. To this day, I can say that some of my best friends were my teammates. During my time, we were Big Ten champions in '56 and '58, won the Rose Bowl twice, and were national champions in 1958. I couldn't even think of having played anywhere else. To be a Hawkeye meant everything to me. It still does.

Jeff Langston was set to play in Iowa's first Rose Bowl appearance on January 1, 1957. A severe car accident in December 1956 held him out of competition during that game and the entire 1957 season. Langston returned to the team in 1958. In the 1959 Rose Bowl, he hauled in Iowa's only touchdown reception to help Iowa defeat California.

RAY JAUCH

Halfback/Defensive Back

1957–1959

I remember in the spring of 1957 I walked out to spring practice. It seemed like there must have been 150 guys out there on the field. Evy called us all together and said, "Some people think you're here to get an education. We know why you're here. Buckle your helmets." And we practiced for about three hours. Of course, that was not really the true Evy. Evy did value the education we were getting, but he wanted to let us know it was time to concentrate on football.

At that time, Iowa was only about 10,000 students, and the city was only about 10,000 people, too, I think. It wasn't very big, and it reminded me in a whole lot of ways of Mendota, Illinois, where I was born and raised. Everybody knew each other. Once you got in there, the townspeople were tremendous. They were just outstanding. Guys from all over the town knew you and talked to you on the street. It was just a very friendly place to be.

I think our '57 team was one of the best teams Iowa ever had. We had Alex Karras and Dick Klein, future NFL players, at tackle. We had Jim Gibbons and Randy Duncan, who was a junior at the time. We had two guards, Hugh Drake and Gary Grouwinkel. I went up and played pro ball for Canada, and those guys could have played up there very easily. We had a lot of really good players on that team. We only got beat one game, over at Ohio State, but we were up there very high in the nation at that time. I think it was one of the best teams that Iowa has had for a long time.

Ray Jauch led the nation in average yards per carry in 1958 and led the Hawkeyes in interceptions in 1959.

Playing for the 1958 Big Ten championship team was a real thrill. Early on, I put a lot of time in on the field because we played both ways. We had some guys playing 58 minutes of the game. As far as accomplishments, I didn't even know that I was the team's leading rusher. We didn't pay attention to any of that, and we didn't really care. All we wanted to do was win. It wasn't an individual thing.

I'll tell you an achievement that I felt very proud of, though. Every year the *Chattanooga Times* picked an All-America team of the best blockers, and I made first-team All-America on the *Chattanooga Times'* blocking team. Three fullbacks and I were in the backfield. I thought that was quite good because I was noted as a runner primarily, but I could block, too!

I remember our game with Michigan in 1958. Between Bobby Jeter, Willie Fleming, and me, we had five touchdowns in that game, and I had the longest run from scrimmage in the Big Ten that year—74 yards. There was a picture in the *Des Moines Register* of the three of us together. We looked like a big Oreo cookie—I was in the middle, and Bobby and Willie were next to me. What can I say? It was just a wonderful time. What was hard is that you only carried the ball seven or eight times a game. It's not like today, where some guys carry it 25 times a game. If we carried it eight times, that was a lot. I think my whole junior year I only carried the ball 72 times in nine games. Evy's offense really spread it around. So when you got the ball, you had to make the best of it! I give credit to our offensive line. We had a really good offensive line, and if I had any success, it was due to those guys. I have no qualms about that at all.

We had a great time in Pasadena. We practiced hard twice a day. Evy put us through some pretty good practices while we were there, but we still got to see quite a bit of the area. I had some friends out there whom I visited, and my parents came out. It was wonderful. Just going into that Rose Bowl and playing in the game was a great thrill. Bobby Jeter had a great day. The rest of us were just kind of bit players in it because it was Bobby's day. I was really happy for him. Bobby was always one of my good friends. We came into Iowa together in the same year. We were on the freshman team together and played together three years. I started a charity in my hometown to help support football in the community. Bobby would always come every year when I'd have celebrities come in. He was just a wonderful guy, and he was a good friend in college and afterward.

I was a cocaptain my senior year with Don Norton. It was very special because Don and I were roommates and great friends. It was a great honor to be recognized that way, because there is no greater honor as a man than to be recognized by your peers. I could tell you a lot of stories about Norton, but I don't think I'd better! Don was a special person. When I was a freshman, I never missed a class and I got pretty good grades. We were at two-a-day practices my sophomore year when Whitey Piro came up to me and said, "Ray, you don't have a roommate, do you?" I said, "No." Whitey said, "Hey, I've got a guy I want you to take care of and get him to get up and go to class. I want you to room with Don Norton." I said, "Why, sure.... I'll do that. I'll try and help him." So Don and I roomed together. Well, I was supposed to change Don, but it didn't work out that way. My grades went to heck, and it took me two years to get back on my feet again and graduate. I didn't change Don, Don changed me! Don was a great guy, though. You never knew what Don was going to do. We loved him. Anything could happen when you were with Don.

I started coaching in '62. I always knew I was going to be a football coach. Evy's wing-T had blocking rules—trapping and pulling ends, tackles, and guards. I always used the wing-T blocking rules in all the teams I coached as part of my playbook. As far as Evy goes, I learned from him to keep 'em off balance. Don't let them get too happy. When you play football, you always have to have a little pressure on you. Evy was a tough guy, but he'd fight for his guys. He wanted us all to be successful off the field, too. He had a big heart.

In 1964 I was Iowa's freshman coach, and in '65 I was the defensive backfield coach for Jerry Burns. I loved Iowa City, and it was nice to come back. But then Jerry was let go, so we were all left out on the street. I went back up to Canada to work for a guy named Neill Armstrong in Edmonton, and I was in Edmonton for 12 years. It was an unfortunate thing that happened to Jerry. In his case, things just didn't work right—it's too bad. Jerry was a really good coach—he knew football.

Bump Elliott interviewed me twice for the Iowa head coaching job in 1973 and in 1978. I don't know for sure, of course, but I got the feeling that I could have had the job either time. But I was in Canada and I had a good thing going there. I didn't really want to leave Canada at that time. It just didn't work out right in my mind.

Coaching to me is coaching. Whether it's high school football or professional football or arena football or whatever it is, it's still coaching. The basics of football don't change. Once it gets in your blood, you either like it or you don't, and I've always enjoyed it. I've coached in a lot of different places. Right now I'm still coaching football. I coach at a high school in North Carolina that just started a football program. There's a young guy who's just starting coaching here, and maybe I can help bring him along a little bit. Ninety percent of the kids on this team have never played football before. They didn't have a clue what was going on, so we had to start from scratch.

All I can say is my time at Iowa was the best time of my life, bar none. There was no greater thrill than to come out of that tunnel and hear that Iowa fight song and run out onto that field. We had great friends. There were great people, and all the great guys in that community were wonderful to be around. I think you can change the title of this book to *The Best Time of Your Life*. That's being a Hawkeye.

After a successful college career, Ray Jauch spent 21 years as a coach in the Canadian Football League, including 14 seasons as a head coach. Jauch was twice named CFL Coach of the Year, and he won two Grey Cups, one as a player and one as a head coach. He has also served as a head coach in high school football, NAIA college football, the Arena Football League, and the USFL.

CHARLIE LEE

TACKLE

1957–1960

I ATTENDED SAN JUAN HIGH SCHOOL in Fair Oaks, California. As a 16-year-old senior, I had several scholarship offers to play football. I was also a good baseball player and was offered a contract out of high school to play with the Pittsburgh Pirates. They offered me a $2,000 signing bonus, but my dad said, "No way! You're going to get your education." Joe Murtaugh, my high school social studies teacher, had a connection to Iowa and told the athletic department about me. I was granted a full scholarship, largely based on the word of Murtaugh. In those days, college coaches rarely asked for films, nor did they send scouts to watch players at the high school level. I did go on to play baseball at Iowa until Coach Forest Evashevski made it clear he wanted me to devote my time to football. That was the end of my baseball career.

Freshmen were not eligible in 1956 to play varsity football. Nevertheless, my freshman year was a memorable one. Our team went 9–1 and won the Rose Bowl by a score of 35–19 over Oregon State. My family and I used my team tickets and watched from the stands.

My sophomore year of 1957 was a breakthrough year for me. At the beginning of the season I wore No. 99. Interestingly enough, another player was listed in the program as No. 99. Each time I entered a game that year, it was announced the other player was taking the field. It was somewhat disappointing to not even get recognized for making the lineup! However, this oddity would prove to be very valuable to me down the road.

In the time Charlie Lee played for Iowa, the Hawkeyes went 37–8–2. Lee played in the 1958 Rose Bowl and contributed during one of the most prominent eras of Iowa football history.

After the first three games my sophomore year, I was invited to attend training table. This was a big deal for football players. My first road trip was to the Ohio State game. I received a phone call to join coaches Bob Flora and Archie Kodros on their plane to Columbus, as the team plane had gone on ahead. This private summons was a very big deal at the time. Our 1957 team finished the season 7–1–1 and was ranked sixth nationally at the end of the season.

As a junior in 1958, I played about half the time, as Coach Evashevski used a platoon system. In those days, players played both offense and defense, so Evy had two units that alternated in and out. The Air Force Academy tied us early in the season, and then we lost 38–28 to Ohio State. However, we won the Big Ten outright and qualified for another Rose Bowl trip. We defeated California by a score of 38–12 and received the Grantland Rice Award by the Football Writers of America for recognition as national champions.

Our record my senior year was 5–4. I had an outstanding season and received many postseason honors. Now comes the interesting part. At the end of my senior year, the Iowa athletics director had me listed as a candidate for another year of eligibility since I did not see action as a sophomore. (Remember, each time I took the field my sophomore year, I was announced by another name.)

Anyway, the Big Ten granted our petition for another year, much to the delight of the Iowa coaching staff. The 1960 season was a huge success. Our record was 8–1, with the only loss being to Minnesota. The team rebounded after this loss and trounced Woody Hayes and the Buckeyes 35–12. The season ended with a 28–0 shutout of Notre Dame, in which I intercepted a pass and returned it to the 1-foot line. Minnesota had just lost to Purdue, so Iowa and Minnesota each had one loss. But, since Minnesota won the game against us, the Gophers got the nod for the Rose Bowl. In those days a Big Ten team could play in no game other than the Rose Bowl. Today, a season like we had in 1960 would have landed Iowa in a BCS game.

During the postseason, I was invited to play in the All-American Bowl in Tucson, followed by the Copper Bowl in Phoenix, and finally the Hula Bowl in Honolulu. Since players were invited to bring their wives to these bowl games at no expense, my college sweetheart Ralphene and I went together. In fact, we moved our wedding date up six months to December 10 in order to make this trip our honeymoon. Ralphene's mom worked a miracle and put together a lovely wedding in only three weeks! The bridesmaids wore gold velvet and the groomsmen wore black tuxes. The groomsmen just happened to be five of our linemen, so we had to send to Des Moines to get tuxes large enough. We didn't really plan to have Hawkeye colors, it just kind of happened that way.

Our honeymoon started with a mid-December trip to Houston, Texas, to watch the Bluebonnet Bowl as guests of Bud Adams of the Houston Oilers. I signed with the Houston Oilers on this trip for a yearly sum of $8,500. That was big money to us! From Houston we went on to the other three bowl games, and we won each of those three games. We were gone three weeks, all expenses paid, and came home with more money in our pockets than we had seen in a long time. Our picture was on the front page of the *Des Moines Register* sports section, saying, "Football pays for this honeymoon." What a honeymoon it was.

And what a collegiate football career it was. I entered the University of Iowa as a freshman in the fall of 1956 as one of 105 freshman football players. I graduated in June 1961, having spent five seasons with the Hawkeyes. A quote from Iowa's media guide says, "From 1956–1960 Forest Evashevski led Iowa to four finishes in the top five of the national rankings, three Big Ten titles, two Rose Bowl appearances, and the 1958 Football Writers' Association National Championship." Talk about being a part of Iowa's Glory Years!

I graduated in June of 1961 and reported to the Oilers' training camp in July. After being at camp for 10 days and assessing the situation, I decided to return to Iowa. I was offered a job as an assistant football coach at Central Missouri State College in Warrensburg, Missouri, and was able to complete my master's degree in science while at CMSC.

After receiving my master's degree, I accepted a job as head wrestling coach and assistant football coach at Bella Vista High School in Fair Oaks, California. I taught and coached football and wrestling at Bella Vista for 32 years before retiring. During those years, I mentored hundreds of young men, both athletes and nonathletes. I got to see my son, David, become California's first three-time state wrestling champ. He went on to be a three-time All-American in college and the NCAA 167-pound national champion in 1989. I was and am very proud of him. I also especially enjoyed taking kids under my wing who were not the so-called "successful" and "popular" kids of the school. I would take them fishing, out for a hamburger, or find other ways to spend quality time with many of these young men who needed it most. It was gratifying to me.

I spent five full years at the University of Iowa, and played four years during the days when freshmen were not eligible. I had the privilege to contribute during one of the most prominent eras of Iowa football history. Forest Evashevski, more than any other person, made Iowa's success possible. He insisted upon excellence, could not accept mental mistakes, and had the respect of every player I ever knew. That's not an easy thing for a football coach. His admonition, "It's no disgrace to lose, but it is the rankest kind of shame to be outfought," inspired me and guided me through many locker room talks of my own during my 32 years of coaching.

The memories I have of the Iowa fans cheering for their Hawkeyes as we walked from the Field House to the stadium on game day and the pride and support we all felt from those fans linger to this day. When I call myself a Hawkeye, I think not only of the Iowa team, but of the whole state. My grave marker will be at a small cemetery in Mt. Pleasant, Iowa, my wife's hometown, and I intend to have a symbol of the Hawkeyes engraved in the right corner along with the words, "On Iowa."

Charlie Lee played tackle during the pinnacle of Forest Evashevski's success in the 1950s. He was on the team during both of Iowa's Rose Bowl championship teams of 1956 and 1958. Iowa had a record of 37–8–2 during his career, which spanned a total of five years. Charlie passed away in September 2010 after a long illness. He lived in California with his wife, Ralphene.

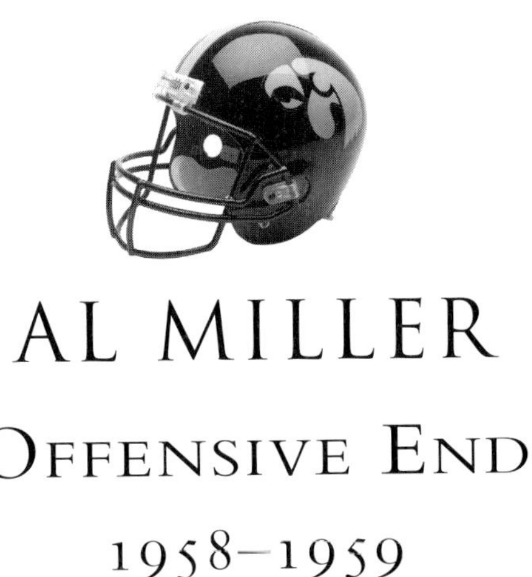

AL MILLER

Offensive End

1958–1959

Growing up in Michigan, it was perfectly natural to gravitate to Big Ten athletics, especially football. The Rose Bowl was all my buddies and I could focus on—no offense intended to girls and cars.

Our high school [Flint Northern] and others in the area had produced several gridders who starred in the January classic for Michigan or Michigan State. So, for me, it mattered not which school I'd compete for. Just give me a shot at playing in what's known as the granddaddy of postseason games—the Rose Bowl in Pasadena, California.

Bear in mind, at the time there were only three other college bowls; namely the Orange, Sugar, and Cotton. Just to play in any would be considered quite an accomplishment. But I'm talking Rose Bowl!

The year was 1956, and, while Iowa was busy capturing the Big Ten title, Flint Northern was posting an unbeaten season en route to a state championship. The pieces began to fall in place, as Iowa went on to win the 1957 Rose Bowl in exciting fashion, then joined the list of schools offering a scholarship. Along with Michigan and Michigan State, they included Nebraska, Dartmouth, Indiana, and Delaware.

I had no sense of urgency to make a choice. I was a midyear graduate, which allowed me plenty of time to bulk up while working construction and taking visits. The latter all proved to be as exciting and informative as I could hope for. That first plane ride spoiled me, and I could hardly wait for the next

Al Miller credits Iowa with fulfilling two of his life's goals—playing on a national championship team and becoming a sportswriter.

trip through the friendly skies. Not to mention the fare provided for all the fancy restaurants.

Most friends figured I'd remain in state. With Ann Arbor and East Lansing both less than an hour from Flint, their concerns were obvious and flattering.

It just wasn't to be. The Hawkeyes and Iowa City impressed me the most. Imagine, on the first of three visits, the director of Iowa's journalism school opened the building for a personal tour. On a Sunday! Another surprise occurred that weekend while touring the downtown area. That's when a barber rushed out of his shop to shake hands and greet me, saying, "Al, we hope you'll become a Hawkeye!" Later, I learned the Iowa City newspaper had published a list of incoming recruits for that weekend. Nice touch!

You couldn't discount the Michigan connection, either. Forest Evashevski, Bob Flora, Archie Kodros, and Jerry Burns all played at Michigan and headed the Iowa staff, along with Whitey Piro, who developed a string of outstanding ends.

Simply put, the Hawkeyes were a hot commodity, not only in the Big Ten, but nationwide. It was a time of single-platoon football, and Iowa's recent success was attracting a better class of athlete. The playing field was becoming more level, to say the least.

Although freshmen weren't eligible to compete, from the moment I signed the conference letter of intent, I was ready to hop a train for Iowa City. Freshman ball was boring for the most part, but that all changed on the Monday following Iowa's 21–21 tie at Ann Arbor.

We had just completed warm-ups when freshman coach Jerry Hilgenberg gave us the news—we were going "live" with the big boys. What a rush that provided! Alex Karras, Jim Gibbons, and Randy Duncan were on the other side, but weren't expected to work up a sweat. Either way, most of us welcomed the chance to get our feet wet. It didn't take long.

Soon into the scrimmage, Hilgy called for a counter-pass, where the end would hook over the middle. Quarterback Mike Lewis whipped a perfect spiral. I went high to spear it, then ducked my shoulder and swung upfield before banging into a pair of defensive backs. Man, did that ever feel good, and even more so when Hilgy entered the huddle and said, "Good goin'! Evy liked that!" We were holding our own.

The 1958 season has been well documented. Personally, it satisfied my goal as a player. It also led to an opportunity to complete the second phase of a dream, one that drew attention prior to my high school graduation.

Doug Mintline, an award-winning columnist for the *Flint Journal*, wrote, "If he realizes his goal of becoming a sportswriter, Al Miller will be able to analyze with authority!" Mintline's observation was based on my earning eight varsity letters in three sports over a three-year period. Also, I had worked part-time for the *Journal*, so the staff there was aware of my ambitions.

So, what goes with the writing? Well, Gus Schrader, the *Cedar Rapids Gazette* sports editor who helped recruit me to Iowa, would become my boss, thus extending the dream for another nine years. I believe I earned my stay, but I'm sure the Iowa football connection didn't hurt the cause. The desire to be a part of the action was predominant. Always! I'm grateful for what was afforded me by the university and the *Gazette*, and in the years to come I would serve the Hawkeyes in several volunteer capacities. I call it "Payback Time," a proud time.

Since my Iowa playing days, I've served in numerous capacities for Iowa players and alumni. I served as the Linn County I-Club President, the Iowa Football Banquet emcee, and the Iowa National Lettermen's Club President. In addition, I coordinated the 15-year and 25-year reunions for the 1958 team.

What memories! There are countless stories to relate—Big Ten and Rose Bowl crowns, paving the way for selection as national champions. No other Iowa football team can claim that distinction.

We were fortunate, and I'm sure a lot of teammates share a similar dream. Perhaps more important, Iowa football in the late '50s did so much to implement today's popular phrase, "It's great to be a Hawkeye!"

You bet.

Al Miller was a two-time letterman at offensive end for Iowa in the late 1950s. His 1958 team defeated California in Iowa's second Rose Bowl under Forest Evashevski. Miller currently resides in his home state of Michigan.

MARK MANDERS

Guard/Linebacker

1958–1960

My father, Clarence Manders, was a fine football player in the late '30s. He was an All-America fullback at Drake, one of their first All-America football players. He then went to the pros, with the old New York Yankees football team at first and then with the Brooklyn Dodgers football team. In 1941 he led the NFL in rushing. My uncle, Jack, went to Minnesota and then played with the Chicago Bears for eight years. He was a defensive tackle and a place-kicker. They used to call him "Automatic Jack" because he very seldom missed a field goal or extra point. There was a lot of football in the family, there's just no doubt about that.

Evashevski recruited me at a football banquet after my senior season, where he was there to talk about Iowa football. I met him, and I was just in awe because I'd heard so many things about him. He was exactly what everybody had said. He was a big guy, an ex-football player at Michigan, and he spoke my language pretty good. He and my dad had met a couple of times, I guess, someplace down the line—they were about the same age. I just asked Dad, "Is he a pretty good coach?" And he said, "Oh, yeah. He's a great coach." I asked, "You think I should go to Iowa, then?" Dad said, "Oh, yeah!" There wasn't a whole lot of discussion about it! I had been kind of leaning toward Iowa State because I wanted to go into engineering. But then I found out that Iowa was as good or better than they were, so then there wasn't much choice after that.

There wasn't a whole lot of talent on my high school squad, so I played all over the place—quarterback, fullback, halfback, tight end. I went to Iowa as a fullback, but we had too many backs, so Evashevski [moved me] to the pulling guard position. That was what he did with the extra backs who were pretty good-sized fullbacks. He'd put them in as pulling guards, and we were faster than most of the backs.

We lost the first- and second-string offensive guards in the 1959 Rose Bowl. I was a sophomore, and Evy put me in there. It was pretty special. I got to play a couple of quarters, and that's pretty good for a sophomore at Iowa. I couldn't believe he called my name. I didn't know whether to run out there or what! I was not expecting that, that's for sure.

You see, the morning of the Rose Bowl, John Nocera, the captain of the team, knocked on the door and said the bus was leaving in 30 minutes. We got up and put our shoes on and got dressed. I opened the door to the hall, and there were guys walking by. I went back and got some stuff that I was going to give my dad before the football game. But when I walked out there, the bus had left about 15 minutes earlier than I thought it would.

I was beside myself, of course. I thought I had to get a taxi or something. The doorman said, "The only place you can get a taxi out here is Hollywood Boulevard." So I walked there, and there was a motorcycle officer sitting at the intersection. I asked, "Any chance of getting a taxi to the Rose Bowl? I'm an Iowa football player and I missed the bus." He looked at me and shook his head and said, "You'll never get there now before the football game," because traffic was backed up pretty good. Then he said, "Well, I might lose my badge, but jump on the back of the motorcycle here with me and we'll get you over there." That's how I got to the Rose Bowl. I went down in the Rose Bowl tunnel with the siren on, so everybody knew I was coming, there's no doubt about that!

I didn't get a smile from Evashevski when I walked in, I'll tell you that! I didn't even look at him. I looked at the assistant coach, but I didn't look at [Evy]! I just walked on in and took my clothes off, put my stuff on, and ran out on the football field. I was very, very lucky, and I got the officer's name and wrote him a really nice letter. He said later, "Yeah, I was listening to the game on the radio, and I think I heard your name." I said, "Well, I hope you did!" He was a very nice guy, and he was understanding and got me there.

There were a lot of different things that we changed defensively in 1959, and it worked very well. We kicked Ohio State's butt that year defensively. Sherwyn

Mark Manders was named All-America as a senior in 1960. He was inducted into the Semi-Pro Football Hall of Fame in 1998.

Thorson and I, the two linebackers, kind of roamed a little bit and didn't always stay in the same spot. We just had some really good defensive players—we kept them down so if we got a couple scores, we'd win the ballgame.

The 1960 team was a little different simply because we didn't have a drop-back quarterback. Wilburn Hollis was a running quarterback, and he was a very good athlete. He wasn't the greatest passer in the world, but he got it out there. We had several quarterback sneaks for more than 30 yards, and he could run. Thorson and I would bust a wedge up through that middle, and he'd just take off and fly. We ran the wing-T, but instead of giving it to the halfback, he could fake it and take off the opposite direction. It looked like we were going to go one way, and then we'd just reverse our direction and go around the other end. It fooled a lot of people for the whole season!

We had such great players up and down the line and the backs. We'd get out there and start an offensive drive, and the first series would tell us what we could do with them. We all kind of had a good feeling about ballgames. The only one that year that we didn't have a good feeling about was when we went up to Minnesota and played in that mud bowl up there. Coach [Murray] Warmath kind of put the kick to us, because we were No. 1 and they were No. 2 in the nation. He paid this guy to go out and put the sprinklers on the night before the game. It was just a quagmire out there. I walked out to the middle of the field, and my cleats went clear down under the sod. They had a slow power team, and we had a fast, fluid team. Everything was pretty darn quick, and it slowed us down a great deal. You'd get up to the line of scrimmage, and your feet would go down in the mud, and you could hardly get them to move. I'd like to play that game again. I think about that game a lot. I thought we had it in our pocket, because they weren't very fast, and I thought we'd just run away from them. We spent more time getting the mud out of our cleats than we did playing, I think! It was that bad. [Iowa lost their only game of the year to Minnesota, 27–10.]

Notre Dame and Ohio State were the two most fun and the most rewarding teams to beat. We only lost to Ohio State once in my career. Football was a little bit different then. It was just hard knocks and not that much finesse. You just kicked the guy's butt as best you could, and that was the name of the game. We were taking care of these guys once, and they were complaining to the referee all the time that I was holding them. I told one referee who called me for holding, "You know the difference between a hold and a great block?" He just looked at me like, "What are you talking about?" I said, "That was a great block; it wasn't a hold!" I was a little mouthy back then, but that's all right.

I was named All-America as a senior. It put a smile on my dad's face. That's all I cared about. He read it in the paper, and I didn't have a telephone in those days. My neighbor walked over and said, "Your dad called, and he wants you to call him back." Dad heard about it before I did. He was pretty happy. We were the first father and son All-Americans that the state of Iowa ever had.

We just had a very fortunate time at the University of Iowa. I always think about what I could have done, and there are just not a lot of holes out there that I could have filled. I just didn't have many, although I wish I could have played one more year. At the time, I couldn't think of anything I'd rather do. I had a job and I had a family, and I still went to Iowa. I just couldn't believe that Forest Evashevski would come to my high school and ask me if I'd like to go to the University of Iowa and play football. My dad was pleased, and that was about all it took. It was beyond any of my dreams.

Mark Manders received an engineering degree from Iowa. After graduation, he played three seasons of semi-pro football with the Des Moines Vikings and was inducted into the Semi-Pro Football Hall of Fame in 1998. Manders later went into the electrical contracting business with his father and remained in that line of work for nearly 40 years.

BILL RINGER

Guard

1958–1960

I was born and raised in Flint, Michigan. I attended an elementary school where we played sandlot football by the hour in literally sand and rocks. Then I changed schools and lived about four blocks from the city park, which had 3½-inch bluegrass. It felt like a carpet! From elementary school, I moved to Whittier Junior High School, where they did not have a football program. However, C.S. Mott, who was a rich General Motors philanthropist, provided junior high school kids a chance to play football in the Mott League. So for three years I played quarterback in the Mott League. Of course, all those players were being watched by local high school coaches. I was invited my ninth grade year to join the Flint Central Indians two-a-day practices in August. As a 10th-grader, I made the varsity team. After the first game, I played the rest of the year as corner linebacker. The next two years I was the starting quarterback and had all sorts of success punting and running. We had a great time.

So I sort of sailed through high school as a high school quarterback, punter, and extra-point kicker until I came to my senior year. We had kind of a so-so year, and I didn't give much thought to college until a Michigan graduate encouraged me to go to Michigan. I thought that was a pretty good idea because I had followed Michigan ever since junior high school. So that was where I was going to go.

My senior year summer I was working as a camp counselor at Mott Camp for underprivileged boys. One day I got a call that they announced over the loudspeaker system. "Counselor Ringer, will you please come up here? Forest Evashevski is on the phone." Even if you have plans to go to Michigan, when Forest Evashevski calls, you answer!

I received an invitation to visit Iowa along with Al Miller, who was also from Flint and going for his second visit. So I went there with offers from Michigan, Dartmouth, Michigan State, Wyoming, and a feeler from Nebraska. I visited and had a chance to talk with Coach Evashevski. We visited the stadium, where assistant coaches Archie Kodros and Whitey Piro had one of the quarterbacks throw passes to us. They were checking us out to see if we had agility and speed I'm sure.

Al Miller and I were talking on the airliner on the way home from our Iowa visit. I said, "Al, you've already signed up and made your intent known. Can you give me one good reason to go to Iowa?" And he said, "Yeah, and all you have to do is answer two questions—do you want to be with the best? Are you good enough to be one of the best?" I thought about that and thought those were two great reasons to go. I wanted to be the best. If I couldn't be the best, I wanted to be part of the best. And that went a long way toward why I chose to be a Hawkeye in 1957.

At the end of my freshman year at Iowa, I was told by Whitey Piro that I didn't make it as a quarterback. He said, "No offense, you're a good athlete, but you can't throw the ball 40 yards." I said I couldn't even throw the ball 40 yards with a tailwind! "But, we think you have potential as a receiver," he said. "You've got good hands and you're very fast." And I replied, "Sounds good to me as long as I keep my scholarship." So I went into spring practice at right end wearing No. 85.

Then in the fall of 1958 Evy asked me to switch to guard and told me one of the guards, Gary Grouwinkel, would teach me. So, as a sophomore I played third-team as a guard.

Here was my training on how to play guard. "Gary," I asked on the first play, "what do I do?"

"Pull right and turn up at the end," he said. So I did, and we went back to the huddle.

"What do I do now?" I said. "Pull left and turn up at the left end," he said.

The next play I asked, "What do I do now?" "Trap left," he replied.

I then said, "What do I do next?" "Trap right," he answered. I had four plays of indoctrination on how to play guard. I spent the rest of the time trying to survive during my development into a Big Ten guard. The next time I saw Grouwinkel was at a reunion in 2006.

During one of these two-a-day practices that sophomore year, Coach stopped scrimmage. He went over to the bleachers, sat us down, and said, "Men, where's Bill Ringer?" I said, "Here I am, Coach!" He said, "Men, I want you to know Ringer is going to play somewhere for me. He's a hard-nosed kid who is in great shape. He hits, he's fast, and he's willing to do more than expected of him. That kind of man is going to play for me somewhere." And so right away my first inclination was, *Gee, that's just wonderful.* Then all of a sudden it hit me—maybe that's not so wonderful! Some other guards didn't seem to be putting out the effort our coaches expected; they were just sort of there. But now they had learned what the model of effort was for Evy. The rest of two-a-day practices and any scrimmage I was involved in my sophomore year I would normally get hit two or three times. It was sometimes people running across the field to nail this guy who Evy thought was so good. His little talk got the other players going and sure toughened me up. That was apparently Evy's way of getting us ready for Big Ten football. I now recognize it as a great psychological move on his part. I went on in the '58 season to play guard as No. 85 in the Rose Bowl, and the team finished No. 1 in the nation.

Evashevski was a superb psychologist. He appeared to have a thinking process that was not subject to being influenced by chaos. As you know, a football game is chaos. He was just somewhere above all that, somehow making sense out of the chaos. Getting ready for the Rose Bowl during 1958, one of the players went to our team captain, John Nocera, and issued a complaint against Evy and his coaching staff. John took it to Evy, and Evy acted on it immediately. We were four days into two-a-day practice before the season when this complaint reached him before lunch. After lunch, he invited us into the Hillcrest Library. We were pretty well beat physically, and we were mentally exhausted. And here one man had the courage to stand up to Forest Evashevski.

What a tense situation, we were damn near on the edge of mutiny. But here's how Evy handled it. Sitting on the edge of a table, he said, "I understand there's a player who says that psychologically and physically he's a wreck because of the heavy scrimmaging and riding of this coaching staff and our harassing him. And I have personally abused all of you men with the amount of combat you've been subjected to. Is that the complaint?" Many of the players nodded yes. Evy said, "Who's the player who feels this way?" Much to his credit, the player said, "That's right, Coach." All eyes were on this player. Evy, in a slow, almost fatherly tone said to him, "Do you know how many days until the Michigan game?" The player said no. Evy said the exact number of days, and then said, "There's going to be 100,000 people at Michigan. They're going to all be screaming at you. I only have one question: if you can't take the abuse of six men, how in the world do you ever expect to perform in front of 100,000?" You could just feel that whole room relax. And the player admitted, "That's pretty logical."

Evy said, "Okay, report to the stadium later in your uniforms and helmets." We thought, *Oh my goodness, we're going to get it this afternoon.* Instead, we spent the whole afternoon playing crazy relays. We expended more calories in those two hours, and were invigorated, not drained, and it just blew our minds. We thought we were at the end of our ropes. Well, we were not physically or mentally exhausted, nor at the end of the rope that afternoon. That's just classic Evashevski—he took a negative mind-set of the team and turned it 180 degrees.

The rest of that season was a whirlwind. It was one of the most enjoyable things to do, just watch that Iowa team roll. I was on the travelling squad and went to Ann Arbor when we beat Michigan for the first time in Evy's career. What a thrill. My hometown paper recognized Al Miller and me as being from Michigan, and the sportswriter was nice enough to say, "And Bill Ringer made the last tackle." I know Evy enjoyed the Rose Bowl victories, but I have a feeling that game was extra special to him.

The heartbreak of 1958 was the tie against the Air Force. Those kids were small, fast, and on the attack. I'll never forget that game. Another one I'll never forget is the game against Ohio State and Woody Hayes. I was a third-team guard, and Evy always wanted the first three teams ready to go in. I was near the coach and observed trainers haul a couple of our players out who were glassy-eyed and staggering, having been physically abused by the Ohio State line. Three of our guards were taken out, and I thought, *Man, if one more guy gets hurt, I'm in there.* And that was a great day of reckoning for me. I decided on that day I did not want to play football. There was no need to run into a meat grinder. And that's a sophomore talking. So I just sat there realizing I was completely yellow. And the coaches had good sense and started putting tackles in to play guard. It was significant to my experience at Iowa to never forget that game, to know that I could be yellow.

Our Rose Bowl experience later that season was really something. When we arrived in California, Evy said, "You've got four 50-yard line tickets. I've made arrangements for 35 white 225 Buick convertibles for your disposal. I only request that you don't do anything to discredit yourselves." He said, "We're going to have a nice banquet with Bob Hope, and you've got beautiful living accommodations here. This first week I encourage you to go do and see after practices, and we'll get down to business the second week. And by the way, I realize this may be the only opportunity some of you men will ever have to be in California, so have a good time."

The next day, we got up and had two full scrimmages, one in the morning and one that afternoon. Evy just beat the tar out of us. So he gave us all our freedom, and then he took it away by literally putting us in a condition that by night we didn't want to be out past 11:00 PM. We couldn't physically partake in all the partying at our disposal.

The second week of Rose Bowl preparations, Evy called us together and said, "Okay, is everybody here having a good time?" We were a resilient bunch, and everybody was bubbling with all the places they had eventually gotten to visit. He said, "Now set all that aside. The University of Iowa, representing the people of Iowa, has sent you out here, and we've had a first-class time. Now we need to knock it all off and get serious about this football game. Now is the time to get serious." We did. And we also had a great Christmas party at which the university presented each player with a Rose Bowl watch and binoculars. Mrs. Ruth Evashevski topped off our gifts with two sports shirts that were wrapped beautifully.

On game day before we went on the field, he said, "It's time for you men to think about the fact that Iowa needs to be repaid for providing you a program to be involved in and a first-class education. And they're not asking anything in return. It's about time we gave them something as thanks." People were clawing at the walls. Let's go play football! And, of course, everything else about the game is history, and Iowans got repaid.

So then in 1959 I came back for my junior season. Unfortunately, I didn't even make the traveling squad, but I did participate on the scrimmage team as a Mau-Mau. During two-a-day practices a few years earlier, the scrimmage team appointed themselves the "Mau-Maus." The name "Mau-Maus" originated from an African tribe in a movie—they were fearless warriors. You

During his Iowa career, guard Bill Ringer played on two Big Ten championship teams and in the Rose Bowl.

were first-team, second-team, third-team, a Mau-Mau, or a sideline stander. That's how the 60 people broke out. We Mau-Maus were scrimmaging against one of the finest offenses in the United States two days a week. What an opportunity to build our football skills.

One thing about Evy is that he never swore. The thing that was worse than any four-letter word he could have used was, "Confound it!" You lived in fear of him saying "confound it." If he said "confound it," you probably were going to lose your position and never play again. And each fall he would make a point of explaining that he could forgive a physical mistake, but he said he could not forgive a mental error.

After one year on the third team and one year on the Mau-Maus, I was going back for my senior year of 1960. After eight weeks in summer Army ROTC basic infantry training at Fort Reilly, Kansas, doing long marches carrying a 60-caliber machine gun in 100-degree weather, I was hard as a nail.

I was in shape, really good shape. The third day of two-a-day practices, I heard, "[Earl] McQuiston, get out of there!" He was playing right guard on the second team. And Bob Flora yelled, "Where's Ringer?" I got called up to the second team, and I never left that spot during the 1960 season.

Part of the reason I moved up is the player ahead of me couldn't remember the plays. This was somewhat understandable. As an example, here was one of Evy's plays: 131 counter criss-cross, bootleg to the right, pass, guards opposite. That was one of 370 plays. To me, that says a lot about Evy. He was detailed and intricate. That play had deception in it; linebackers see the action to the right, and they see the guards pulling to the left. That was the key to Evy's running offense—deception! If you could cause the defense to think for a split second, our halfback would be on his way to the goal line.

There were two memorable games for me in 1960. First was the Ohio State game. Remember that Ohio State game in 1958 when I decided I was yellow? As a senior, I was playing second team (Evy played two teams that rotated). I had no fear. I was fast, small, and fearless. I was playing on one of the best teams Iowa has ever had. Why would I now be concerned about these big brawny guys from Ohio? We were faster and smarter. Our second-team unit drove to the 5-yard line, and on second-and-goal the play off the left tackle was called.

And here's the inside story: the scouting report I read pointed out to me that the tackle and linebacker over the right guard were Academic All-Americans. They were huge men, and mean, and I made a mental note that these people were also smart. So I was on my way to the line with this huge man lined up in a goal-line stance in front of me, and I decided to double my spacing. There was a chance they would think the ball was going over center and I was trying to create the hole with this spacing. And they bought it. The linebacker yelled, "Over center, over center." The ball was snapped, they filled in over center, and I filled in on them. Touchdown off left tackle! Because of me having been yellow two years earlier, that drive was my redemption. I was participating against Ohio State linemen on an even keel with the best in the nation, and here I was able to dupe them.

In 1960 we won every game except Minnesota. We old-timers will never forget the loss, but we have a lot to be proud of in that 1960 season. We finished 8–1, were co–Big Ten champions, and judged to be the No. 2 team in the nation. Then, in 2010, someone judged us to be Iowa's all-time best team to date.

Years later Coach Evashevski and I shared a lot of football thoughts with each other over coffee in his home in Petoskey, Michigan. During one of my visits to his house, I brought a photograph showing Wilburn Hollis running the ball in the end zone on a quarterback sneak during the 1960 Purdue game. He was going off the right shoulder of the center and was being aided by a tremendous block on a defensive tackle. This photograph shows everybody doing their job, and Hollis stepping into the end zone. I was the right guard blocking that big Purdue tackle.

I took the photo to Evy with the idea that he'd sign the back of it, which he did. I said, "Coach, what do you like best about this action photo?" He said, "Well, obviously the blocking is commendable, but that's not the most important part." And I said, "What do you mean?" He pointed to those Iowa fans in the background. He said, "That's the important part—those fans, and the fact that that stadium is full." One of the legacies of Forest Evashevski, I think, is how highly he regarded the Iowa fans. He planted the seeds for full stadiums because he held in reverence the University of Iowa, the state of Iowa, and the Iowa fans. He provided them with winning teams and appreciation.

In closing, my personal and family life, work life, community life, and church life have all benefitted from my experience as a student and athlete at the University of Iowa. Soon after my Iowa experience, I married my high school sweetheart from Flint, which brought the birth of our son. He and his wife are truly blessings. Barbara Ringer and I have been married 48 years and have two wonderful granddaughters. Finally, it's been our enduring love of our Lord that has meant so much throughout our life and especially in our retirement.

So, what does it mean to me to be a Hawkeye? It means to be indomitable.

Bill Ringer moved from quarterback to receiver to guard in his time at Iowa. He played on two Big Ten championship teams and lettered his senior year. Ringer currently lives in Vincennes, Indiana, with his wife, Barbara.

The SIXTIES

WILBURN HOLLIS

Quarterback

1959–1961

I GREW UP IN A TOWN they called Possum Trot, Mississippi. It's kind of a little crossroads in the old South. But I went to grade school and high school in Boys Town, which is located outside of Omaha, Nebraska. I think there was a priest who came into my life and somehow got me involved with becoming a part of Boys Town. I've read letters he wrote to Monsignor Wagner, who was the director of Boys Town, saying he had this kid who could really benefit from an opportunity to go to Boys Town. There was correspondence back and forth, and finally Monsignor Wagner said, "Okay, send him to Boys Town." So that's what I did. I started grade school there when I was probably nine or 10 years old, and I was there until I was about 18.

I spent a lot of time at Boys Town playing football under Coach Skip Palrang. He was one of the best high school coaches in the world and coached the Boys Town football team from the 1940s to the 1970s. He's been noted in all kinds of articles about how great he was as a high school coach. When I moved out of grade school and into high school, Coach Palrang said, "What do you play?" I said, "I don't know." He said, "Well, why don't you go down there with that group? They need a quarterback. Go play quarterback for them." You see, we had enough kids to field about 18 teams. So I said, "Okay." I went to the different group and said, "Okay, I'm quarterback." That's how I started playing quarterback for Boys Town. I went on to make high school All-America.

The way I ended up at Iowa was somewhat of a fluke. My senior year, there was a fellow Boys Town citizen who went to the University of Iowa. His name was Charlie "Deacon" Jones. He was a great decathlon athlete and actually ran in the Olympics twice for the U.S. He was out practicing at Boys Town and asked me what I was going to do after high school. I said I'd probably get a job as a machinist. Boys Town was a vocational school, and we were all trained to become proficient in different trades we could use after high school. Deacon said, "Why don't you just come down to Iowa and see if you can get a scholarship to play football for them?" I said, "Okay, what do I need to do?" He said, "Why don't you grab some of your high school game films and bring them with you to show to the coaches?"

Monsignor Wagner arranged for me to get a ride down to the university. I took my films to the Iowa coaching staff and asked if they could take a look at them. The two coaches I met were Jerry Burns and Jerry Hilgenberg. I asked them to let me know what they thought because I wanted to go to the University of Iowa. That was on a Friday, and on the following Monday I got a call, and they said, "We'd like you to come to the University of Iowa. If you would like to, we'd give you a scholarship."

The funny thing about it was that Coach Palrang had us running the exact same offense at Boys Town as Iowa did—the wing-T. That's when they had Bob Jeter, Willie Fleming, Kenny Ploen, Randy Duncan, and all those guys. It was generally a running offense, and we used the very same one at Boys Town. That was a big help, and it was a great deal for me.

Like everyone back then, I sat out as a freshman in 1958. I began playing some as a sophomore in 1959. I didn't get to play against California in the 1959 Rose Bowl, but we started the 1959 season in Berkeley against California. I scored the first touchdown of the season as we beat Cal even worse than we did in the Rose Bowl. Olen Treadway was the starting senior quarterback. With Don Norton as his main receiver, Treadway set some Big Ten records as a passer. Every once in a while they'd take Treadway out and put me in at quarterback. As a sophomore, I was a little nervous working with this senior All-American in Norton, but I got past that. I ran for a couple hundred yards on the ground that year and got my feet wet mostly. We started out 2–3 in 1959, but we won three of our last four to finish at 5–4. It was a step down from our Rose Bowl team of the previous year, but we lost some real close games. In addition, we beat Ohio State in Columbus, which hadn't happened very often. They were our only loss the year before. I had a good day running and even threw a touchdown against the Buckeyes.

I took over as quarterback in 1960. One game that comes to mind my junior year is when we were playing at Michigan State. I think we were behind by a point or two with five minutes left when we fumbled in our territory. I'll be darned if we didn't get a fumble right back and run it in for a touchdown. Then we scored again on an interception. As we got back to campus, the students were all telling us they'd shut their radios off before the game ended and thought that we lost. That stands out as a really good game.

Another game I remember that year was against Wisconsin. It seems like my junior year we had a lot of close games that we won in the last quarter. We were playing Wisconsin, and I threw a touchdown pass to one of our receivers, but the tight end was offside, so they called it back. We called almost the same play again, and I threw it down the middle to one of our halfbacks, Sammie Harris. He tipped the ball from the defender and caught it as he fell on his back in the end zone. It was really a thrilling game.

The only disappointing game that season came when we played at Minnesota and we were both undefeated. We were ranked No. 1 in the nation and they were ranked No. 2. They had a great quarterback named Sandy Stephens.

At one point in the game, our center snapped the ball to me, and I backed out to hand the ball to the running back, and this big ol' defensive guard from Minnesota crashed the line. He hit me in the back of my heels, knocked me down, and I didn't get the pitch off to the halfback. Otherwise our back would have walked into the end zone. We ended up losing 27–10, so Minnesota went to the Rose Bowl and we didn't. We had gone two years earlier, so the rules back then were when two teams tied for the championship, the most recent team to have gone didn't go again. So that kept us out of the Rose Bowl. To this day, I sit and think, *Boy, if I just would've pitched that ball.* That's really the only play in my career that I think about over and over. If I could've taken it back, that's the one I would've taken back and tried again. We all have those things in life we'd take back. I had some great plays in my life playing football, but that wasn't one of them.

We rebounded the next week to pound Ohio State and then Notre Dame by a combined score of 63–12. Even though we didn't make the Rose Bowl, or any bowl for that matter, we still shared the Big Ten championship. Beating the Buckeyes and Irish to end the season like that took some of the sting

With Wilburn Hollis at quarterback in 1960, Iowa spent three weeks at No. 1 and won the Big Ten title with an 8–1 record.

off the Minnesota loss. The Notre Dame game was Forest Evashevski's last as Iowa's head coach. I was selected to the All–Big Ten team my junior year. Surprisingly, no Iowa quarterback had ever been selected first team as a junior, so that was a nice honor. I also received third-team All-America from the United Press.

We started out our senior year ranked first in the nation under Jerry Burns, who was promoted from assistant to head coach. The first game, though, we lost our All-America halfback, Larry Ferguson. Larry was very fast, and he was a smart football player, very confident. He was a really tough competitor, so losing him hurt.

The second game we beat a strong Southern Cal team by a point when one of our halfbacks broke up a play at the end of the game. This was unfortunately the game I broke my wrist and had to sit out the rest of the season. One of our really good tight ends got hurt, and then one of our tackles got hurt. So Jerry Burns started out with a team ranked No. 1 in the nation and within a few games lost four of his key players. Possibly the worst part of that whole scenario was me getting hurt because my backup was a passing quarterback as opposed to a running quarterback like I was. At the time, the Iowa offense was based on a running attack. My replacement was a different style quarterback, so they had to revamp the whole offense. They had to put people in roles they weren't used to, and they just didn't have a whole preseason camp to get ready for a new offense. They had one week, and that hurt our team badly.

My injury occurred when I got my hand jammed backward. The way I understood it, back in those days, if you played more than a certain percent of the second game, you would not get an extra year. I exceeded that percent of the second game. The injury seemed like no problem when I did it in the first half, so I didn't think much of it. It just seemed like a sprained wrist, so I played the whole game, and that was it. In reality, I had broken a small bone in my wrist. That'll teach me to tough it out.

I was in terrible misery on the flight back from Southern Cal because it started swelling up. I think with all the adrenaline going, I was able to shrug it off during the game. They were actually going to switch me to halfback, and then they tried to get a medical redshirt, but our request was denied.

There was a lot of speculation that I'd gotten in a fight after the game later that week, because nothing was said about it until Friday before the next game. We didn't tell the press or anybody that I had a broken wrist.

I didn't handle it too well at first. I started skipping class and really turned into a loner. And I thought, *Man, what am I going to do?* So finally I just said, *Look, you can't let this thing get you down.* So I kind of got things turned around and started going to classes again and got my head straightened out.

Even though I got hurt like that, I was drafted by the football Cardinals, so it turned out to be okay. I played for the New York Giants for a year, and then I played for the Steelers for a part of a year. Then I played in a continental league, which I guess would be equivalent to the Canadian Football League these days as far as ability. I played for the Charleston Rockets in the Continental Football League for about six years and set a lot of records playing.

Looking back, I was very fortunate to be around so many talented people at Iowa. It was not only the players, but also the coaches. I had a really, really strong feeling for Evashevski, and Jerry Burns also. I felt really strong and close to those guys. Evashevski was a fantastic coach. He stuck by you, and I really adored the guy. I played my heart out for him. The thing about Evy was he wouldn't let you down. He was in your corner all the way. He was there for you all the time. I recall one time when I was a sophomore, I threw a pass against Wisconsin that got intercepted and ran back for a touchdown. That was Wisconsin's winning score, and the fans got all over Evashevski. "What are you doing with a sophomore in there, what are you doing with Wil Hollis in there?" And Evy said, "Hey, this kid's only 19 years old. I'd go with Wilburn Hollis all the way. He's our quarterback and I'll stick with him." And the fans never questioned it one bit.

And Jerry Burns was the same way in a different kind of manner. Evy would give you hell if you needed it, but he really was in your corner if you needed it. That's what I respected so much about him. He's the only Iowa coach to ever win the Rose Bowl. He had a relatively short tenure there, but his record was impeccable. He was a super leader, just like my high school coach. He demanded discipline, conditioning, and attention to detail, and that's what he asked you to do. If you did it, you won. And he won a lot of accolades at Iowa, rightfully so.

I think we had the same kind of fan base as we have now. The one thing I've noticed about the Iowa fans is they are so loyal to the University of Iowa. I just love the Hawkeye fans. Ever since I played my sophomore year and came out of that tunnel to see those Hawkeye fans screaming for us, I loved our fans. And so it will always be with me. They are just great. I go to all the games myself now. If the snowflakes start falling, once in a while we may take off a little early, but boy we're down there. We're there for the Hawks. And that's the way it is.

Every time I go to a game I think about those kids coming out of that tunnel. Then I think back to what it was like for me to be out there doing the same thing. I think about Evashevski, Burns, Jerry Hilgenberg, Wally Hilgenberg, Bill Perkins, Jim Winston, and all those guys I played with. I think about what a great honor it was to be with them and share the great tradition that represents Iowa football. That was the most wonderful thing, to be a part of the Hawkeye tradition and loving the Hawkeyes the way I do and the way my family does. Just being a part of that whole aura of the Hawk, the wonderful Hawk. And I guess that's all I can say. It's a wonderful feeling.

Wilburn Hollis ascended to the starting quarterback position as a junior and helped lead Iowa to one of its most successful seasons in 1960. He rushed for two touchdowns against Wisconsin in 1960 and threw the game-winning touchdown with 52 seconds remaining in a 28–21 victory. That performance earned him National Back of the Week honors from the Associated Press, and Iowa was elevated to No. 1 in the nation after the win. Iowa spent three weeks at No. 1 and won the Big Ten title with an 8–1 record. The 6′2″, 200-pound Hollis earned All–Big Ten and third Team All-America honors. Hollis currently resides in Marion, Iowa.

MIKE REILLY

GUARD/LINEBACKER

1961–1963

IT WAS A PRETTY EASY SELL—figuratively speaking—to get me to come to Iowa. I had a cousin play for Iowa in the 1940s. I was a Hawkeye fan; my mother and father were both great Hawkeye fans. All through junior high and high school I went to Iowa games regularly. If I had an opportunity to go to the University of Iowa, I was going to do that. I briefly entertained an offer from Notre Dame, but I was never really serious about that. When Iowa contacted me about playing there, I was very happy to oblige.

I was impressed with Forest Evashevski. As a high school kid, I looked at his record, and it was very impressive. He was still coach during my freshman year before Jerry Burns took over our sophomore year.

I wasn't eligible to play in 1960. We had a very good team that year with Larry Ferguson at running back and Wilburn Hollis at quarterback. They tied for the Big Ten championship.

After my freshman year, Coach Evashevski stepped down, and Jerry Burns became head coach. Fair or unfair, there were some big expectations placed on him his first year. We were ranked No. 1 in the nation. I thought Jerry Burns was a good choice to follow Evashevski, but he had a lot of people who wanted him to maintain the level of success Evy had. I appreciated Coach Burns and was proud to be part of his program.

We won our first four games in 1961, but injuries to Ferguson, Hollis, and Jim Winston took their toll. That was a downer, as it would be in any team

In 1963 Mike Reilly was named Iowa's Most Valuable Player, first-team All–Big Ten, and first-team All-America.

who has its top players sidelined. With the shock of those guys getting hurt, you just hope that you can meld everything together. Obviously we didn't do quite as well as everybody expected. After our four wins, we reeled off four straight losses before we ended the year by pounding Notre Dame.

My sophomore year I backed up a couple of guys at right guard and linebacker. I was just very fortunate and happy that I could be part of the Iowa program. I kept my head up and said, "Hey, when my chance is there, I'll take advantage of it." I started a game or two my junior year, but was relegated to second team until my senior year.

As a senior, the game that probably stands out most was against Wisconsin. They were ranked second in the nation, and though we got beat 10–7, it was a hard-fought game. Back then they didn't count the number of tackles, but somebody said they watched the film and I had close to 30 tackles in that game. I was Big Ten Lineman of the Week after that game.

The captains my senior year were Wally Hilgenberg and Paul Krause. Wally was a great player, and he had excellent speed for a linebacker and guard. We played both ways at that time; I was right guard and right linebacker, and he was left guard and left linebacker. He and I worked well together straight across the board. I was happier than heck to have him as my teammate. Krause was just an unbelievable athlete. He was a great center fielder in baseball, and he obviously had a great career as a football player. He was about 6′3″, but he was a bean pole. We called him "Skinny." He could run and jump and overall was probably the best athlete on the team. Wally and I did pretty well as offensive guards, but I think we both enjoyed defense a little bit more. We were the same year in school and were very good friends.

After I left Iowa, I went on to play pro football with the Bears and Vikings for six years. I was able to sign my contract on George Halas' desk. That was a neat experience.

Some people say they don't remember me playing for the Bears. Here's my normal response: "Did you ever hear of Dick Butkus? That's why you never heard of me." I played behind Bill George, who was an All-Pro player my first year and then Dick the following four years.

My sixth year, I say I died and went to heaven and went up to Minnesota for one year. I rejoined Wally Hilgenberg and Paul Krause in playing for the Vikings. Minnesota played in the Super Bowl that year, in 1969, and I'm so glad I was able to finish my career up with Wally and Paul. Jerry Burns was even an assistant coach in Minnesota at that point.

I then came back to Dubuque, Iowa, where I grew up. I decided I had had enough football for a career and went into the advertising business.

Soon after, I began broadcasting Iowa games with Ron Gonder. We did that for 18 years on the radio and then one year on television. Ron and I hit it off really well and had a great 19 years together. When we first began during the Bob Commings era, wins were hard to come by. Then Hayden came on the scene. I told Gonder many times I was happy we stayed together long enough to do Iowa games during the Hayden Fry era. That was really exciting. Hayden is a great guy, and I wish I could see him more often. He did a great deal for the university.

Ron and I were broadcasting when my son, Jim, played linebacker at Iowa. I was able to broadcast all of his games. Jimmy didn't have a scholarship offer, but after Hayden called me, I said, "Jimmy, you can't beat the opportunity to go down there and give it a chance. Go take a chance, because if you never try, it sure won't happen." I knew damn well Hayden would provide him an opportunity because of his history with walk-ons. Hayden encouraged walk-ons and had so much success with them. From 1985 through 1988 Jimmy wore the black and gold and played very well.

In all, I had three sons who went to Iowa: Steve, Jimmy, and Bob. Bob played football his freshman year, and Steve played golf.

What it means to be a Hawkeye is hard to explain. In short, it was overwhelming. I was so fortunate to go to Iowa games with my dad in the early 1950s. That was probably the biggest thrill I had as a kid. I was so comfortable living in Iowa City for four years. The whole college atmosphere is great in Iowa City, and it has down-to-earth people. I grew up that way, and I appreciated everything in Iowa City because it was first-class.

I don't want to belabor it, but I could go on forever telling you how great it was to be a Hawkeye. Our family was very Hawkeyes-oriented. With my cousin in the 1940s, I'm part of three generations in my family to have played for Iowa. There are a lot of good memories over those years, and I'm just happy that I was fortunate enough to be part of it. You couldn't ask for anything better.

In 1963 Mike Reilly was named Iowa's Most Valuable Player, first-team All–Big Ten, and first-team All-America. Reilly and teammate Wally Hilgenberg comprised one of the best Big Ten linebacker duos in the 1960s. After his professional football career with the Bears and Vikings ended, he spent 19 years broadcasting Iowa football games. Mike still lives in his native city of Dubuque, Iowa.

SILAS McKINNIE

Running Back

1965–1967

I AM FROM INKSTER, MICHIGAN, which is a suburb of Detroit, and I went to Dearborn Heights' Robichaud High School. Later, Tyrone Wheatley went to the same high school and broke all my high school records. My high school coach, Keith Emerson, was like a second father to me. He was a great guy who gave me great advice. My father and mother trusted him to help me with my decision-making process on where to go to school.

I grew up near the University of Michigan, but I was a running back, and they wanted to make me a wide receiver. Andy MacDonald, the running backs coach at Iowa, recruited me to Iowa City. Coach Emerson and MacDonald played together in college at Central Michigan, so there was a connection. Both MacDonald and Jerry Burns were from this area. In addition, quite a few kids from Michigan, including Paul Krause, had had success at Iowa, so it was easy for me to make that decision.

Jerry Burns was a player's coach. He was really good with the veterans, but he was really hard on the young guys. You had to earn your way to become a vet. Coach Burns was an excellent football coach and an excellent offensive mind. He really knew football and offensive football in particular.

One thing that was attractive about Iowa then was the media projected Iowa to go 9–1 my sophomore year in 1965 and go to the Rose Bowl. We went the opposite and went 1–9. But at least from a talent standpoint, we were supposed to win more games because we had six to eight guys drafted off of that team.

So they fired Coach Burns and brought in Ray Nagel. It was a big change for our football team, and I'm not sure we had all the players to fit what Coach Nagel was trying to accomplish. We were really void of talent, because we were a senior-heavy team in 1965. Dave Long, Bill Briggs, Gary Snook, Karl Noonan, Cliff Wilder, Al Randolph, John Niland—all these guys graduated after the 1965 season and ended up in the NFL. That's a pretty big hole of players when you think about it. Plus, while it was an excellent coaching staff, Nagel brought in a totally different offense and defense.

I think that change in coaching systems and the loss of talent after my sophomore season were big reasons why the team didn't win much in my last two years. There were a couple teams like Notre Dame and Michigan State that were just so vastly superior to us talent-wise. When I was a sophomore, we were playing Michigan State on TV, and the only thing that my friends back in Detroit remember is that I came through a hole and George Webster took my head off. It was like a highlight film! But for most of our games, I honestly felt we were in such good physical shape and prepared so well that if the game could go on for a fifth quarter, we'd have a chance to win.

It was really an honor to be named team captain as a senior because those are the guys who you've been in the trenches with. I respected my teammates. We were in it together, and I really prided myself on always practicing hard. I never missed practice or games. That was one of those things that I got from my high school coach. It didn't matter how beat up I got in the last week's game. He did a great job with me mentally in getting me to understand that there's a difference between injury and pain, and I carried that with me to college.

In three years, I only had four fumbles. One of those was against Ohio State, and that was legitimate. I got hit in the rib cage, and the ball went all the way across the field! He really put a lick on me and actually put me out of the game. The other three fumbles all came in one game. We were playing against Miami in 1966. It was humid and sticky down there. On one of those fumbles, I was in traffic, and Ted Hendricks physically took the ball from me. He was called "the Mad Stork." I haven't blocked him yet! He was the hardest guy on the field to try and block.

The most memorable game of my career was when we played Indiana in 1967. We had them. They lined up to kick a field goal, and we knew that they weren't going to kick that field goal because a field goal didn't mean anything to them. I won't say who rushed in there and lost containment, but the Indiana player who was holding the ball wheeled around and got the first down.

Running back Silas McKinnie was named team captain his senior year and led Iowa in rushing all three years he played for the Hawkeyes.

Then they went down and scored a touchdown and beat us 21–17. That was the year they went to the Rose Bowl, and we had them.

Frank Gilliam has been helping me with some life decisions ever since he coached me in college, and we are still very close. Eddie Podolak and I stay in touch, too. Ed Podolak was probably the best all-around athlete I have ever played with or been around. He was a great competitor, and he made me better. He and I became very good friends.

Coach Fry did a great job at Iowa. He had a great commitment to the program. He recruited good players, but he also had good coaches. They did things the right way, and then it's really nice when you transition and you get a guy like Coach Ferentz in there who has those same kinds of values. He keeps his coaches and never gets too high or too low. There's great stability.

I absolutely love going back to watch games in Iowa City. I go there as much as I can and probably more than I should! It was a great honor to be an honorary captain. It wasn't something that I expected. I was really pumped up and was able to go with my grandson. Even though he was young, that's something he'll always remember, because he got to shake Coach Ferentz's hand before the game and wish him good luck. That was a neat experience. These coaches always make you feel like you are a part of the program.

When I first made the decision to go to Iowa, I was 90 percent sure it was the right decision. I knew after I got there that if I had to do it all over again, I'd do the same thing. I was a little bit homesick when I first got there, like most people are. But I thought the people—and I'm not just talking about athletes—were really good people. It is so much a part of me. I grew up 20 minutes from the University of Michigan, and I always wanted to go there. I ended up going to Iowa, and now it really almost feels like I grew up 20 minutes from the University of Iowa. That's how I feel about it. I have such a great comfort level there. I have a great love for that university, for the people that I played with, and for the coaches I played for. It's just such a big part of me and who I am.

Silas McKinnie led Iowa in rushing all three of his years in uniform. He was the first Hawkeye to accomplish this feat in more than three decades. After graduating in 1968, McKinnie played five seasons in the Canadian Football League. He later spent two decades as a college basketball coach. McKinnie is currently a personnel scout for the Detroit Lions.

JON MESKIMEN

OFFENSIVE GUARD

1966–1969

OUR HIGH SCHOOL TEAM IN CEDAR RAPIDS was undefeated our last three years. Except for one tie our junior year, we made it a clean sweep. They moved me to halfback as a 5′11″, 220-pound senior. We had a lot of depth and a really good team coached by Ted Lawrence.

Coach Lawrence became a freshman coach at the University of Iowa after my senior year. I was being recruited by Iowa State, Notre Dame, and a couple other Big Ten schools at the time. I thought Iowa was the school I wanted to come to, and when Coach Lawrence came to the university, my choice became even easier. Coach's son, Larry, was one year behind me and our quarterback at Jefferson High School. He wound up playing at Iowa also.

When I came to Iowa, I was a fullback for one day. I'd kind of eaten my way out of the fullback position to an offensive guard position, and that's where I played each year in college.

My freshman year of 1966 was the first year freshmen were allowed to play in games. I played in two games my freshman year, but most of the time we were bag-holders. It was really unbelievable to come out of that tunnel the first time—or any time for that matter—and have 50,000 to 60,000 people screaming and yelling for you.

I did not play in the first game my sophomore year. The second game, I played the second half and did pretty well. The first game I ever started was the following one at Notre Dame. They had a big defensive tackle by the name of Mike McCoy, who wound up playing with the Green Bay Packers. He was the first guy I had to block. We came out of the tunnel, and there were only about 200 Iowa fans. All the rest of them were for Notre Dame. A guy by the name of Terry Hanratty was the quarterback at the time for Notre Dame, and Ara Parseghian was the coach. Needless to say, I was shakin' in my boots.

That day we got the opening kickoff, drove it down the field, and scored to lead Notre Dame. Those were the last points we scored that day. We missed the extra point and then lost 56–6. Not much went right after that opening drive. Regardless, it's pretty memorable since it was my first start at Iowa.

We went 5–5 my junior year. We really kind of turned the corner. Ed Podolak had played really well, as had Larry Lawrence at quarterback. Our defense was playing a little bit better also.

During spring ball after that season, we had a boycott here at school, and all but four or five of our black players walked off the team and would not practice. Some outside agitators had come to Iowa City to stir things up. They were telling our players they weren't being treated equally and fairly, but that was really not true at all. Nevertheless, a group of players walked off, and then the coach kicked 'em all off for good. That took our entire defensive secondary, including four starters and two of the backups. Those who stayed were Denny Green, Ray Cavole, Ray Manning, and a couple others. Some stayed, but losing that group of players did hurt.

The Vietnam conflict was also going on at that time. We had riots on campus. Some students were walking downtown and throwing bricks through windows, and the riot police were here. For the sake of the students, they let us go home. That was another distraction that interfered with our trying to become a better football team. There were some interesting happenings in the late 1960s, that's for sure.

Our senior year we averaged 26 points a game, so we moved the ball really well. Unfortunately we also gave up 28 points a game, so we had some real shoot-outs. One game in particular was against Purdue. We were behind 35–31 with two seconds left and no timeouts. We completed a pass to the 2-yard line. All our receiver had to do was fall into the end zone, but in the process of catching the ball, he accidentally put a knee down. That was the game—we had it in the bag and let it get away. That was a tough one, and we still had four or five games left in the season. That game just kind of deflated us. There were a couple games where we played really well but just gave up too many points.

Jon Meskimen was named first-team All–Big Ten both his junior and senior seasons, and team captain in 1969.

I really enjoyed every part of game week. Probably the most exciting moment was being a cocaptain my senior year while we went out on the field to meet the other cocaptains. Big Ten football is good football, and one of the things I'm most proud of is saying that I played in the Big Ten.

The friendships you make along the way are important. You don't do too much with the freshmen when you're a senior, but on your way up, you sure learn to respect the seniors and the juniors and those people ahead of you, and you want to play your best for them also. A lot of them are still my best friends to this day. My best friend was my freshman roommate, Mike Cilek. He was a quarterback, and we played against one another in high school. I always had to kid him that my high school team beat his 59–0 when he was a senior in high school. I was the best man in his wedding, and he was the best man in mine. We've continued to be friends for almost 50 years now, and our wives have been good friends. I wound up teaching one of his daughters in school, too, and that was special.

My freshman year was Ray Nagel's first year. There was talk of Evy returning, but he remained as Iowa's athletics director. I've always had great respect for the coaches we had. Coach Nagel was a lawyer and a mild-mannered man. I went to talk to him my senior year. I said, "Coach, I've been here three years, and you've never really come in and tried to fire us up or get us going." He said, "Well, it's my philosophy that when students get to college, they can get themselves ready to play." After that week, I said, "Coach, you mean you don't think Woody Hayes ever goes in the locker room and yells and shouts, slams the lockers, and gets his team fired up?" He said, "Well, it's just a difference in philosophy, and I don't think I have to do that."

That happened to be the week we were playing Northwestern. The year before we had played Northwestern, and they had scored a touchdown in the second quarter. They came back with an onside kick that went right by me. I thought it was going too high and was going to go out of bounds or the end behind me would come up and get it, so I went forward and blocked somebody. They retrieved the ball and drove down and scored again. I'll be darned if they didn't come back with an onside kick again, and the end behind me again took off downfield and they received the ball and drove down and tried a field goal just before halftime. We never had an offensive play the entire second quarter.

So the next year the coaches had been showing us that quarter of football all week long. Coach Nagel, on Saturday just before the game, had that canister of film. He was wavin' it around and said, "We've shown this to you all week; we do not want this to happen to us again. We need to be ready to play." He tried to open up the can of film, and he couldn't get it open. So he paused the speech and was standing there struggling with this can of film, and we all started to snicker. He finally got it open and threw the reel up against the wall and said, "Let's go play football!" That was the day we beat Northwestern 68–34. Ed Podolak ran for 286 yards on the ground and set a Big Ten single-game rushing record. Something worked that day, but he never tried that speech again.

When I was a senior, I wanted to play in the pros, but I was too short. I weighed between 235 and 250, so I had the weight to do it. But the Dallas scout told me, "You've had a great career; you've played real well; but our shortest guard right now is 6′4″ and weighs 260. Are we gonna replace him with somebody who's smaller and a little lighter, or are we gonna look for somebody who's bigger?" It's a business when you get to the pros.

Afterward, I stayed on two years as a graduate assistant coach at Iowa. I was able to finish my degrees before I moved on to become a high school head football coach in Cedar Rapids. I was there five years and came back to Iowa City West High School. I was head coach at West for seven years. Since then, West High has grown with Iowa City, so now instead of being the smallest school in the league, it's the second-largest high school in the state. They've had several state championships and a lot of good athletics. Hopefully, I started some of that. When I was done with football, I continued on as a physical education teacher until my retirement.

What does it mean to be a Hawkeye? It means pride in the university and pride in Iowa. I've taken a great deal of pride in trying to continue the legacy of the sports and people here at Iowa. I live just a mile and a half from the stadium. On game day I can go outside and hear the crowd. There are probably 10,000 people who tailgate and don't even have tickets to the game. Saturday is game day in Iowa City. When there's a home football game, everybody takes a great deal of pride in how the Hawkeyes do. I was with a salesman just this week, and he said Iowa ranks in the top 10 in college merchandising sold around the country. We have an avid fan base. If you want to see what Big Ten football is all about, just come to Iowa City.

Jon Meskimen played offensive guard in the late 1960s. He was named first-team All–Big Ten both his junior and senior seasons, and team captain in 1969. After his playing days were complete, he stayed at Iowa for two years as a graduate assistant coach. Later, as a high school head coach, he started a Special Olympics program for his school. Meskimen did that for 26 years and took athletes to three World Special Olympics games. He currently lives in Iowa City.

The SEVENTIES

BILL WINDAUER

DEFENSIVE TACKLE

1969–1970, 1972

PLAYING IN THE BIG TEN DREW ME TO IOWA. I went to Mendel Catholic High School, which is on the south side of Chicago. As a Catholic League kid, I probably could have gone to Notre Dame. But Iowa had a great tradition, and that's why I decided to come out here. At that time, Iowa was doing okay. Ray Nagel was a really good coach. He had a great staff and was pulling a bunch of good players together. Iowa was slated to do pretty well right when I was coming in. Plus, I didn't particularly want to go to a big, giant school. I liked Iowa's size and wanted to get away from the hustle and bustle of the big city. I liked the more low-key atmosphere of Iowa.

Forest Evashevski, who had won the Rose Bowl at Iowa as a young coach, became the athletics director. I think there was sort of a battle between him and the coaches he brought in, mainly because he wanted to keep a lot of control over what was being done and everything. I think that was not such a good atmosphere for a coach, to have your athletics director trying to run the show. That may be the way some coaches are where they don't want to give up the reins even after they're through with their coaching days. As a player, you don't really get into the politics a whole bunch, because you're just a player. You just do what they tell you to do. You play your hardest and try to be as good as you can be. But you could sort of sense that there was something happening. Roughly half our coaches were old Evashevski guys, and the other half of the coaches were the ones Nagel brought in. I would imagine there was some conflict even within the coaching staff that made it difficult for things to progress as well as they probably should have.

There was a lot of campus turmoil, rioting, and unrest on campus, with Vietnam, the discrimination problems, and the assassination of Martin Luther King. As an athlete and a football player, you mostly kept your nose to the grindstone and didn't get involved in that kind of stuff. For most of us, we wanted to focus on playing football, going to school, and probably drinking a beer or two along the way, but we were stuck between a rock and a hard place.

Then the majority of the black players on the team got together and boycotted practice because of the unrest that was going on within the black community. A lot of guys got kicked off the team, and that put us on a downward spiral. Here again, you're out there playing and doing what you can do, but it causes a lot of uncertainty. This affected not just Iowa guys but anyone from about the mid-1960s through the mid-'70s. There was about a five- to eight-year time span in there when there was not a really good atmosphere within college athletics.

What was interesting is that some of us were so young that we didn't even know all the boycotting players that well. You knew the guys in your recruiting class and maybe some of the guys from the year before, but you really didn't know much about some of these older guys. You didn't know their personalities, and you didn't hang around together much. So then we were set in a room and told, "Okay, now you vote thumbs up or thumbs down on whether these guys get to come back." Well, how the hell do you do that? But by hook or crook, some of the guys got voted back on and some of them didn't. Meanwhile, we tried to keep living life as football players. That's the world we lived in.

We were 18- and 19-year-old kids, when you think of it. All of a sudden, you're thrown into the most volatile kind of world and just trying to figure out how to handle it. With Vietnam, guys who didn't have the grades were getting drafted. Because I was in school and my grades were fine, I wasn't getting called in, but I would have been on a helicopter and off to war if I wasn't in college and didn't have grades. That was the other pressure on a lot of us to compete. Tomorrow, you might not even be here. You might be in the jungle somewhere shooting somebody or getting shot yourself. I had a really good high school buddy of mine, Jack Dalton. He was a senior captain of the wrestling team and a wonderful guy, but he was killed on my birthday in Vietnam. That's the other thing we were faced with. It was a pretty interesting time.

My first two years were with Nagel, and then I was redshirted in 1971 because of an ankle injury. With Frank Lauterbur coming in, I was sort of like a grad assistant that year. The new coaching staff relied on me a little bit, just to acclimate them to players' names and things. I played in 1972 as a fifth-year senior, and thank God I got out of there before the 1973 season. They lost all of their games, and it was just a total disaster. It was not the most enjoyable circumstances for any of us at that time, but we just sort of survived the situation, and that was it.

You remember the big games like Michigan or Ohio State because it was always a great challenge. You remember playing against Franco Harris and a lot of these other phenomenal football players. You got yourself up for the game and played your hardest. If you won, that was great, but if you just played a good game, that was acceptable, in my book anyway. My senior year, we played against Penn State. Joe Paterno was even coaching then! Flying out to Penn State and playing against them was a big challenge and a great experience.

For some reason, we seemed to always have a knock-down, drag-out rivalry with Michigan State and Minnesota. I don't know why, but it seemed like those two always gave us tough, close games. Duffy Daugherty was the coach at Michigan State at the time, and they just played tough, hard-nosed football. Minnesota did the same thing. We just banged it out with those guys. There was no chance of really going to bowl games back then. There was the Rose Bowl, but we never got even close enough to sniff a rose. Since you didn't worry so much about going to a bowl game, every game during the season was sort of like your bowl game.

I don't think anybody comes out of football without being damaged. I would say that during my college career, I probably had 12 concussions, sometimes even to the point where I didn't remember a game. You're playing the game, but you don't remember the game. I have buddies who remember almost every play of every game they were ever in, but I remember very little of any specific game. I've had a knee replaced and metal put in my toes to fix a bad turf toe. I go through the airport now and buzz really bad at the metal detectors! I've had probably 10 surgeries on my elbows, knees, and ankle. It does take its toll on you, but that's part of the game. I don't think anybody escapes it unless you're a backup kind of guy. It's a really tough thing to go through, but I don't think anybody complains about it. You understand it's there. If you're a war horse, you're a war horse, and you just do it. I'm not complaining at all. I've had a good life.

Defensive tackle Bill Windauer was drawn to Iowa because of its winning tradition and made Iowa City his home during his years in the NFL.

My wife and I moved back to Iowa City to make it our home base when I was playing in the NFL. I was selling real estate while I was training and playing, but once I got through with football, I really didn't want to be a real estate salesman. I started working with the University of Iowa Foundation as a fund-raiser, raising money for scholarships. Right now I'm raising money to build a new addition to our dental building. I enjoy doing it because I like people. I was able to stay here in Iowa City and enjoy a city where there's no rush-hour traffic. It takes me about five minutes to go home in the evening. All my kids were athletes, and Iowa City was a good place to bring them up.

Hayden Fry came in and rekindled the tradition that had been lost for a while. He built a solid base, and then Kirk [Ferentz] was able to come in and continue that. Sure, they had their tough times, but I'm so proud of them because now they can go to bowl games almost every year. They play that well. Two thousand nine was a phenomenal year, the kind of year you really want to cherish. I'm just happy these kids are having this experience. Down the line, they'll be thinking about it just the way I am.

Being a Hawkeye means carrying on the tradition from the early years and great people like our Heisman Trophy winner, Nile Kinnick. To be a part of that kind of long-term tradition is incredible. Maybe my teams weren't that great, but you're part of a bigger place and a great university. Last year, the University of Iowa Hall of Fame inducted a guy named Fred Becker. He was the first football player to be a first-team All-American for the University of Iowa, and then he got killed in World War I as a soldier. You think of that tradition, and we represent what those guys represented. For me, anyway, being a football player means being a part of the bigger brotherhood of football players and athletes at the university and living up to the standards set by the Nile Kinnicks and the Fred Beckers. That's what makes me proud, that it's a tradition that I'm trying to carry on, and it'll go on forever. I don't know what football will be like in 100 years, but hopefully 100 years from now there will still be an Iowa football team. We'll always be a part of that.

Bill Windauer played defensive tackle for four NFL teams after graduating from Iowa. He has served as a fund-raiser for the University of Iowa for 24 years and is currently the director of development for the University of Iowa College of Dentistry. His son, Bobby, was a decathlete for the Hawkeyes, lettering in track at Iowa in 2007 and 2009. "He got a letter jacket and a letter ring," Windauer said. "I was really proud of him because that's the heritage. He's following me in a way."

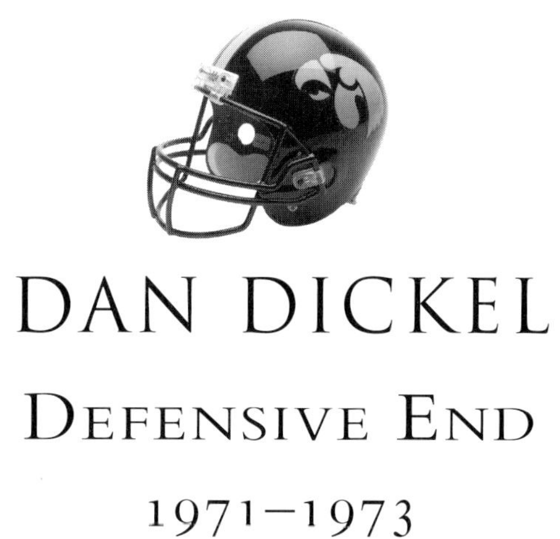

DAN DICKEL

DEFENSIVE END

1971–1973

I GREW UP IN KALONA, IOWA, which is just about 20 miles down the road from Iowa City. I went to Mid-Prairie High School and played several sports. I played basketball, and my senior year, we played in the state championship game against Paullina. We finished runner-up, unfortunately! I also ran track in high school. In football I was a wide receiver and a defensive end.

There were 26 recruits in my class, and I was the last one offered a scholarship. They didn't recruit me, actually, until they watched me play basketball in the state tournament. That's what I was told. My recruiting trip was my driving up to watch a spring practice, eating with a coach and another recruit, and driving back home. That was it.

I didn't have any other Division I scholarship offers. I had been looking at a lot of Division III schools. Back then, there were a couple of players from Iowa who had played Division III football who had also played basketball. For example, Vern Den Herder was at Central, and he played both football and basketball, and he had made it with the Dolphins. I guess in my mind I was going to go and play both sports in college, but then when a scholarship offer came along from Iowa, that was definitely what I wanted to do.

Ray Nagel was the head coach my freshman year, but freshmen were still not eligible to play. I think it was my junior year when freshmen were first eligible, so I just played three years on the varsity. Frank Lauterbur came in when I was a sophomore. He had come from a very successful program in Toledo. I remember him coming in and saying how some of the bigger guys were going to cut weight so we were going to be faster and quicker than everybody. I remember thinking, after playing Ohio State, that we not only were smaller, but we weren't any quicker either! It was kind of interesting.

My first year under Lauterbur, we were 1–10. Early in the year, a defensive end who was ahead of me, Ike White, got hurt. Then I got my opportunity, and that was it. I started ever since then. My first start was against Indiana that year. I just know things went well. I had a good game, and that's about it. That's a long time ago.

We were 3–7–1 my junior year. The tie was against Michigan State. I remember the Michigan State coach, Duffy Daugherty, announced after that game that he was retiring at the end of the season, so that was kind of interesting. But my whole junior year went very well for me. I led the Big Ten in tackles for loss in 1972, and yet the next year when the Big Ten record book came out, my name wasn't even listed anywhere among the guys listed for tackles for loss. It was quite interesting to me how that ever occurred. It was just one of those things, I guess.

I was named team MVP in 1972. Our head trainer, Tom Spalj, had become sick late that season. The team banquet was scheduled for shortly after the season. After the season and before the banquet, Spalj passed away, and he was a young man. So they moved the whole banquet and changed it, and it wasn't much of anything, really. I remember being surprised when they awarded me that—I hadn't even thought about being the MVP. The thing I suppose I got out of that more than anything was it just gave me confidence that I could play the game fairly well and that maybe I would have an opportunity to go on and play after college.

My senior year was the real disaster—0–11. I think we should have really seen it coming. Like I said, when I was a freshman, 26 of us came in as recruits. My senior year, there were only six of us left, and I was the only defensive player. When you don't have the senior leadership, which obviously we didn't, that's really tough. Things just didn't click that year, and it was hard—it really was. Before practices, I remember just having to convince myself that I needed to go out there and do my best. And that's about all you can do.

I'll be honest, I just came to Iowa with the thought of playing football. Then I learned that, obviously, you needed to get the work done in the classroom, too. My second semester as a freshman was my poorest one, but after

Defensive end Dan Dickel was named Iowa's team MVP as a junior in 1972, and he was selected as the captain of the 1973 Hawkeyes.

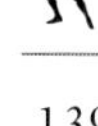

that, I did well in the classroom. I got my degree in elementary education. I guess I was pretty much a student-athlete, and that was it.

I used to say I went from the worst college team to the worst professional team. My first year in the pros with the Baltimore Colts, we were 2–12. Howard Schnellenberger was our coach, but he got fired in the locker room after the third game of the year by Joe Thomas, the general manager. Thomas then became the coach for the rest of the year, and it was pretty much a joke. Then the next year, Ted Marchibroda came in, and we won our division three years in a row. We had really good teams, one of the best in the NFL, but we were beaten in the playoffs—twice by the Steelers when they were at their prime, and then once by the Oakland Raiders when they were really good. I spent four years with Baltimore, and I finished up my last year with the Detroit Lions.

After that, I went right to Kewanee, Illinois, and became a high school coach. In September of 1979, Lauterbur was coaching with the Los Angeles

Rams. He called me and said, "We'll guarantee you a spot on the roster," because somebody had gotten hurt and they needed help. But I had already started coaching, and in my mind, I was done. Well, that year the Rams played in the Super Bowl, so I missed an opportunity there! But that was all right.

This is my first year in 47 years that I haven't been out on the football field. Last year, I helped somebody else who used to coach for me, and then this year I stepped away from it. However, I'm going to Turkey to coach an American football camp. I'll be over there for 12 days, so that will be my football fill for the year!

It's been a real joy to watch the Hawkeyes over the years. I have developed a good relationship with Coach Ferentz. When you know people personally, you just feel all the better for them when they have that kind of success.

I'm just thrilled to root for the Hawkeyes and watch them do well. Regardless of where I am, I'm proud to say that I'm an Iowan and a former Hawk player. Many times I've said that when I was a captain, it was maybe the worst team in Iowa history. But that hasn't stopped me from being proud of being an Iowa Hawkeye football player, there's no doubt about that.

As a sophomore in 1971, Dan Dickel made 18 tackles in his first start, a 14–7 loss to Indiana. The following year, he recovered two fumbles in a 6–6 tie against Michigan State, and he had 18 tackles and a forced fumble against Wisconsin in Madison. Dickel finished with nine sacks, five fumble recoveries, and four forced fumbles in 1972, and he led the Big Ten in tackles for loss with 15 that year. After the season, he became the first junior in eight years to be named Iowa's team MVP, and he was selected as the captain of the 1973 Hawkeyes. Dan Dickel later spent more than three decades coaching high school football and coached Highland-Lone Tree High School to a Class 2A state runner-up finish in 1997.

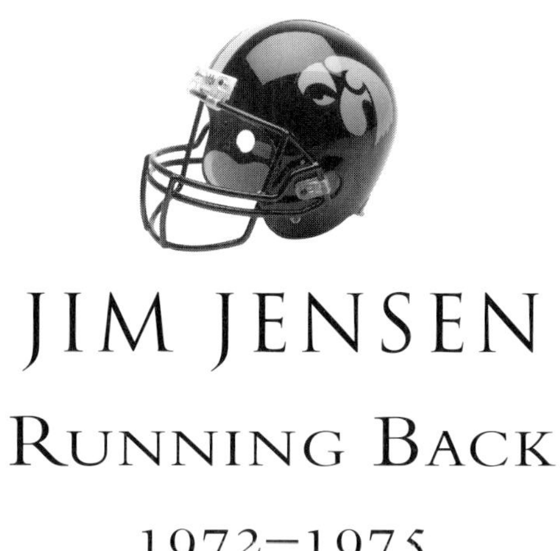

JIM JENSEN

Running Back

1972–1975

The days of my youth were filled with exploring new places, competing in sports, and running. I learned early on I could run fast, and usually my outdoor activities involved running. I grew up in Davenport, Iowa, which is 60 miles east of Iowa City. The Quad Cities, as the Davenport metro area is called, had tremendous sports programs and had always produced high-quality athletes.

The biggest factor that led me to sign with Iowa was the head coach, Frank Lauterber. While he hadn't been at Iowa for more than one season, I knew he wanted me to succeed and he had my best interests at heart. I trusted him each time he shook my hand and looked into my eyes and said, "We want you to be an Iowa Hawkeye, and I'll do everything I can to make you a great one." I couldn't say that about any of the other coaches I had met.

During my recruiting weekend to Iowa City, it was a visit to an art class that still makes me smile the most. My Hawkeye veteran player escort was Tom Cabalka, and assistant coach Steve Szabo was there as well. Part of the weekend was set aside for academic purposes, and because I had noted on my paperwork that the fine arts were of interest to me, the two accompanied me to an art class on campus.

I could tell during the drive over to the art college that Tom and Steve were a little leery about why a football player would have any interest in the arts. That was a passion of mine, I explained. The two curriculums typically don't mix very well, and I wasn't getting much understanding from Tom and Steve as we walked into a large, high-ceilinged, atrium-type room with students perched at drawing tables.

The art instructor paused to welcome us, then continued with his instructions to the students: "Okay, everyone, this will be a quick one-minute sketch, so keep your eyes on the subject and try and capture the main lines first. Ready? Go."

On his command, a robed girl who was sitting in a chair on a table in the middle of the room gracefully stood up and dropped her robe to the ground. Entirely nude, she assumed a pose with one hand on her hip, and the students began to furiously sketch with their charcoal. Tom and Coach Szabo were awestruck for a moment, but then they turned and gave me an incredulous look. I simply winked at them and turned back toward the nude model to enjoy another sublime 30 seconds of natural scenery.

The car ride back to the football offices was entertaining to say the least. According to my chaperones, I had gone from being an artsy-fartsy geek to being the smartest recruit they had ever met. "No friggin' wonder he wants to take art classes!" they were rumored to have said to several others that weekend as they recounted their trip to the art school.

Coach Frank Lauterbur, or FXL, as he liked to be called [short for Francis Xavier Lauterbur], came to Iowa from the University of Toledo, where he had turned a mediocre team into a conference champ. He was familiar with the Midwest high school talent due to his previous recruiting efforts, and he was able to bring along prospects like Bobby Lawson, Andre Jackson, Rod Walters, and Joe Devlin.

The 1972 season was exciting because I was entering a whole new level of football competition and I couldn't wait to show everyone what I could do. College football teams were comprised of the best players from across the nation, and as a freshman, we had to adjust to being placed at the bottom of the food chain. Most of us had spent the prior two years as the stud in our hometowns, so there was definitely an adjustment as we were thrown into the mix of a team full of veteran Big Ten players. As much as it was exhilarating, humility was expected and learned in the same breath.

The 1972 Hawkeye team had popular veterans like Kyle Skogman, Craig Darling, Bill Windauer, and Brian Rollins. It was intimidating for an 18-year-old kid to look across the line of scrimmage and realize you would be pitted against a player you had heard about on the radio the prior season.

As a freshman, training camp began with rookies being placed on the "meat squad" until they proved themselves. It was brutal, but everybody knew it and accepted it.

I was fortunate my freshman year because I had the ambition and luck to survive some hardships and make it to the varsity team halfway through the season. It didn't happen right away as I had hoped because of injuries. First it was a foot problem that came from playing in artificial turf shoes. Then, because I was tall for a running back at 6′4″ and hadn't yet learned the art of lowering my shoulder at contact, I developed two hip pointers. Hip pointers come from being hit at the point on one's hip where the quad muscles connect to the hip bone. I was on the meat squad at the time, and the trainers would wrap my hips with bubble wrap to protect the injured areas. The bubble wrap, worn under the football pants, considerably expanded my hip dimensions, and defensive coordinator Ducky Lewis sarcastically exclaimed one afternoon during practice, "Jensen, you look like the great pumpkin taking a handoff!"

Eventually, I healed enough to have some stellar games on the JV squad. I had a big game in Minnesota, even after being hit in the gonads by a kickoff ball that skidded off the wet turf during pregame [warm-ups]. Then at Illinois I ran around and through the Fighting Illini. In those days, the JV squad traveled by bus, which made for some long days and nights. The Illinois trip was especially long, as my buddy, Rob Fick, somehow hooked me up with a bottle of Sloe Gin for the trip home. I did my best to be every inch of a knucklehead rookie and drank it within 45 minutes. Before we even got across the Illinois state line, the bus felt like it started doing cartwheels, and I puked out the back window.

When we finally arrived back in Iowa City, the JV coaches looked at me and my red-stained sweater vest in disgust as I got off the bus. They knew I would have hell to pay with FXL the following week. To add insult to injury, JV trainer John Streif chased me down with a car full of players as I attempted to walk back to my dorm room and sleep it off. I had complained of a head injury during the game earlier that day, and he thought the red on my vest was blood I had vomited due to a concussion. I had to finally tell him the truth that I had gotten drunk on Sloe Gin and it was booze rather than blood on my vest. It was a hard lesson learned.

It was ironic that the week I was elevated to the varsity squad was the same week FXL pulled me aside before practice to discuss the Sloe Gin episode.

FXL had a routine of walking around the room before practice and talking to each player. It was his style, and he had a great personal rapport with each of us. As I sat back and leaned against the wall, I was hoping he would just say his routine words to me and continue on by. But he didn't. He asked me to meet him in the film room down the hall. It was a long agonizing walk as he followed me there. He sat me down and looked at me for a moment with his steely eyes and said, "Would you care to explain what happened last weekend on the JV bus?"

I remember it took everything I had not to become a blubbering, repentant idiot. He had barely finished talking before I launched into a heartfelt soliloquy of why I had done a really stupid thing. I had of course practiced the speech many times over in my mind, but however I managed to say it, FXL solemnly looked at me when I was finished and said what we would hope any knowing father would tell his son: "You know, Jim, we were all young once and we've all made some stupid mistakes. I believe you've learned a lesson here, and I know it won't happen again."

He extended his hand to me, and I shook it as if it was the last human hand I would ever touch. We both got up and walked back to where the team was waiting and uneventfully all trotted out to the practice field. That was the day FXL earned the lifelong respect of a young impressionable football player who would never forget his words of wisdom and trust.

My freshman season ended with our team having a 3–7–1 record. Compared to FXL's first year in 1971 when they were 1–10, the 1972 team had tripled its productivity. Emotions and expectations were high as 1972 ended and 1973 began.

Another reason I chose to go to the University of Iowa was because Coach Lauterber assured me I could run track as well as play football. I actually had garnered more acclaim as a trackster in Iowa high school competition and was on multiple state championship teams and was a state champion in the high hurdles, the pentathlon, and the mile medley relay event. My senior high school year at the Iowa State outdoor meet I won the 120-yard high hurdles and placed high in four other events. I loved track, so being able to compete collegiately was important.

I injured my neck during spring football, but injury and all, I still managed to attend classes and take part in my physical education curriculum. The injury also kept me from taking part in the outdoor track season, but the important thing was I completed my first year of college with passing grades

Running back Jim Jensen's career highlights include a 202-yard performance against Indiana, which was the second-best single-game total in school history.

and I earned varsity letters in two sports. It was a tumultuous freshman year, but through all the trials and tribulations I had become a bona fide Hawkeye letterman. And, I was excited about the prospects of returning for my sophomore year in the fall.

The year before I attended Iowa, its football team was 1–10. My freshman year our record was 3–7–1, so the vast majority of the players, coaches, fans, boosters, and media thought we were on our way to building a winning tradition because we had won three times as many games and eked out a tie. An air of optimism existed when training camp began in August of 1973 and, personally, having been through the drill before, I was more confident as a player heading into my second season.

We had had a tremendous recruiting class in 1972, and many rookies played well enough to earn a varsity letter. We had a great core of returning first-year veterans like Andre Jackson, Joe Devlin, Rod Walters, Mark Fetter, and Rod Wellington, and we did our best to assume the leadership roles our coaches continually demanded of us. FXL did a good job of instilling in us the desire to make Hawkeye football the pride of the nation as it had been in the past, and I thought our attitudes were right on target. Even though we lost key starters, our sophomore class was fortunate to have second-year veterans like Dan McCarney, Warren Peiffer, and Earl Douthitt at our sides.

When the 1973 Iowa Hawkeye football season began, the whole state was expecting the improvement to carry over from the prior year. The coaching staff was in its third season, and the great rookie class from the year before had logged a lot of playing time. The veteran players now had an improved supporting cast. Hawkeye fever gripped the state.

My neck had healed relatively well during the off-season, and I was in great shape for training camp. My speed and strength had improved, my familiarity with the fullback position had increased, and I was really excited about not having to be on the meat squad! There were no returning juniors or seniors at fullback that year, so it was either going to be Phil Haymen or myself as the eventual starter at that position.

Who would have ever guessed that by the time 1973 was over, the Hawks would have lost every game and FXL would be fired? Or that three times during the season our opponents would score more than 50 points? None of this was imaginable at the beginning of the year. The 1973 season was the year that the Hawkeyes were to break free from the shackles of mediocrity and reclaim their honor.

But the first three games of the season found us playing against Michigan, UCLA, and Penn State—all perennial powerhouses. While most teams today begin the season playing easy nonconference teams, we began the season playing the top teams in the nation. We were chewed up, spit out, and tread upon as our season began 0–3. We played Michigan at home in front of a sold-out crowd and then traveled to UCLA and Penn State in a matter of two weeks. West to east, it was a lot of time on the road, and we had plenty of wounds to lick on the plane flights home.

Looking back on the UCLA game, I was thrilled at the time to travel to Southern California and play in the legendary Los Angeles Coliseum. The sight of palm trees along the roadside and the Pacific Ocean to the west really had me excited to play football. It was an evening game to boot, and I loved playing at night. In addition, there's something intoxicating about growing up in the Midwest and being able to visit California for the first time. It almost seemed like it was too good to be true. *Life really can't be this nice,* I remembered thinking. It wasn't—we lost 55–18.

We traveled the width of the United States in a matter of eight days as we went from Los Angeles one Saturday to State College the next. We jumped from the proverbial frying pan into the fire in the midst of a week. UCLA was a powerhouse, and Penn State ranked right up there with them. The Penn State score wasn't nearly as bad as UCLA, but a 27–8 loss is still a loss. Besides the score, what hurt the team the worst was fellow sophomore running back Phil Haymen fractured his neck in the early part of the game. Phil and I had been rotating at the fullback position, and we took plays from the sideline into the huddle.

But as I stood on the sideline and watched him take a dive handoff and hit the interior Penn State defensive line, I noticed that he dropped his head prior to impact, similar to what I had done in spring ball. It was a massive collision, and when the bodies had all gotten up off the ground and cleared away, Phil still lay there motionless. Needless to say, I had major flashbacks to just six months before when it was me laying there on the field with a jammed neck. I watched as the trainers and team doctor rushed out onto the field and knelt around Phil trying to determine the extent of his injury. Once they had carefully rolled him onto his back, I saw them ask him to move his arms, squeeze their hands for any sign of motor or strength loss, move his legs, etc. There was a hush on the sideline as his teammates held their breaths hoping he would sit up and walk off the field. Within a few minutes, Phil was helped to his feet and walked with assistance to our bench.

Because I had recently survived and overcome a similar injury, Phil's misfortune jarred a sense of gloom into my psyche that day. Not only because he was a good friend and teammate, but also since it could have been me who was hurt on that play. It was but a fleeting thought, though, as FXL turned and looked at me with his steely eyes and said, "You've got to get the job done, Jens. Let's get back in there and make something happen."

I nodded my head in understanding, snapped my chin strap back on, and ran out to the huddle. Thank God the adrenaline of a 20-year-old overrides any attempt of common sense from controlling the mind. Minutes later I was oblivious to the fact we were all fragile mortals, and I played football that afternoon in Beaver Stadium as if there were no tomorrow.

At the time none of us knew, including the doctors or trainers, that Phil had sustained a fractured first cervical in his neck. It was a shock when we finally learned the seriousness and saw him in a halo traction apparatus at the hospital. When I went to visit Phil, it was a sobering experience. As I slowly opened the door to his darkened room, I looked in and saw his 6′3″ body lying face up on the bed with a metal ring around his head and a series of pins inserted into his skull. I took a deep breath and attempted to be as optimistic and light-hearted as I could be. Phil was always easy-going and he gave me a big smile when he heard my voice.

The two of us had been former all-state contenders in high school football and track and had battled each other for the starting fullback job in Iowa City. We were the same age and were teammates, competitors, partners in crime, brothers, and friends all rolled into one. He and I probably shared the most common bond on the Iowa football team that year, so it was an emotional afternoon when I stopped by to see him. When our eyes met as I was leaving, there was an unspoken understanding that it could have been either one of us there on the hospital bed that day.

As the 1973 season played itself out, the losses kept mounting and frustrations kept growing. The last time a Hawkeye team had been winless was in 1889, when they played a single game against Grinnell College. Each afternoon when we would meet for a beer after practice at the Wagon Wheel Saloon in Coralville, someone always ended up saying, "Of course we're gonna win a game. Every team in the Big Ten has to win at least one game!"

As the season went on, it was inevitable that the head coach would come under fire from many fronts. FXL ended up being terminated before the season was over, and we were mentally wounded by the fact that the man we loved and trusted had been fired. I was personally torn apart because Frank had always been good to me and lived up to his word.

Football at the University of Iowa in those days was lean in the winning column and a trying experience. There isn't a lot a person can do to shine up the fact that experiencing an 0–11 season was anything but painful drudgery. Looking back, I can say I learned important lessons about attitude, working through adversity, discipline, and the importance of hope. But that's about it. Winning less than 10 games during a 44-game college career is not something to be proud of or brag about. Facts are facts. The Iowa Hawkeyes never did give up, though, and an important motivation at the time was knowing that when we took the field at Kinnick Stadium on Saturday, the crowd loved us and cheered us all the way through each game to the end. We were loved and supported by the fans, in spite of the scoreboard, and that fact made an indelible mark on my soul I have never forgotten.

The 1973 season was a good season for me, personally. I was the leading rusher that year, and on the awards chart in the locker room hallway, I had accomplished many personal goals and surpassed many running back milestones. For each goal players achieved that season, we were awarded a gold star for our helmets. Mine was practically covered by season's end. But, with the exit of FXL, his achievement awards went by the wayside and no one was ceremoniously commended for their efforts. The only performance records that remain are the archived statistics of rushing yards, passing yards, tackles, win-losses, etc. It was almost like the 1973 season never existed.

Of course there were fun times during those FXL years. The few times we were victorious were like national holidays in eastern Iowa. Their scarcity made them even more so. Iowa City on a Hawkeye victory weekend was like no other experience one could imagine.

Strange as it may sound, college and professional sports alike were evolving by leaps and bounds and entering new territory in the early 1970s. Water breaks were considered a luxury and unnecessary, and concussions were treated with smelling salts. Coaches would also walk through the training room after practice and deride players who were getting rehab treatments for injuries, explaining that there was a difference between pain and injury. That usually meant if it hurt, you still needed to practice and play. Otherwise you were a pussy and were letting the team down. Those days were definitely part of an unenlightened era of football history.

Bob Commings was named Iowa's head football coach at Iowa the season after FXL was fired. Many of us were surprised a high school coach could be elevated to the ranks of a Big Ten college coach, but Commings' arrival did generate excitement again. Perhaps the biggest upset of the era was when we beat UCLA 21–10 in the second game of the 1974 season. It was an improbable victory, and Hawkeye fans went completely nuts in celebration. Students swarmed the field and pulled the north end zone uprights out of the ground. They then lugged them to the top of the east stands and threw them over the edge. No thought was given as to who might be underneath the stands 100 feet below, and luckily no one was injured.

Commings, however, couldn't manage more than three wins a year in 1974 and 1975 even though there were five of us drafted in the 1976 NFL Draft.

Though I led the team in rushing during the 1974 season as I had done in 1973 also, Coach Commings wanted to move me to tight end. I resisted his effort to put me at that position and learned—for right or wrong—coaches don't appreciate players who won't cooperate. Even though I led the team in rushing two years in a row and eventually played seven seasons as a running back in the NFL, Bob Commings wanted to move me to tight end.

By season's end I had the highest yards-per-carry in the Big Ten, and I set a stadium rushing record in Bloomington, Indiana, with 202 yards in a victory over the Hoosiers. The Dallas Cowboys drafted me in the second round of the NFL Draft that year, and I was the leading rusher for the North in the Senior Bowl in Mobile, Alabama.

After four years of being a University of Iowa athlete, I was able to graduate with a degree and be proud of the fact that I had earned eight varsity letters—four in both football and track. Those were memorable years in my life, and it still gives me great pleasure today to say, "I'm proud to be a Hawkeye!"

Jim Jensen led Iowa in rushing in both 1973 and 1974. He finished with 1,661 yards and nine touchdowns in his career. He also lettered four times in track while at Iowa. Jensen is a native of Davenport, Iowa.

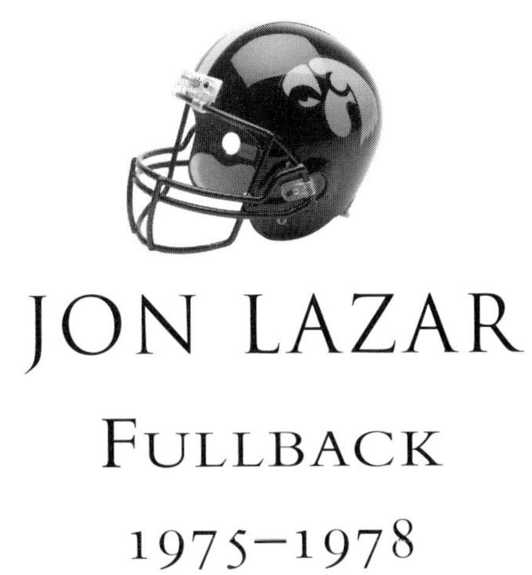

JON LAZAR

FULLBACK

1975–1978

MY STORY STARTED LIKE SO MANY OTHER KIDS' IN IOWA: I wanted to play football for the University of Iowa.

My brother, Keith, took me to my first Iowa game. We sat way high in the stands; so much so that the players were hardly seen without a good pair of binoculars. I don't remember who they played, but I do remember my brother talking about the Hawkeye players as if they were gods. That was my perspective as a young Iowa boy. I imagine that's similar to the way today's youth think of current Iowa players. I know it may seem strange to classify an Iowa football player as a god of sorts. After all, they're only 18- to 23-year-old kids. But if you know Iowa, then you know how many of us feel when we get a chance to see or talk to an Iowa athlete.

Growing up in Tama, Iowa, I saw other players from the community go to Iowa. That influenced me to follow in their footsteps. One player in particular was Mark Fetter. As a freshman in high school, I began watching Mark throughout his high school career, and that alone was such a treat for me. I wanted to be like Mark Fetter. Thus, the drive to be a good player began with the drive to be like Mark. Countless times I watched him play and practice. I studied his actions and tried to simulate him both on offense and defense. I also remember seeing numerous coaches and recruiters trying to land this *Parade* All-American for their schools. Mark went to Iowa and played for Frank Lauterbur through one of the toughest times to be a Hawkeye player or Hawkeye fan.

Another big influence for me to play football was the pressure from my family. All my uncles, my father, and brother were also good athletes in their time. My uncle and cousins were playing football at Illinois. My father played football at Northwestern for a year before heading to war. One cousin was the starting quarterback for Illinois, one was a linebacker at Illinois, and one uncle signed to play for the Chicago Cubs before being killed in the war. I definitely had the lineage to become an athlete of some sort. I could have played baseball or basketball at a small school, but football was my love.

I ended my high school career at South Tama listed as one of the top 100 running backs in the nation. I also achieved first-team all-state and Scholastic All-America honors. I was chosen for the Iowa Shrine All-Star Game, in which I was awarded the offensive MVP award. Each of these honors helped generate a large number of football scholarship offers. I narrowed my list down to four schools: Iowa, Iowa State, Minnesota, and Nebraska. I wanted to play at a school that would allow my family to see me play. Most of my cousins were close enough to make that drive, as well. I eliminated Minnesota and called my good friend, Tony Dungy, to let him know I was not coming to his school. I called Nebraska and told them I was not even going to make the trip, as I liked what I saw at Iowa and Iowa State. I felt both programs would be a good choice, and it was nice knowing I had a full-ride scholarship awaiting me at each school.

So it came down to deciding between the in-state schools. You have to understand that all of my family played football in the Big Ten, and I had a feeling deep inside that I would follow in their footsteps. Iowa State made a bid for me. They had seen me for three years at their football camp, and I knew all their coaches very well. A lot of great coaches were on the staff at Ames, including Earle Bruce. When he showed up to sign me to go to Iowa State, I signed the letter of intent. That letter eliminated all other Big 8 schools. It still left the door open for Iowa to sign me. When Iowa heard I signed with Iowa State, the pressure came in hard. I received calls from family members, my brother was not speaking to me, my father was upset with me, and kids from school were upset. The only ones speaking to me were the Iowa State kids. I had a lot of influential people call me to talk with me, and it was quite an experience for an 18-year-old kid. With that said, I signed with Iowa and became a Hawkeye.

Fullback Jon Lazar fought through serious injuries as a freshman to finish with 1,225 yards in his career, which at the time was 10th on Iowa's all-time rushing chart.

Coming to Iowa was quite an experience. I recently told Dave Beckman, my old running backs coach, that I should've arrived in Iowa City a bit more subtly than I did. Forget the flamboyant act, with the nice car and pretty girl. I would have been better off arriving in a beat-up Chevy, parking three blocks away, and blending in with the crowd. He told me not to think that way. "You were who you were at the time, and that was the important thing," he said. Believe me, trying to compete with players three years older than you in the weight room can be daunting. In addition, having a self-inflicted target on your chest didn't help my cause!

I took a physical beating my freshman year, with numerous stitches, a separated shoulder, and a major surgery where I almost lost my leg. Not many know I was rushed into emergency surgery for a blood clot that stopped the blood flow from my knee down. With no blood reaching my feet, they were burning as if a soldering iron was touching my toes. An inch of my fibula actually had to be cut out of my leg to relieve the pressure and allow proper blood flow again. I lost some speed and was lucky to ever play football again. For me, that was the biggest obstacle I faced playing at Iowa. That was a very scary ordeal, but I wanted to play football and I wanted to be a part of that team. That was me.

After the surgery, I was lost as to where I would really fit in and what I could actually do as a football player. I had no idea if I would be able to contribute. The world "bust" went through my mind, and that was something I did not want to be known as. That was always present in my thoughts for a period of time. That summer, I lived in the training room, doing rehab and lifting weights for hours. Therapy and weights were all I did in hopes I would be able to play or at least dress for games.

I felt going into camp my sophomore year I was about 70 percent, healthwise. But with my new body, thanks to all the weight-training, the coaches decided to move Tom Rusk to middle linebacker and me from halfback to fullback. That put me into second-team fullback behind Nate Winston. We called him "Mr. Motion," which is funny now because I never knew why they called him that.

Our first game was against Illinois in Champaign. They just installed new Astroturf, and I remember the nasty turf burns I had after that game. I played on the special teams covering kickoffs and punts. Nate started that game, and I played the last quarter when the game was out of reach. The next Monday, the coaches had me running with the first-team offense—they wanted more speed at that position. Syracuse was going to be my first test as a starter. Syracuse had a pretty good team and had played Penn State well the week before. I had one touchdown and 65 yards rushing in my first start, which earned me that position for the rest of the year.

Earning that position as a young kid really brought a lot of attention to me on and off the field. It seemed wherever I went, everyone knew who I was and watched what I did. I'm not sure I was ready for that attention so quickly, but it goes with the territory. I had to get used to it. I contend that playing at Iowa is unlike many schools, because we have no pro teams in our state. More people are drawn to the Hawkeyes than any other team in the state. This is why so many see Iowa players as if they are bigger than life. We have an audience of dedicated and intelligent fans who love these teams. There are downsides, but it presents a very special opportunity for student-athletes.

Some of my career highlights certainly don't compare to many players' highlights in this book, but I had my moments. My first memorable moment was as a freshman against Southern California. I was running down on kickoff coverage when USC's Paul Rice returned the ball. As he ran the kickoff out, I hit him right under the chin with my helmet running full speed. All I heard was a big pop. The collision ended up knocking his helmet in the air about five feet high and the ball shooting up about 10 feet. We recovered and took an early lead on the No. 5 team in the country. I only did the kickoff team my freshman year. I wished the coaches would have redshirted me, because that extra year would have made a huge difference.

I had a two-touchdown game against Michigan State as a junior. In that game I ran a fake punt in for a 40-yard touchdown. It was a pretty neat play. I was lined up in the gap about three yards off the line of scrimmage when the ball was hiked to the up-back, Tommy Grine. He caught the ball, ran up to me, and stuck it under my rear end. He then spun as if he were running an option. All the MSU players ran after the fake, as I stood there waiting to run. As I stood there, a defensive end grabbed my leg. I jumped up in the air trying to get out of his grasp and lost my shoe. I then ran down the opposite sideline with Ty Willingham in pursuit. I could barely stop running through the end zone as I was stopped by the railing to the stands, minus one shoe, of course.

I also vividly remember the Iowa–Iowa State series renewal in 1977. I felt a lot of pressure for that game and wanted to show ISU I was worth my weight as a player. A mistake was made on my part prior to the game, however. I chose a new pair of shoes with a pimple cleat that would grip the turf and give me more traction. I wanted any advantage I could get to stick it to the Cyclones. Well, the grip was too good. On a burst through the line, I made a cut and sprained my ankle. I was still able to go, but I hated the fact it was happening in such a big game. I did score on the 11-yard run to put us up 12–10, but then broke up the middle for a 13-yard gain and again tore up my ankle. This time it was bad, and I was unable to play the rest of the game. I left with seven carries for 41 yards and was out for the next game.

Beating 11th-ranked Penn State 7–6 in State College was also quite a highlight. A few years ago, I was sent a DVD of a live broadcast of that 1976 game. I had not seen film of that game in 30 years. The neat thing about that game is the announcer was the famous Ray Scott with Joe Paterno's brother doing color commentary. That game gained us some national attention.

The funny thing about playing Division I football is that on any given Saturday, the game can go either way. After Penn State our emotions as a team were high, and the next week we went to Los Angeles with confidence to play highly ranked USC. Well, talk about running into a buzz saw. We went into that game as the top Big Ten team defensively. Offensively, we were about sixth. USC beat us 55–0. Talk about letting the air out of your sails! Going from hero to goat in one week's time was tough. I cannot tell you how embarrassing it is to walk the campus on Monday knowing you let your university down. Ouch.

When we were in Los Angeles having lunch one day, Coach Commings was sitting there with us. We stayed at the St. Bonaventure, which is the glass hotel you always see in the movies. I said something to him and remember not getting the nice and encouraging response I normally got. All of a sudden, he stood up and ripped the entire team about falling into the L.A. spell. His face became beet red, and he spit chewing tobacco as he yelled. I remember sitting there and not moving. The waiters and waitresses just kept doing their jobs as he stood there screaming and yelling at us for not being ready. He was right. The one thing about Coach Commings is that he had the entire team's respect. He was a tough man who was full of lessons. The one thing he taught me was to face adversity head-on. I know he passed away from cancer several years ago, but I still remember him as if it were yesterday. His words echo through my mind, and I am sure a lot of players who played for him feel the same way. I think this is where it becomes more than a game.

Several years ago, I was the honorary captain for an Iowa game. I was invited back, and a good friend named Bill Ranes was to accompany me. For personal reasons, Bill could not make the game as planned. I was captain anyway and loved being back on the field after all those years. Well, Coach Ferentz told me since Bill could not make that game, he would give me sideline passes for another game. I asked him what game would be good for him, and Coach Ferentz said, "Ohio State would be a good game." I agreed on the spot. Bill and I made the trip to Iowa City when Ohio State was ranked No. 1 in the nation. As the team walked down the tunnel, Bill and I walked alongside them like two children. Even having started for three years at Iowa, I still felt like a child for that brief moment. It brought back so many memories for us. This is typical of the way the current coaching staff treats past players; they really embrace Iowa's teams from the past. I cannot tell you how wonderfully I was treated, and that was something he certainly did not have to do for me. Coach Ferentz is a first-class person and coach.

A large part of football is the feeling you have for your coaches and brothers who you fought beside each Saturday. Several years ago I ran into our offensive tackle, Barry Tomasetti. He told me it was a pleasure to play football with me at Iowa as he knew he could count on me to be ready and give my all. That was good to hear. My good friend Mike Frantz, who was a tight end at Iowa, once told me if he were to go into battle, I would be his first choice. Those are compliments that any person would be proud to hear. It meant more than scoring any touchdown, getting a win, or making a big hit. It is the respect you earn from your peers. I am a proud Hawkeye!

As for me, I lived a dream and loved every minute. Those memories will never leave my soul until the day I leave this earth. I can only tell all Iowa fans that I know we didn't have the winning seasons they've enjoyed the past few decades, but it was a pleasure playing for such a great fan base. The Iowa fan is the best, and I thank you for being so good to us through some difficult times.

The Iowa football experience provokes many images in my mind. It is the site of the stadium with fans streaming in and the sound of the man yelling, "Programs!" It is the tailgating set up for blocks around and the sound of the sirens as the team busses stop at the curb. It is the sound of the train as it pulls to a stop with the eager Hawkeye fans on board. It is the sound of the band with the drum corps beating a football beat. It is the collective voices of Zabel, Gonder, Brooks, and Mitchell that we all listened to each football Saturday. It is the banners plastered on the press box showing each respective radio station. It is the Big Ten team flags blowing in the wind from the top row of the stadium. It is the kids collecting in the knothole section. It is the cheerleaders, band, and Golden Girl during each halftime performance.

Not many will ever understand why Iowa football holds such a place in our hearts. It is something in our blood and soul as a human being. You cannot truly explain the Hawkeye experience to anyone without them experiencing it firsthand. I have heard many people tell me they were a fan of another team, but once they attended an Iowa game they became Hawkeye fans. That's something we can all be proud of. When we are gone and another generation of Iowa fans emerges, I know they will also agree this experience is special. There is something about being a Hawkeye and following these teams. I will certainly cherish the years I have left, but one of the best things that's happened to me so far was becoming a Hawkeye.

There were no Big Ten titles for me. There were no huge honors, but I'm good with that. I was a Hawkeye. And with that said, I will rest content.

A native of Tama, Iowa, Jon Lazar led Iowa in rushing from 1976 to 1978. Highlights of his career include beating 11th-ranked Penn State in State College and defeating Iowa State in the renewal of their annual series. Jon now lives in North Carolina, where he runs his company, ReMan Technology. He has two children.

The
EIGHTIES

CHUCK LONG

Quarterback

1981–1985

You know, to this day, I don't know how Hayden Fry recruited me to play quarterback at the University of Iowa. I really was not very heavily recruited coming out of high school at all. I came from a high school program in Wheaton, Illinois, that relied almost exclusively on an option running game. We threw the ball maybe five times a game, tops. Think of those great Nebraska teams of the 1980s and '90s under Turner Gill, Tommie Frazier, Eric Crouch, et al. I was told later that all of the film the Iowa people used to evaluate me fit on one reel! In fact, given that the number of scholarships currently offered today has decreased substantially from my playing days, I'm not even sure that I would have been recruited at all by today's standards.

Yet, one thing we did do as a team in high school was win. In fact, we won an Illinois State championship during my junior year in 1979. Now, Coach Fry only had two years under his belt when I was being recruited in 1980, and he was working hard to turn around a culture of losing that had been prevalent at Iowa for the better part of 20 years. Maybe he was thinking that a quarterback who had won extensively in high school could serve as a role model for the rest of the team at the college level? I honestly don't know, but whatever Coach Fry saw in me, I am truly grateful that he gave me the privilege to play for the Iowa Hawkeyes.

Coming out of high school, there was never a doubt in my mind that Iowa was where I wanted to be. The only other schools that had serious interest in me were Northwestern and Northern Illinois. But Iowa was head and shoulders above both of these schools, in my mind. My official visit to Iowa came in December. In those days, you typically weren't offered a scholarship until the Sunday of your weekend visit, and I was desperately hoping that Coach Fry would make me that offer, and fortunately for me, the offer was finally extended.

Iowa was by far and away my first choice. I just fell in love with all the people associated with the Iowa program, fell in love with the campus. Of course, Coach Fry was a great salesmen, and his staff was just tremendous. I loved the whole package at Iowa and was thrilled to have the opportunity to play football at a Big Ten university.

My very first game as a Hawkeye in 1981 was one I will never forget, even though I played very little that first year, as it essentially was a redshirt year for me. It was a sultry day at Kinnick, and the Big Red of Nebraska were in town. Iowa had lost to Nebraska 57–0 the year before I arrived and, needless to say, expectations weren't very high on the Iowa side for this particular game. Yet, we went out and played our guts out and earned a hard-fought 10–7 win, which was certainly Coach Fry's signature win up to that point in his Iowa career.

Based on that monumental victory, it was very apparent that the program was being turned around. Somehow, someway, you just knew something special was brewing. Of course, we went on to upset nationally ranked UCLA and Michigan on the road that year en route to Iowa's first Rose Bowl since the 1958 season. That was an unforgettable season for me, and I wasn't even playing!

Probably my two greatest personal highlights happened during my senior year in 1985. We were ranked No. 1 in the country coming into the Big Ten opener against Michigan State, but found ourselves down 31–28 on the game's final drive. We had driven the ball to the MSU 2-yard line and called timeout with 31 seconds left. It was our last timeout.

I came over to the sideline to consult with Coach Fry about the next play. The play selection was 100 percent Hayden Fry's call. I remember it vividly as we discussed it on the sideline. Coach Fry said, "Hey, Charlie, what I want you to do is fake this handoff up the middle and I want you to keep it and go around end." I tried to talk him out of it, because I knew if they tackled me in bounds, with no timeouts, the game probably would be over. "Don't worry about it, Charlie, you're going to get in. Now go out there and do it,"

Chuck Long holds school marks for yards passing, completions, touchdown passes, and total offense in a game, season, and career. He started at QB the third game of his sophomore season and finished his Iowa career starting 44 of the next 46 games. *Photo courtesy of Bob Rasmus*

he said confidently. When we came back to the huddle, I didn't even tell the rest of the team it was going to be a fake. I was the only one who knew it.

Sure enough, I came around the corner after faking to Ronnie Harmon, and no one was there. I don't think I ever scored an easier touchdown in my entire career. Every Michigan State defender collapsed on Ronnie, and I had an easy stroll into the end zone.

Then, two weeks later came the historic No. 1 versus No. 2 matchup at Kinnick Stadium against Coach Bo Schembechler and Michigan. It was such an honor and a thrill to be a part of that great victory. It probably was my greatest moment as a player at Iowa. The game had everything. Hollywood couldn't have devised a better script, even if they tried. I remember the tension mounting as Michigan made futile attempts to ice our kicker, Rob Houghtlin. There was nobody who was better under pressure than Rob, and he confidently nailed the kick.

When that kick sailed through the uprights, the way the stadium was at that moment, I will never forget it. The celebrations went all the way into the night. I remember sharing the victory with our great fans that night downtown. It was a real magical moment, that is for sure.

We had mixed success in bowl games during my time at Iowa. We pounded Texas in the Freedom Bowl, which was a very gratifying win, not only for us, but also for Hayden Fry, who of course is from Texas. However, one of the biggest disappoints of my career at Iowa was not being able win that Rose Bowl, not only for ourselves as players, but also for Hayden.

Thankfully for me, the good times far and away outnumbered the bad during my time in black and gold. I was fortunate enough to play with so many great teammates. Although it is so difficult to single any individuals out, guys like Jonathan Hayes, Hap Peterson, Scott Helverson, and Mike Haight were all guys from my class who I had real close relationships with—many of them actually became my roommates in school.

Although they were just a little older than me, guys like Bob and Mike Stoops were both very influential personalities on many of the teams I played on. It was also a great thrill just to be on the same team as future NFL Hall of Famer Andre Tippett. Andre was a senior when I was a freshman and was a tremendous force on that 1981 Rose Bowl team.

When you're young, you're very impressionable, and there was one other older guy on the team when I was a freshman who left a lasting impression on me. Mel Cole was a starting linebacker and a great leader. Mel would give these passionate motivational speeches every Friday before games that were just outstanding. Not only what he said, but the way he said it really fired everyone up to go out there and play. He is one of the great motivational speakers I have heard, even to this day, and there is no question that any of my teammates from those teams would certainly say the same thing.

One of the great memories I will always have is the experience in New York City related to the Heisman Trophy. Honestly, the Heisman Trophy was something that I never gave much thought to until after our regular season was over and December hit. My focus during the year was on helping the team win, but to have the opportunity to go to New York and represent my team and my school was a tremendous thrill and honor. Consequently, I always viewed the award as more of a team award than an individual award. I never dreamed about winning the Heisman Trophy, never even thought twice about it growing up. I was always brought up with the idea of team first.

All the hype and build-up over it was also overwhelming, and when it was all over, I definitely felt a huge sense of relief. I can honestly say that there wasn't one shred of disappointment in coming so close and not winning. Losing out to Bo Jackson has allowed me the opportunity to get to know Bo, and that has been really neat, too. If you are going to lose something like this, losing to an athlete and person the caliber of Bo Jackson isn't so bad. It was the closest Heisman vote in history, right up until 2009, and it was fun being talked about every year at Heisman time. But coming so close and not winning has never been something I have dwelled on or regretted at all.

The thing I am probably most proud of from all my playing days is the fact that we did more than just turn the program around. Sure, Iowa had the 20 non-winning seasons and it was great to break through and get to those first bowl games in the early 1980s. But, together, we were able to do something much more difficult: sustain the success once we had climbed that mountain. That is something that I think is immeasurably more difficult to do than just turning things around.

I think everybody knows Iowa is not an easy place to recruit. There simply is not the population base that there is in the eastern states in the Big Ten like Michigan, Ohio, Pennsylvania, and even Illinois. This means that Iowa must resort to getting players out of state—and you really need to battle with so many other programs to get the out-of-state kids. Or in so many cases at

Iowa, they took the kids who no one else wanted and were able to get the absolute most out of those kids through coaching and development.

The success at Iowa needed to come just as much from coaching and developing players as anything. The art of developing and coaching college football players is something that I believe nobody did any better than Iowa back in 1980s. You look at that famous Hayden Fry coaching tree that has grown so large over the years. The list goes on and on and, of course, includes Kirk Ferentz. Why do Hayden Fry's coaches and his former players get hired? Because Iowa has a proven track record of coaching and developing great football players.

The ability to coach and develop football players is one of the things that makes Iowa so unique, I think. My hat goes off to the coaching staff and players from the late 1980s, right through to today's group under Kirk Ferentz, for being able to sustain a long period of greatness in Iowa Hawkeye football.

I don't know who is credited with development of the phrase "It's Great to Be a Hawkeye," but when I really sit down and think about the essence of what it means to be a Hawkeye, there is no better way to put it than this time-honored phrase. It was such a magical time in my life. It was so magical that, in a way, you are almost afraid to go back because you want to remember it just the way it was, back in the 1980s.

I did find the time to be able to take in the homecoming game back in October 2009 against Michigan. It was the first time I had been back in 10 years. Kirk allowed me to speak to the team before the game, which was a great thrill for me. I had the opportunity to participate in tailgating as a fan and soak in the entire experience. My wife and I had a blast. It couldn't have been a better weekend. The whole thing is worth every last penny of that ticket, that's for sure.

I am so thankful that it all worked out for me, to be able to go to the University of Iowa, especially given the way I was recruited. It's funny how fate seems to work sometimes. Yes, I have vivid memories about how great things were there. But looking back on it, my feelings toward the University of Iowa are just as warm today as they were then. I took not only a wealth of football skills from my experience at Iowa, but life skills...things I use almost every day personally and professionally. I'm not sure if anyone could ask anything more from their college experience than the experience I had at the University of Iowa.

Chuck Long is the Big Ten's all-time leader in passing and total offense. He was a consensus first-team All-American his senior season, while finishing second in Heisman Trophy balloting, winning the Maxwell Trophy and Davey O'Brien Award. He also was a two-time consensus first-team All–Big Ten selection. Long was drafted in the first round of the 1986 NFL Draft by the Detroit Lions (12th overall pick) and spent six seasons in the NFL. He was inducted into the College Football Hall of Fame in 1999. He served as defensive backs coach and quarterbacks coach at Iowa before serving as an assistant at Oklahoma from 1999 to 2005. Long was head coach at San Diego State from 2006 to 2008 and is currently offensive coordinator/quarterbacks coach on Turner Gill's staff at Kansas.

MIKE HAIGHT

Offensive Line

1981–1985

I GREW UP IN THE SMALL FARMING COMMUNITY of Dyersville, not too far from Dubuque. I suppose Dyersville is kind of famous for at least a couple things. A good sized Catholic church, known as the St. Francis Xavier Basilica, is located there. I happened to be an altar boy there from third grade to 10th grade. I think that they decided to have me "retire" because I was bigger than all of the priests. Also, the famous baseball field from *Field of Dreams* is still located there. It is about two miles from where I lived.

Although Beckman High School wasn't really known for producing a lot of great teams, we had an absolutely awesome talent pool of kids come through school. Some chose to play only baseball. Some chose to play everything, like I did.

Even though Iowa football had experienced some rough times in the '70s and even in the early years of the Hayden Fry era, there was a lot about the University of Iowa that appealed to me coming out of high school. First of all, being a small-town boy, I couldn't imagine being too far away from home. I also had some interest from Iowa State, although they didn't offer a scholarship, they were willing to let me walk on. When Hayden Fry saw fit to offer me a scholarship to play at the University of Iowa, I jumped at that opportunity. I actually had scholarship offers from the Missouri Tigers and the Oregon Ducks. I never even considered either of them because they both were too far away, plus I didn't know anything about them at all.

My first year at Iowa in 1981 was the year Hayden Fry turned the program around and went to the Rose Bowl. I didn't play a whole lot in my freshman year, only one play, but that year was certainly very memorable. I arrived at Iowa with a great group of other freshman who would eventually help bring the program to even greater heights in the mid-1980s. Guys like Chuck Long, Hap Peterson, Jonathan Hayes, Owen Gill, and my roommate, Kelly O'Brien, to name a few.

My first college football drill as a tight end was against an outside linebacker named Andre Tippett. Not knowing Tippet was a senior who was an All-American with a black belt in karate, I was thinking that I would just go "lockup" on him and try to run-block him. I found out that it wasn't quite that simple. Tippet grabbed me by both of my arms, picked me up, and threw me on my head. Then he said, "Welcome to the Big Ten, freshman!" I guess you could say I learned from one of the best right from the get-go!

With the Hawkeyes, I will never forget the feeling I had when I got to dress my first game as a freshman. Coming out onto that field in that famous Hawkeye swarm, feeling the electricity, it was just absolutely amazing. Your hair stands up on your arms and the back of your neck. Just thinking about it, wow, it's happening to me right now!

The following season, a few other tight ends came into the program, and the coaches decided to move me to offensive line and redshirt me my sophomore year. Evidently I had rocks for hands and couldn't catch the ball. It wasn't much fun on the scout team that year getting my butt kicked by the likes of Mark Bortz, Dave Brown, George Little, Paul Hufford, and Larry Station, among many other tough defensive players. I only weighed maybe 215 pounds at the time they moved me to offensive line, so that wasn't the best experience for me. I was basically fresh meat. I was about ready to call it quits because I just didn't want to be an offensive lineman. Fortunately, my dad convinced me to work through it and not be a quitter. Thank God I listened.

It was really an honor for me to have gotten to play for both Coach Fry and Coach Ferentz. Coach Fry really liked people a lot. He liked being the center of attention. Some people can handle that, while some can't. Actually, I think both Coach Fry and Coach Ferentz can handle this quite nicely. They both can control a crowd quite well. Coach Fry comes up with different stories, different tall tales, some of which are true, while others may not be so much! Coach Ferentz, on the other hand, doesn't spin any yarns or anything

Mike Haight converted from tight end to offensive line after his freshmen year in 1981. His junior year, he was selected to the AP's first-team All–Big Ten squad.
Photo courtesy of Bob Rasmus

like that, he tells you the way it is. Kirk is as honest as the day is long, that is the way he was as a coach and as a person.

Having had the opportunity to play for Coach Ferentz in the 1980s and see how he conducts himself now as head coach, I see very few changes. I think Kirk handles himself very well on the sideline. I'm proud of him to see how he keeps his composure, particularly when things are going badly, which hasn't been too often. These days, it seems you see so many coaches jumping up and down, throwing hats or headsets and screaming at the referees. That is definitely not Kirk and it definitely is not the University of Iowa.

Coach Ferentz is a player's coach. If he didn't think you were holding up your end, he'd let you know. Kirk is much more apt to talk to you one-on-one rather than ride you constantly in front of your teammates. Sometimes, you might get a foot where you don't really want it, but he is going to do it and then he is going to move on. Probably the thing that he detested the most was if someone lied to him. I do remember one player lying to him in '85. Not only was that kid running laps around the turf field in Kinnick, he ran up and down every stair in Kinnick Stadium each day! And that went on the whole season. You don't lie to Kirk Ferentz, that's for sure. As for that kid, he is probably still running somewhere!

Not only did I have great relationships with my coaches, but I was also fortunate enough to have some tremendous teammates. Our offensive lines during my time at Iowa were absolutely like a band of brothers. It was so much fun to be together on the field, off the field, in the locker room—it was just unbelievable. Now this family surely had its problems every now and then, but in the end, we all recognized that we were on the same team and looking to achieve the same common goals.

In some sense, I think that we were closer than today's Iowa football players because we lived together in the athletic dorms for our entire time in school. Things are different now because the athletic dorms are no longer allowed, per NCAA regulations. In many cases today, guys on the team might go out on their own, go off to live with other friends, high school buddies, girlfriends, or maybe live by themselves. They are not living side by side with their teammates, so the closeness is not there. As a result, I think you lose some of the close camaraderie that we had. Then again, two guys living in a 10-foot by 15-foot room for four or five years could get a little on your nerves sometimes!

I have always heard that when you get your chance, don't blow it. By the time I got my chance, it was my fourth year in the program in 1984. I eventually became the No. 1 offensive tackle. That was the year we had beat Texas 55–17 in the Freedom Bowl. Iowa had just lost seniors John Alt, Tim Hanna, Joel Hilgenberg, Jon Roehlk, and Joe Levelis from the previous year. I don't think too many people thought we would have a very good offensive line, but I feel like we proved the doubters wrong and did a fairly decent job for Chuck Long and our running backs, including Owen Gill and Ronnie Harmon. I personally credit it to my fellow offensive linemen and, of course, Kirk Ferentz, who was our positions coach.

Of course, the 1985 Iowa team was most memorable to me. We just had a great group of guys on the team. Mark Sindlinger, Dave Croston, Mike Flagg, Hap Peterson, Kelly O'Brien, Jeff Drost, Larry Station…I could go on and on. As an offensive line, we knew that we could count on the defense and they, in turn, knew they could count on us. It was a complete team both offensively and defensively. There was no finger pointing or anything like that. On top of it, our special teams were spectacular.

Now that I am in my daily grind of life, I actually have to pinch myself sometimes to remember that I actually was an Iowa or NFL football player. It is still pretty cool when people come up to me and talk to me about that great game in 1985 when Iowa was No. 1 and Michigan was No. 2 and we beat them 12–10 in the final seconds with a field goal by Rob Houghtlin. Or maybe they want to talk about the Michigan State game that same year. That was when Chuck Long scored on that naked bootleg at the end of the game while holding the ball high up in the air in one hand. Most people may not know this, but the year before against Michigan State, Chuck ran the same type of play, but the officials called it dead because they didn't see that he had the ball. There was a fake to Ronnie Harmon who got piled up on the line of scrimmage. Some people thought Chuck did that to be a showoff, but actually he wanted everyone to see that he had the ball to be sure that the play wasn't going to get blown dead again. I remember Hayden Fry being a little upset about the ball being held up over Chuck's head as Chuck stepped over the goal line alone and untouched. I think he got over it really quickly, though!

A big thing that both Coach Fry and Coach Ferentz look for in a future Hawkeye is the quality people right up front with big hearts who want to excel. They want someone who can come in and be a part of the team and be a leader both on the field and off the field. That was just the way it was or you weren't going to be there very long. I think that was the biggest thing that helped me move on beyond the University of Iowa, not only as a football player, but as an individual. We had a lot of quality leaders off the field as well as on.

The Iowa program also taught me to remember where I came from. After I was finished with each season in the NFL, my wife, Polly, and I came back to Iowa City. People would ask us, "Hey, how come you came back to Iowa? You both could go anywhere!" We'd say, "Hey, this is where we want to be. Not only are our friends and our family all here, Iowa is where it all started and made us what we are today."

Hayden Fry is full of wisdom and had some classic sayings, but the most memorable thing I think I ever heard him say is, "Once a Hawk, always a Hawk." Hayden was singing this particular tune from the day he started recruiting me in 1980 right up to the day he retired. I've been done playing Iowa football 25 years now, and I still very much feel the same way.

Coach Ferentz goes out of his way to make the former players feel as welcomed as possible. In fact, all former Iowa football players are more than welcome to come back to the practices, to the games, to stop in and see the coaches or new facilities. It has never been anything like, "You've had your time here, move on, please!" or, "We don't want you around anymore, don't bother stopping." That is not the Iowa football way. I, as a former player, appreciate that big time. After 25 years, it makes me feel like I'm still an important part of the Iowa football family. I'm proud of the Iowa football tradition, the players, the coaches, everybody. It is great to see the success being carried on. It truly is great to be a Hawkeye!

Mike Haight's senior year came during the memorable 1985 season when he was named the Big Ten's Offensive Linemen of the Year and was an honorable mention All-American by AP and UPI, along with the AP and UPI first-team All–Big Ten teams. He was drafted in the first round of the 1986 NFL Draft by the New York Jets (22nd overall). He spent six seasons with the Jets before finishing his NFL career with the Washington Redskins in 1992. Haight currently lives in the Iowa City area.

LARRY STATION

LINEBACKER

1982–1985

GROWING UP IN OMAHA as a Nebraska Cornhusker fan, I knew very little about the University of Iowa football program. This includes the team, the coaches, the fans, or its history. I remember before my senior year in high school occasionally seeing an Iowa football score on television, but no thoughts or emotions registered in my mind at all. I felt no connection to Iowa football. The University of Iowa and Iowa State University were equivalent to me then. In my mind, the Iowa football program could have been 1,000 miles away instead of being located in a bordering state. It wasn't until my senior year in high school when Iowa, as part of the recruiting process, invited me to attend their last home game of the year. That's when I first learned about what it meant to be a Hawkeye. The game I attended was Iowa versus Michigan State on a cold day in November. At that time, Iowa was still in the hunt to go to the Rose Bowl, but the only way Iowa could go was if Michigan beat Ohio State and Iowa beat Michigan State. While watching the Michigan State game with the other Iowa recruits, I remember the energy level in the stadium being so high. Even though it was cold, the fans were so fired up that I barely noticed the blustery weather conditions. It was an electric atmosphere.

I recall the exact moment when I felt as if I had become a Hawkeye. That moment occurred on the first possession of the game. Michigan State threw a pass to their tight end out in the flat, and Bobby Stoops came up and hit the

Larry Station was selected to the all-time University of Iowa football team in 1989 and was inducted into the College Football Hall of Fame in 2009. *Photo courtesy of Bob Rasmus*

tight end so hard that the ball flew up in the air. As the ball came down, it landed on Bobby's back as he raised his arms in celebration. Andre Tippet intercepted the ball off Bobby's back and began to run the ball before being tackled. It was that one play that virtually made me a Hawkeye on the spot. I knew where I wanted to play.

As the game went on, I saw that Iowa's defense, in particular, played with such emotion and tenacity. I could see myself being a part of that. Until that game, I had never seen such a high degree of effort and intensity put forth by an entire defensive unit. What came to my mind as I watched the game was that they played the way I played. Even the offense gave that same type of effort throughout the entire game, which was very inspiring to watch.

I felt the genuine appreciation that the fans had for the players' efforts. At some point during the second half, the announcer said that Michigan had beaten Ohio State. The crowd in the stadium became frenzied because they all knew that Iowa was now in control of its own destiny to go to the Rose Bowl. The energy that the fans radiated was contagious; by the time the game was over, I felt like I had I been a Hawkeye fan my entire life. The Hawkeyes had won and were on their way to the Rose Bowl.

It was at this game that I felt Iowa would be the best fit for my aggressive, never-quit style of playing. And to have fans who appreciated the effort the players put forth influenced my decision to commit to Iowa. This feeling was in stark contrast to what I had experienced when attending a Nebraska football game earlier in the year. There were times when the Nebraska fans booed both the players and also Coach Osborne during their loss to Penn State in Lincoln. It made me feel bad for the players and coaches.

Now that I felt a connection with the Hawkeye players and fans, I had to confirm there would be that same bond with the coaches by meeting them personally. So on a cold January weekend, I took an official visit to the University of Iowa. There, I met a number of players and all of the football coaches. I felt the same sincerity in the coaches' desire to work in conjunction with the players to make them the best that they could be. I wanted to be part of that. I felt I could trust their knowledge and that they would support me in becoming the best player I could be. I sensed that they were competent in that respect, as well. That feeling from the Iowa–Michigan State game stayed with me in regard to trusting the fans would be supportive of players as long as we gave an all-out effort. I also felt I could trust the other players to give their best effort along with me and never quit, giving 100 percent effort no matter what the game score was. I knew then and know now that this is what it means to be a Hawkeye.

Being a Hawkeye has had a lasting impact throughout my life. The lessons I learned during my time at the University of Iowa both on and off the field influenced decisions I have made in my personal and professional endeavors. As a father of three, I have integrated these lessons into my parenting practices. Additionally, being a Hawkeye has provided me with many opportunities such as becoming a member of the 2009 College Football Hall of Fame. It all started with my decision to attend the University of Iowa. I'm forever grateful I did.

Larry Station had perhaps the most decorated career of any Iowa linebacker. He was All–Big Ten three times and consensus first-team All-America twice. He holds the Iowa record for career tackles. Station led Iowa to the 1986 Rose Bowl against UCLA. He was selected to the all-time University of Iowa football team in 1989 and was inducted into the College Football Hall of Fame in 2009. Station still resides in his hometown of Omaha, Nebraska.

QUINN EARLY

Wide Receiver

1984–1987

When I was around eight years old, I told my mom I was going to play in the NFL. At the time, she kind of laughed and patted me on the head, but she learned later that I was pretty serious about it. My parents got divorced when I was around 12, so I primarily grew up with my mother in a town called Great Neck, which is on Long Island, New York. She basically went back to school and had a full-time job so that she could support us, so I was pretty much a latchkey kid. I'd go to school and go through my sports, and then I'd come home and cook for myself and do all that.

I played lacrosse my freshman year of high school, but after that I focused on track, football, and basketball. I was all-county in football and basketball, and I was all-state in track. The biggest schools that recruited me for football were Iowa, Penn State, Boston College, and Syracuse. I was recruited around the country by most schools for track, but I wanted to play football and run track. I didn't want to get put on a track scholarship and maybe play football.

One of Iowa's biggest selling points was the fact that they had a good art program, which is what I was looking for. Also, I was a Pittsburgh Steelers fan, and I loved those Pittsburgh Steelers uniforms that Iowa had. I guess when you're 18, that's kind of a big selling point! Another selling point was that when I went there, Iowa had a lot of kids from the East Coast. The Harmon brothers [Ronnie and Kevin], Nate Creer, and Devon Mitchell all were from out here.

After graduating from Iowa, wide receiver Quinn Early played 12 seasons in the NFL for the Chargers, Saints, Bills, and Jets. *Photo courtesy of Bob Rasmus*

Coach Fry was a great teacher and a great motivator. He really knew how to bring the best out of himself and his players. Fry used to say, "Quinn, I know you like to go out and drink soda pop every now and then"—and when he said soda pop, he meant beer—"but you gotta take it easy and learn to stay out of the bars." Another thing he used to say is, "Now, when we go on this trip, I don't wanna see any nose rings or ear screws." He didn't want us wearing jewelry or any of that stuff. He wanted to keep it on the professional level. Coach Fry was a big believer in psychology. He was a great motivator, and I really enjoyed playing for him and growing from a boy into a man in that program. It was an awesome experience.

I remember when I first got to Iowa, we had one of our first scrimmages. I caught the ball, and Larry Station wrapped his arms around me like he was my grandmother giving me a big hug, face mask to face mask, and drove me into the ground. I had a stinger in my neck and didn't get back to normal for about two weeks. That was kind of a "welcome to college football" moment for me.

Even though I didn't play that much, my favorite win of my Iowa career was probably when we were ranked No. 1 in the nation in 1985 and Michigan was No. 2, and they came in to Iowa City. Rob Houghtlin kicked that last-second field goal, and all the fans stormed the field. That was a pretty big deal. I had a couple of pretty big games personally at Iowa, but I think overall for a team win, it was pretty awesome to be a part of that. You know, every time we won a big game, Coach Fry would make everybody do the Hokey Pokey. That was the first thing we did when we got to the locker room, and I never heard the Hokey Pokey so loud! Everybody was doing it—the trainers, the coaches, the ballboys, and everybody. Everybody was jumping all over one another. It was awesome.

My game against Northwestern in 1987 was a game where everything just went right. I could close my eyes, stick my hands out, and the ball would just fall right. At one point, I ran a post pattern, and when the ball came in, the safety and the corner were right there. We all jumped, and they both missed it and hit each other. I had my knees up, and the ball went through my hands and landed in my lap. It was just one of those days where everything went right, and I guess I was kind of in a zone that day. They actually took me out of the game in the fourth quarter, or I might have kept going.

Ronnie Harmon, Jonathan Hayes, and Devon Mitchell mentored the younger guys like me, so I thought it was my job to kind of mentor younger guys like Merton Hanks. I think that we led by example. Robert Smith and some of the other guys and I used to stress to all those younger guys the importance of making sure you're in class, making sure you're doing well in school, and things like that. Merton was a great football player. He was really quiet and just let all his talking get done on the field. It was funny, though, when Merton got to the NFL and he started doing that whole chicken dance. I'd just laugh because I knew in college that wasn't him at all, but sometimes in the NFL you have to do something to separate yourself from a marketing standpoint. He did a good job of that. I'm really proud of Merton and his career.

Bill Snyder was my position coach. He was the one person I would have to give most credit to, from a teaching standpoint, for my success. As a freshman, he was hard on me; he was hard on the young receivers. As a group, we would be the first ones on the field and the last ones to leave the field. He actually had one of the ballboys take statistics during practice on how many catches and drops each receiver had. At the end of practice, he would post those up on the bulletin board for us all to look at. That really made us competitive as to who caught the most passes and dropped the least amount of footballs. We spent countless hours on film work. We'd be the last ones going home in the evening. He was on us about everything that we did, including going to class and being where we were supposed to be. When I was 18 years old, I hated the guy. Robert Smith and I were the best of friends in college, and we would both sit around after practice talking about how much we hated Coach Snyder!

As I continued to train and learn, I realized what he was trying to accomplish. The biggest thing that I noticed was any receiver under his tutelage—it didn't matter how tall, short, fast, slow—could develop into a quality receiver there. It was tough love. He worked you and expected a lot out of you, and he yelled at you in practice. But all of a sudden, I was doing things I never even imagined on the football field, and that's because he pushed us. By my junior year, every time I saw Coach Snyder, he just had a big smile on his face, and all he had to say to me was, "Good job, Quinn." That's because of the work ethic that he instilled in me. By my senior year, I'd go into his office, and we would just shoot the breeze. He didn't have to coach us much anymore—he was just there. He knew that we knew.

Later, I wrote him a letter and told him how much I appreciated him and how much he helped me with my work ethic. I carried that with me to the NFL, and that's a huge factor in the fact that I played 12 years there, because nobody worked harder than I did. That's the most valuable lesson I learned from Coach Snyder. There might have been people who were bigger, stronger, faster, or more talented than I, but nobody worked harder than I did, and that took me a long way. A coach appreciates the kid who works harder than everybody else more than the kid who has loads of talent but is lazy.

Coach Ferentz was the offensive line coach when I was there, and he has done a phenomenal job as Iowa's head coach. He's always been a great coach. Like Coach Snyder, he expects a lot out of his players. I know that the kids love him, and they love him in the community. He sets a really good example, not just how to be good football players but how to be successful young men in the world. I think that's just as important working with athletes. He's done a great job with that team.

One of the biggest things that I remember about being at Iowa is growing out of being a boy and becoming a man. I remember having to get along with others who came from different homes, backgrounds, and upbringings, and I remember learning from each other. That's not even really talking about football—that's just the living part of it. From a football standpoint, I talk about adopting that work ethic and learning that what you put into it is what you're going to get out of it. That's how I live my life today, and that's what I try to instill in my children. Those experiences were awesome. Lastly, I learned that the bus waits for nobody.

I made a lot of friends, and again, I was pretty much molded by that experience. It was just a great thing. I have nothing but good memories. What it means to be a Hawkeye has just always been a commitment to being the best that you can be. It's about family, community, giving back, and just having a winning attitude.

Quinn Early led the Big Ten in yards per catch as a junior in 1986. The following year, he had a Big Ten record 256 yards and a school record four touchdown catches in a win over Northwestern. His 95-yard touchdown catch in that game was the longest reception in school history, breaking the record that he had set the year before with a 93-yard reception. He currently lives in San Diego, teaching martial arts and coaching high school football.

CHUCK HARTLIEB

QUARTERBACK

1985–1988

I CAME FROM A FAMILY OF FOUR BOYS, and we were one of those families that played sports year-round in Woodstock, Illinois, located near Chicago. As we went through high school, we found our best sport was football. It was what we all wanted to play in college, and fortunately all of us were able to earn scholarships in the Big Ten. Jim, John, and I went to Iowa, while Andy went to Wisconsin.

I was an example of a kid you never wanted to give up on because I had a very average junior year in high school. I kind of came into my own my senior year and caught some attention as we won the state championship. I didn't necessarily think I was going to be capable of earning a Division I scholarship until my senior year, so I didn't have the big ego, thinking I could go anywhere I wanted. To the contrary, I was just hoping I could play college football. As my senior year went on, I received about 12 to 14 offers. I wanted to go to the school that was the most successful on the field, threw the ball enough, and was a good academic institution. The University of Iowa in 1984 was heads above the other choices I had.

I can't emphasize enough how unique the people of Iowa are. I was basically a Chicagoan from a more urban environment, and how outgoing, supportive, and understanding Iowans appeared struck me immediately on my recruiting visit. From the assistant coaches that Coach Fry assembled, to the training staff, academic staff, and boosters, they were great.

The first day I was there on a recruiting visit, I met a successful businessman in Iowa City named Earl Yoder. Earl and Edna Yoder were friends for life for me, and it didn't matter if I actually played or not. They were just committed to helping people who chose to play for the Hawkeyes. It wasn't financial, it was just friendship, support, and advice—a dinner away from home. They were so reflective of the kind of people whom we ran across and got to know while we were at Iowa. I think athletes who chose the University of Iowa were really happy with their experience because of the people they got to be associated with. I've heard many times how it doesn't happen that way in other university cities. There is a truly unique heart and spirit to being a Hawkeye.

I think so many of Coach Fry's players and recruits had the mentality of an underdog, that we had to kick, scrape, scratch, and claw for every victory, and that's reflective of what Iowans are all about. The way Coach Fry approached games was it was going to take every ounce of effort, every ounce of team unity, and all the faith in the world to believe we're going to get it done. And that is so much more of an enjoyable challenge than a "we expect to win" or "we know we're going to win" mentality. I really appreciated being on that side of the fence. We were a really tight-knit unit. We were always together, one unified group, and maybe as symbolic as any of that is how we purposefully came out on the field holding hands as the swarm. There wasn't anybody sprinting away, hot-dogging it or waving to the crowd; we came out as one complete unit on the field and off the field every time. That goes back to what being a Hawkeye is all about. That was our approach.

Kinnick Stadium is an awesome stadium. The fans are basically on the sidelines, and it can be really intimidating for the opponent. The fan base was outstanding—sellouts every single weekend and tremendously supportive and loud. Iowa fans are more loyal and exuberant than typical college football fans.

You'll find so many guys who had success at Iowa but were not blue-chip recruits. They weren't the *USA Today* All-Americans who were used to being on the front cover of newspapers. We were an eclectic, hardworking group. Coach Fry molded us in the '80s, kept going in the '90s, and I think Coach Ferentz has found the exact same blueprint for success. He doesn't always want the kid who's getting recruited by Florida or USC; he wants to find the undiscovered kid no one else knows about and who fits the program.

Some people ask whether I felt pressure playing just two years after Chuck Long. I tell them you had Bill Snyder as quarterbacks coach, Kirk Ferentz as offensive line coach, and Hayden Fry as head coach. The pressure was to perform for them. Coach Snyder was extremely challenging in his expectations, and he wanted every single ounce of effort out of you. I just wanted to have games that Coach Snyder said, "Excellent game, you made the right decisions and right throws. You showed great leadership and we got the 'W.'" The standards Coach Fry and Coach Snyder expected out of the quarterback position were the main reason why you go from Long to Vlasic to Hartlieb to Rodgers, etc. We had a string of very successful quarterbacks. Coach Fry was an ex-quarterback, and Coach Snyder was an ex-quarterback. We were very lucky to have great coaches during that span who knew how to run a passing game.

My first game action was against Iowa State in 1986. I completed five of six passes in a reserve role. I was extremely nervous ahead of the game because I knew I'd probably get a chance to play. Up until then I always wondered, *Can I execute in front of 70,000? Will I have the poise to get it done?*

I was very nervous throughout the couple series I played, but I did just fine. That really got me over the hump. I knew I could do it when it counted. That was an important game for me because it was my third year and it was time for me to get some confidence going and understand whether I could play this game or not. It helps take the nervousness off the first time you get smacked, but we were playing Iowa State, so I didn't get hit too much. I played just a couple times that season.

Nineteen eighty-seven presented a unique quarterback competition. Tom Poholsky, Dan McGwire, and I were very equal. We all had our positive and negative traits. Coach Fry started McGwire in the season opener, Poholsky the second game against Arizona, and me against Iowa State. It was tough and somewhat controversial, but we worked through it over a three- or four-game period. One reason I had an opportunity was because McGwire got hurt in the Big Ten opener. I started the next game at Wisconsin and had a good game.

That same day, my brother Andy was on the other side of the ball, facing me as a linebacker. That was a really unique, special experience, and a lot of our family was there. Not many situations occurred in Big Ten football where you have your brother on the other side of the ball. To win that game, go up against him, and win the quarterbacking job was a great experience.

From that point forward, Coach Fry basically said it's mine unless I have a big misstep. I executed well the rest of the season, and everyone kind of got into a flow. I think we went 8–1 the rest of the way, won our bowl game, and

Quarterback Chuck Hartlieb earned both All–Big Ten and honorable mention All-America honors his junior and senior seasons. *Photo courtesy of Bob Rasmus*

finished in the top 15. We had a great nucleus of players with Quinn Early, Herb Wester, and guys like that. It was a great year.

To most people, the Ohio State game was the signature win of 1987. The fact that Coach Fry had never won there, and then losing in 1985 when we were No. 1 in the nation made it an especially big game. We knew Coach Fry wanted this one more than anyone else. He wanted to beat Ohio State in Columbus. To win that game in the fashion we did was a once-in-a-lifetime experience.

I remember going out on the field with about 1:50 to go in the game. One hundred thousand fans were screaming as loud as they could in that two-minute drill. I just remember going out really poised. Coach Snyder had coached us up so well. I knew we had eight to 10 plays and just needed to slowly move the ball down the field. We completed some passes and had a penalty and a fumble. It was a little messy there, and we got ourselves into a deep hole sitting at fourth-and-23 with 16 seconds left.

We called timeout before that last play, and I'll never forget Coach Fry, as I came off the field for the timeout, look at me in the eye and say, "Charlie, what do you want to do?" I knew I wanted to get the ball to Marv Cook, and I knew it was going to be hard because they would have him well covered. Regardless, I said, "Coach, I really think we should do lion 75 Y trail. Let me see if I can look them off and get Marv down the sideline." He said, "We'll do it, let's go."

Marv was covered, but we had practiced being able to throw behind a man-to-man coverage. Sure enough, Marv adjusted to the ball and made a tremendous play and catch to get seven. And I'll tell you, I was screaming out the plays and it was just deafening. When Marv crossed the goal line and the referee's hands went up, you could've heard a pin drop. It was so quiet. We had shocked them so much. It was amazing how quickly it went from sounding like a rock concert to there being nobody in the place.

I had a very unique game relationship with Marv. We understood each other so well it was almost as if we could play catch blindfolded. We always knew we could count on each other. He would get open where I needed to put the ball. We had a lot of chemistry out on the field and completed a ton of passes. Quinn Early was also a remarkable talent.

While 1987 was by all means a success, 1988 defined frustration. It was just one of those years that it wasn't meant to be. *Sport* magazine had us ranked No. 1 in the country, but we could never get the ball rolling. One primary reason was injuries. I think there were only two guys on the offensive side who played every game in '88. Marv Cook sat out four or five games, Bob Kratch was hurt, we lost our center for a while, our tailbacks got hurt, and it was just really difficult. I injured my ACL in the middle of the season. Going to Hawaii, we were confident, but we just lost our legs in the second half. I threw a touchdown in the corner of the end zone to go ahead with about 30 seconds left in the game. We all thought it was a touchdown, but I'll never forget that late flag crossing my face. A hometown ref called a very controversial holding penalty on us. I had never seen anything like that before. The touchdown was negated, we missed the field goal, and that really set us off on some negative events the rest of the year. The three ties were frustrating beyond belief. Sometimes things don't go your way no matter how hard you try.

As difficult as 1988 was at times, it was still a tremendous honor to be named captain that year. It's an incredible feeling to come out of the tunnel first and see 70,000 people all have their eyes on you. The noise is deafening, and that players were able to prompt that kind of reaction is remarkable. It's almost impossible to not let your guard down for a moment and take it all in. I wish every single Iowa football fan could experience that. It's an emotional moment.

I was one of those kids who found a way to excel at Iowa, but didn't necessarily have the talent to excel in the NFL. I was very happy to play one year with the Houston Oilers. While I think I had a good enough arm, I measured only 6′, and my footwork was very average. I had a great experience being the No. 3 quarterback but did not make it to the second year and got cut. I was ready to start a family and get started in the business world. It was difficult, but I didn't really look back after I made the transition from football to business. It was wonderful to experience the NFL, but I moved on pretty quickly. I was so thankful for what I was able to accomplish at Iowa.

It all started with Coach Fry giving me an opportunity. I learned a tremendous amount about life by how he approached the game of football on and off the field. He had a great understanding of people, how they interacted with each other, how critical unity is, and how communication among a group is important. Anyone can say they understand people, but few people truly do. He identified winners in his program, and there's nothing more exemplary than the type of assistant coaches he had over the years. He was just a unique person from a management standpoint. Coach Fry was able to identify and surround himself with talented coaches, and each of them benefitted from being so loyal. He knew we needed to do it differently. He knew we needed to come out with guns loaded and not play it safe. He, along with Bill Snyder, really revolutionized the passing game in the Big Ten and broke up the "big two and little eight." I'm forever grateful I was a part of that.

Chuck Hartlieb grew up in Woodstock, Illinois. As quarterback, Hartlieb left Iowa ranked second in school history in career passing yards and still owns nine school passing records. He is well known for his last-second touchdown pass to Marv Cook at Columbus, Ohio, in 1987. He currently resides with his family in Des Moines, Iowa.

BRAD QUAST

LINEBACKER

1986–1989

I HAD NO IDEA HOW OVERWHELMING the recruiting process would be when I started. Recruiting has completely changed since I went through it, and there's even more pressure on the athletes today. It's just kind of interesting how you're 17 or 18 years old and you're trying to make a decision of that magnitude as you're being pulled a dozen different directions.

I took five official school visits: Illinois, Michigan, Notre Dame, Iowa, and UCLA. My fun trip was UCLA. I went out to Los Angeles to get a look at what the university was like. It was good, but I was a Big Ten guy. Michigan was recruiting me heavily, and I got a phone call from former President Gerald Ford. He was a University of Michigan football player, so he called and then sent a letter with the presidential seal. Bo Schembechler, Hayden Fry, and Lou Holtz all came to my high school. You come home from meeting with each school, and you say, "Geesh, I want to go there." Then you take the next trip and you say, "I want to go there, too."

In the end, Iowa really sold me. I felt very comfortable talking to Coach Fry, and with the Iowa fans and the university less than four hours from my house, it worked out very well. So I became a Hawkeye.

I'll never forget when I first started my freshman year. I was looking at the depth chart and said to my dad, "Oh my gosh, I'm fifth-string strong-side linebacker. There are four guys ahead of me. What's this all about?"

Brad Quast came to Iowa as a football and scholastic high school All-American out of Des Plaines, Illinois. He became one of the few linebackers in Iowa history to start all four years. *Photo courtesy of Bob Rasmus*

I had to work hard and scrimmage and try to do the best I could to compete every day. The great thing about Iowa is the type of people Coach Fry recruited. I was 18 years old, and I had fourth- or fifth-year seniors helping and instructing me where to line up and where to drop in coverage. All the while, I was competing for their jobs. It can make your head spin, because as a linebacker you have to learn everything about the defense—what they're doing in front of you and in back of you. You're the quarterback of the defense.

Through the preseason, I slowly worked my way up the depth chart. I remember sitting down with Coach Alvarez when he said, "Listen, I'm not going to redshirt you. You're going to get some playing time this year as a true freshman." The first couple of games, I played a bunch but didn't start. Before the first Big Ten game, he called me before practice and said, "Quast, I'm going to start you against Michigan State." I said, "Really?" He replied, "Yeah, we're on national TV. How do you like that?" I was fortunate enough to become a freshman All-American in 1986 and a starter for the rest of my career.

Coming out of the tunnel my freshman year was just awesome. Sometimes you're playing in front of 100,000 fans, and you're thinking, *Damn, I have goose bumps.* I have goose bumps simply recalling this. Players should cherish that moment because you can never get it back—ever.

My junior year [when we played] in Manhattan, Kansas, I had a 96-yard touchdown interception. At the time it was the longest in Iowa history. I think I still lead all Iowa linebackers for career interceptions, and I'm, like, sixth in interceptions for all Iowa players.

Playing Minnesota was always fun because I knew Darrell Thompson pretty well. We went on recruiting trips to Michigan and Iowa together, so we had a bond in that way. We were always like, "Hey, where are you gonna go?" We were going back and forth in our decisions. I always had a bunch of tackles against Minnesota, and it was usually a great game for linebackers because they didn't pass much, and you knew you were just going to pound their guards and tackles. I still talk to Darrell occasionally.

My roommates for more than two years were Mark Stoops and Peter Marciano, and I still talk to them. I do business in Iowa City now, and Matt Hughes organized a really nice reunion. There must have been about 80 guys back from Hayden's time all the way to Kirk's present class. We rented out a bar and had a good time. I saw tutors who I haven't seen in 20 years. And the trainers, such as John Streif and Ed Crowley, were there, who were so important. It's a great group of people who were so vital in my growth and development into a man. They taught us how to develop through the good times and the bad times.

One thing that makes athletics so special is that 20 years later, your teammates and football associates can literally sit there and talk all night over a couple of brewskies. We can just sit there and talk about stories and the crazy stuff we did in the dorm rooms or in the locker rooms, or stupid stuff we pulled in the library trying to study. It's just fun and it never gets old. It all comes back as if it were yesterday.

After Iowa, I went to a couple of all-star games and then got drafted by the New York Jets in the 10th round. I got hurt and spent half of 1990 on injured reserve. I couldn't stay healthy. It seemed like I was always dinged up in college, too. I missed time my freshman year because of my neck. I broke my hand my sophomore year. I always missed a couple games here and there.

After 1990 I played in the NFL Europe for Barcelona. That was great because the Olympics were going on there and it was like a paid vacation. Then I signed a two-year deal with the Philadelphia Eagles for 1992 and 1993, but I ripped up my knee in 1992. I had three surgeries that year and then I had my physician redo my knee in 1993. At that time I had had a total of eight knee surgeries in my career—five on my left and three on my right. I was done; I just couldn't pass any physicals. Doctor [James] Andrews agreed, "You're done." I'm due for a knee replacement here in a couple of years, and I'm only in my early forties.

I think of the University of Iowa as a top-tier program, and I don't think it gets the recognition it should. The talent level is much better than perceived. They win with class, lose with dignity, and produce good quality individuals. They produce great student-athletes and great people in the community.

Iowa wants kids who are going to be good team players and just work their tails off. We did the things we had to do, won a lot of games, and had a great experience. And then the fans—I think the fans are crazy. They're passionate and dedicated. Everyone knows how Hawkeye fans travel; they travel all over the place. They love their Hawkeyes.

It was funny, when I went to the 2009 Penn State game, there were probably 10,000 people at the Hawkeye Huddle. My kids, Zach and Shane, were with me, and Zach wore my old No. 35 jersey. I wasn't drawing attention to myself, but associate athletics director Mark Jennings got up and acknowledged me and a bunch of other former players. I mean, they still recognize and remember players like myself! As I was walking to my seat in the stands, someone said, "I remember the Kansas State run." They remember it vividly, and my boys were going, "Geeze, you did play football, didn't you?" Shane said, "You were pretty good, I guess, huh?" And I said, "I did all right." He replied, "I thought you were just making that stuff up."

My four years at Iowa went by so quickly. I played right away as a freshman and never seemed to take it all in. It's like I blinked and it was over with. I think it's odd, when you're playing college ball, you don't realize how to cherish the moment. You're trying to rush to get to the next level and sometimes forget to savor your time there. The college experience is the greatest experience ever. Especially now, 20 years later, I'm glad I chose the University of Iowa.

Brad Quast was named the top freshman linebacker in the nation by the *Sporting News* in 1986, and he was an All–Big Ten selection in 1988 and 1989. His 435 career tackles ranks fourth in school history, and his 11 career interceptions ranks sixth. Quast presently lives in Mullica Hill, New Jersey.

The NINETIES

DANAN HUGHES

Wide Receiver

1989–1992

Although there were a couple of guys from my hometown who went to the University of Iowa before me, I had not heard much about being a Hawkeye. I kept an open mind about college throughout the recruiting phase and had several recruiting trips planned to universities across the country. Being from New Jersey, I had pretty much all of the East Coast schools showing interest, but I figured I'd be better served to get away from home. So, although I did visit Boston College, my decision came down to the University of Iowa and the University of Nebraska. The other schools did not really interest me or were too close to home.

I remember clearly to this day when Coach Hayden Fry came to my house to visit with my parents and me. Prior to his visit, I had many conversations and interactions with Coach Bernie Wyatt. He was an East Coast guy, a New Yorker I could definitely relate to. He spoke my talk, and he knew some people in my high school. He really did a great job of connecting with me. He was like "one of us," as people would say in my area. So it was easy to take him in and build a trusting relationship.

But when Hayden Fry came to visit my home, with cowboy boots and all, I thought, *What in the world am I thinking? Is this how they dress in Iowa? Am I going to have to get some new gear to fit in?* Wow! That was the first time I had ever seen cowboy boots in person, much less in my own home. It was cool in a weird kind of way. Anyway, Coach Fry did his thing and won me over.

Danan Hughes was All–Big Ten in 1991 and left as Iowa's all-time leader in career receiving yards. *Photo courtesy of Bob Rasmus*

He sold me on the fact that Iowa was the right place for me. Integrity is everything to me. Mean what you say and say what you mean! When I told him I wanted to play Hawkeye baseball, too, he never flinched! His criteria were that I worked hard, stayed eligible, and kept my grades up. Then the opportunity would be open for me. To his credit, he never backed off from that commitment. In a time when recruiting is more about telling kids whatever you think they want to hear—being an immediate starter, going to the NFL, etc.—he stood by his commitment. I will never forget that. He will always mean a lot to me because he spoke my language.

I remember getting off the plane in Cedar Rapids for my official visit to Iowa, and I have to say, this city kid was taken back a little. I had never seen anything like it. I had never been exposed to farmland, livestock, or anything resembling the views I saw driving from Cedar Rapids to Iowa City. It was refreshing to see more people and city life as we came into Iowa City. I felt more comfortable.

I was intrigued by life, school, football, and baseball in Iowa. Any doubt I had in my mind totally vanished as we entered Carver-Hawkeye Arena that day. I became totally sold! My first encounter with Hawkeye sports involved walking into the arena and watching the wrestling match between Iowa State and Iowa. Now, if there was any doubt about the dedication and fire for Hawkeye sports, it was answered in that match. My first thought was, *Are you kidding me? These people have packed into this arena, standing-room-only, for a wrestling match?* Then I thought, *If they like wrestling so much, they must love football!* I was impressed! I cancelled all the rest of my college visits and verbally committed to the University of Iowa soon after the visit.

After redshirting in both football and baseball my first year, I was blessed with three great years of baseball before being drafted as a center fielder in the third round by the Milwaukee Brewers, and four excellent years of football before being drafted by the Kansas City Chiefs as a wide receiver. I then played six years in the NFL.

I have a ton of great memories from my time as a Hawkeye athlete. Just about every time I run into a Hawkeye fan, they always bring up the "snow angel" play. In 1991 we played Minnesota in Kinnick Stadium after a heavy snowfall. We were beating the Gophers pretty bad, and after scoring a touchdown, I made a snow angel imprint in the end zone. The funny thing is, some of my Iowa baseball teammates were standing right down near the end zone where I did it. I was also fortunate enough to play in the Rose Bowl and Holiday Bowl. I played in the Big Ten championship and regionals for the College World Series as a Hawkeye baseball player.

Every thought I have, every memory I took with me can be summed up in three words: a true blessing. I enjoyed every aspect of my life in Iowa and cannot begin to put into words how much of an impact the people, the university, my coaches, teammates, and friends have had on my life. The values and dedication learned and experienced will be with me the rest of my life. Without God's hand on my life and Him blessing me with my time at Iowa, I would not have accomplished what I have in my life either athletically or personally.

So when the question is asked, "What does it mean to be a Hawkeye?" to me it means everything! I will forever be associated with the best university in the country, the best people, and a great tradition. People may remember me for wearing a No. 3 on my back and chest, but I will always remember them as just the best. I am and will always be extremely honored to be a Hawkeye for life.

Danan Hughes came to Iowa from Bayonne, New Jersey. He played both football and baseball at Iowa from 1989 to 1992. He helped lead Iowa to the 1991 Rose Bowl, and the Hawkeyes finished 10–1–1 the following year. Hughes was All–Big Ten in 1991 and left as Iowa's all-time leader in career receiving yards. He played both football and baseball professionally, including six seasons with the Kansas City Chiefs. Hughes currently resides with his family in Kansas City and works in the banking industry.

MATT SHERMAN

Quarterback

1994–1997

This is classic Coach Fry. My mom was a German teacher for a number of years. Coach Fry came to our little school, which was front-page news. We walked into the guidance counselor's office, and Mom and Dad were there. We were all sitting in there, and Coach Fry started talking German to my mom. I took German, but I had no idea what the hell he was saying. He and my mom were talking German back and forth. Afterward, I said, "Did he just really speak German to you?" And she was like, "That was absolutely unbelievable." I don't know what they said, so I probably should find that out. But that's the type of recruiter he was—he always won over the mom. Even though he was this huge public figure, he was always able to adapt and come down to our level and just have a conversation, albeit in German. He was able to come down and say, "Hey, here's why I want your son, and oh, by the way, have you had bratwurst somewhere?" Or whatever the hell he said, I don't know.

I ended up playing some as a freshman in 1994 and ultimately starting the last two ballgames that season. That season was crazy. I got hurt midway through the year just in practice. I broke a bone in my foot. We actually had five quarterbacks play that year, because a couple of them got injured or just weren't productive. At halftime of the Purdue game, we were down 21–0. I still had a broken bone in my foot, but the doctors worked some magic and I ended up playing, and we came back and—they still had ties back then—

we tied the game 21–21. I started my first game the next week against Northwestern and then started the final game that season against Minnesota.

I never lost to Minnesota or Iowa State in my career, and I was proud of that. See, I grew up in St. Ansgar, a small town of 1,000 people in north-central Iowa. It was a small farming community, nine miles south of the Minnesota border. There are so many Gopher fans in our area. Minnesota wasn't a great team, but they and Iowa State were always big games for me personally.

That Minnesota game in 1994 was unbelievable. One play that was so interesting and showed why Coach Fry is so magical as a coach happened right at the end of the first quarter. There were 18 seconds left, and the clock was counting down. We were in Minnesota's red zone. The book would say regroup, go back to the other end of the field, and let the quarter end. But Coach Fry was in a hurry to get this play off. We called it in the huddle and snapped that thing with two or three seconds left. It was a trick play, a throw back to the quarterback. Minnesota thought that was the last thing we were going to do! Tim Dwight threw the ball, and I made a catch in the end zone. It was an outstanding play, and one where you just look back and say, "How did Coach Fry even come up with that?" We practiced it, but we never thought he'd actually call it. But he called it at a time when no one ever would have guessed or thought it would be the right time for a trick play. I guess that's the beauty of Coach Fry.

We finished strong in 1994, but we didn't go to a bowl game. In the off-season, I didn't think I was big enough or strong enough, so I really worked hard in the weight room. Obviously, it helped me, but I also had some arm issues my entire sophomore year, and I think a lot of it was due to the overuse in the off-season and into the summer. Some games I struggled, no doubt about it. I give Coach Fry all the credit in the world because he easily could have yanked me, but he stuck with me. He just wasn't a guy who pulled guys in and out, and as a player you sure appreciate that because athletics and especially the game of football isn't about one guy. I guess that's where the patience and persistence has to be in you, because if you don't have that, it's never going to work. Coach Fry was wonderful that way.

In the 1995 Sun Bowl, Washington was the No. 2 Pac-10 team. I remember we went down there 10 days early. Coach Fry said, "Listen, I want you to go down there and have fun. Do what you need to do for a couple days, but obviously, be smart and don't get in trouble. Then be ready to work like a normal work week for us." We did that. We went down there and enjoyed ourselves, but then by our second or third day down there, we were saying, "Okay, let's get back to work." I don't think people thought we even had a chance against Washington, but we beat them in absolutely every phase of the game. Were they more talented? Probably. They had better players, but man, we just caught them off-guard. Maybe they didn't prepare right—I'm not sure, but it was a pretty special day. It was a cool win because, as a team, it really did set the tempo for the 1996 season.

Nineteen ninety-six was probably our most talented team. We had some really good players who could play anywhere in the country, and we knew that. We didn't have egos or a lot of conflicts on the team, but there were some challenges, no doubt about it. We were the first Big Ten team to ever go down to Tulsa. Unfortunately, we got beat, and I'll never forget that plane ride home. That was just an awful feeling, because my group from '94 to that point had never lost a game like that, where we were favored and they just outplayed us or we weren't prepared.

That hurt us, and then we were down early against Michigan State. Michigan State was ahead 17–0 at Kinnick, and this was mid-to-late first quarter. It was third-and-26, and things were just going terribly. Well, Demo Odems caught this in-route, and we got the first down, and that set the tone really for the rest of the year, believe it or not. Everything just kind of came together. I remember the pass was just an inch or two over the linebacker's hand, and if he would have tipped it, we would have punted, and there would have been more negativity. But that one play, in my mind, was the point where things just started working. We completed some more passes and got in the end zone. That was the play where everyone in the huddle said, "Now we got it. Let's go." It was a pretty critical play. We ended up winning that game 37–30. That was a game that kind of brought us together and made us believe again.

We beat Penn State on the road that year. I remember waking up the morning of the game and opening up the door, and it was sleeting, raining, and was like 30 degrees. I closed the door immediately and thought, *This is going to be awful today.* I was just convinced we were not going to be able to throw the ball. But we went out and played really well. The funny thing is that we were watching tape of Ohio State–Penn State that week. Ohio State ran a couple plays that absolutely exposed Penn State, so we put them in, thinking, *There's no way these are going to work, because Penn State's going to make the adjustment.* But they didn't, and we completed a couple of big plays

Matt Sherman grew up in St. Ansgar, Iowa. His 24 wins as a starting quarterback rank third among quarterbacks in Iowa history behind Chuck Long and Ricky Stanzi. *Photo courtesy of Bob Rasmus*

that we basically borrowed from Ohio State. That was an unbelievable experience and a fun plane ride home, no doubt about that.

I had never had any major injuries. But my senior year, we were up in Michigan. It was a huge game, 2:30 on ABC. We had those guys on the ropes and should have had them beat. We were driving, and I got sacked or threw it away—I really don't recall. But I got hit and landed on my thumb. I thought it was just dislocated, but it wasn't. I kept pushing it back into place, but it just kept popping in and out. I stayed in and played because—I don't know, maybe the adrenaline gets you. If you ever watch the tape—and I haven't for a long time—you'll see the balls flutter a lot because my thumb really isn't working. It's just kind of holding in place. After the game, I went to the doctor and said, "There's something wrong with my thumb. Maybe I dislocated it." He looked at it and said, "Oh, no, man. It's more serious than that." Here we are, we just lost probably the biggest game of my career, and then I find out that my career playing for the Hawkeyes is probably over.

My thumb was broken. We ended up not having surgery, and I probably wish I would have, because we casted it. That year we ended up going to the Sun Bowl to play Arizona State. I believe the game was on a Friday, and I took my cast off basically on Wednesday of the week. I started the game and tried to throw, but I couldn't even complete an out route. I came out in the first quarter, and we ultimately ended up losing 17–7. Coach Fry wanted me to have an opportunity to go out on a high note, but my arm atrophied so much. It was just weak, and I couldn't get it done. It's amazing how a season can turn on one snap of the ball. For both me and the team, the season took a different path than we wanted it to. You never draw it up that way, but that's okay. It happens.

I love Iowa City, and it will always have a fond place in my heart. I love going back, because Iowa City brings back great memories. I'll drive by the stadium with my three-year-old boy, and he'll say, "Daddy, you played there, right?" It's cool to be able to kind of show him what happened, and obviously, I hope to live through him moving forward! I try to be humble, and I'm not arrogant about it, but I'm pretty proud of what we did. I struggled saying that for a number of years, but looking back now and talking with the guys I played with, it's fun to kind of rehash it. It's a small part of our lives now. Now it's about kids and minivans and all that type of stuff, but it's pretty dang cool to be part of that tradition.

You're always a Hawk. For me, being a Hawkeye was just a dream come true. Telling people that I played at Iowa is something that I was really proud of then and I'm probably even more proud of now. We do it the right way and we don't cheat and we don't break rules. I think people across the country respect the Iowa name. When people hear you played for Iowa, they think pretty highly of that, and not all players can say that about where they played. For me, I was in a fantasy world, just living the dream of a kid from a 1,000-person town. I was fortunate enough to have some success and obviously make a lot of really good relationships, and being a Hawkeye has changed my life more than I ever thought it could.

After college, Matt Sherman played three seasons with the Iowa Barnstormers before settling in Minneapolis and taking a job with Learfield Sports selling Gopher Sports Properties to marketing, radio, TV, and Internet advertisers. "Whenever any of my Iowa teammates ask for a business card, it has a big Minnesota logo on it, and they absolutely can't understand how I could work for the University of Minnesota!" Sherman admits. "But I have great people I work with, and it's a great career for me right now. Coach Fry always believed that no matter who you work for, even if you're working for another Big Ten school, the reality is you're still always a Hawk and a part of this family, and I think that's pretty cool."

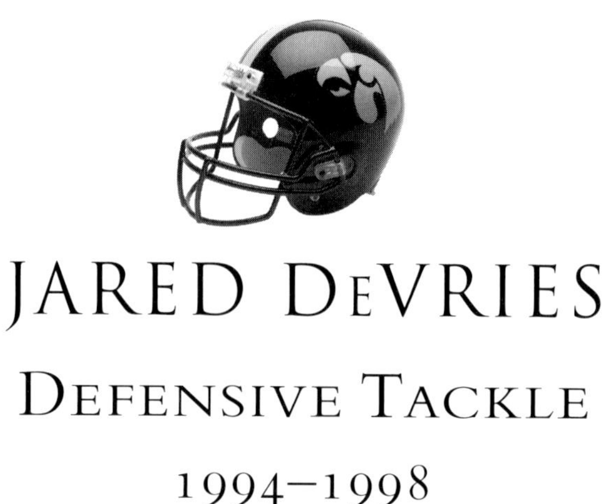

JARED DEVRIES

DEFENSIVE TACKLE

1994–1998

I GUESS YOU COULD SAY I STARTED my football career from somewhat humble beginnings. I am from the small town of Aplington, Iowa. My junior year, my school consolidated with the neighboring community of Parkersburg a few miles to the east and became Aplington-Parkersburg High School. Even after we consolidated, we were still considered Class 1A, which is the smallest in Iowa.

I would not say that I was particularly heavily recruited by colleges coming out of high school. Even though I wasn't even playing for Coach Ed Thomas yet my sophomore year, he was nice enough to forward a tape of me to Iowa, so I was sort of on their radar screen after that. Then, my junior year, I joined Coach Thomas' program. We played a game against St. Ansgar, and Iowa happened to be there scouting Matt Sherman. That night was the first time that the Iowa folks saw me live, and the whole recruiting process got going from there. Coach [Bob] Elliot was the assistant coach at Iowa who recruited me.

As far as I was concerned, if Iowa was going to give me an opportunity, I was going to take it. I had passing interest from schools like Wisconsin and Nebraska, but didn't really entertain them seriously because it was a lifelong dream of mine to be a Hawk. I didn't even take any other official recruiting visits. I had seen all I needed to at Iowa and accepted their offer in short order.

Jared DeVries was a four-year starter from 1995 to 1998. He holds Iowa career records for sacks (42) and tackles for loss (78). *Photo courtesy of Bob Rasmus*

My recruiting class in 1994 was rated as one of the very best in the nation. I came in with the likes of Eric Thigpen, Vernon Rollins, Matt Hughes, Tim Dwight, my roommate Michael Burger, and a bunch of great offensive linemen, like Mike Goff and Jeremy McKinney. We had a great class. Many of us redshirted, but a few played right away. I view all of these guys who came into the program with me as my twin brothers. The rest of my teammates I viewed as my big brothers.

The big brother I'm closest with to this day is Casey Wiegmann. He is from Parkersburg and actually hosted me during my official recruiting visit. If I had any questions at all, I would ask him. He would also tell me a lot of things I never even had to ask about. Another big brother who was very influential to me was Ryan Abraham. He was a senior when I was a redshirt freshman, and he didn't need to waste his time on me back then, but he took an active interest in me and didn't want me to make the same mistakes he made. Both Casey and Ryan kept me out of trouble and headed down the right path. I have both of these guys to thank for an awful lot of my success.

The year after my redshirt year, I came into preseason camp as the backup to Chris Webb on the defensive line. He had some shoulder issues that didn't allow him to play his senior year, so I was thrust into a starting role very early in my career. I wasn't completely sure I was ready for it. I remember coming into my very first game against Northern Iowa and thinking, *Oh my goodness, I get to run out onto the field at Kinnick Stadium for the first time for real.* The excitement and nervousness within me was just palpable. In my first collegiate game, I ended up with three sacks. That is an experience I will never forget.

One of the many things that made being a Hawk so special was having the opportunity to play for Coach Hayden Fry. Coach Fry was a living legend. I grew up as a little boy rooting for the Hawks and seeing Coach Fry all the time in the media, and playing for him really wasn't real to me for a while. But, in spite of all this, he made me feel comfortable at all times and never put too much pressure on me as a young athlete. This is something that I'm grateful for and I think helped spur my development as a football player.

Because of my success on the field my first three years, I found myself with a decision to make coming out of my junior year. I remember that there were a few articles that came out toward the end of the season speculating about my NFL future. Maybe the best memory I have of the great Iowa fans came after our last game that year against Minnesota. After the game, I remember running into a whole mob of fans eagerly expressing their opinion as to what I should do with the "One More Year" chant. At that moment, it really struck me how passionate the fans are about the Iowa program and the players who are a part of it. That type of unwavering support made it such a privilege to be part of the Iowa program.

When I think about family, I think about the Iowa football program. When I think about brothers, I think about my Iowa teammates. Every college experience is great for a kid, but none will top what I experienced at Iowa. Probably most important, the relationships I established at the University of Iowa some 15 or more years ago now, are in many cases still alive and strong today, and I expect them to last a lifetime.

These are feelings I am now so thrilled to share with my wife and my two boys. Up until this past year, my NFL schedule made it very difficult to get back for games. I only made it back for two games in 11 years. But this past season, due to an injury, I found myself with more time, and my family and I were able to take in all except one home game. Prior to this season, my boys had been to a game before, but it was awfully hot that particular day, and I think they were still too young to appreciate the whole experience. It was fun for me to see how much the boys enjoyed the games this year. I look forward to many more football Saturdays in Iowa City with my family. I can only hope that the memories we will share together as a family will come close to the great memories I had during my college years at Iowa.

Jared DeVries was named first-team All–Big Ten for three straight seasons and was selected second-team All-America as a junior by *Football News*, while also being recognized as Big Ten Defensive Lineman of the Year in 1997. DeVries was a consensus All-American his senior year in 1998 after being named first-team All-America by the American Football Coaches Association, Walter Camp, and the *Sporting News*. DeVries also earned MVP honors in the 1995 Sun Bowl and 1996 Alamo Bowl, both Iowa wins. After his senior season at Iowa, he was drafted by the Detroit Lions in the third round of the 1999 NFL Draft (70th overall pick) and has played a total of 12 seasons in the NFL, all with Detroit.

MATT HUGHES

Linebacker

1995–1998

I'm from a small town in Texas. Eastland is about 100 miles west of Dallas and has a population around 3,000. I played running back and strong safety in high school. I was recruited by the big Texas schools and a few out-of-state schools. My connection to Iowa was that Bill Brasier, the defensive coordinator for many years under Hayden Fry, actually graduated from my high school. Plus, Hayden Fry himself was born in Eastland and lived there until he was in second grade. So there were lots of synergies involved that drew me to Iowa.

Yet there was still some uncertainty related to Iowa because of its distance from home. But then my older brother was killed in a car accident my junior year, and when it came time to pick a college, I was looking for a way to get as far away from my past as possible. I had an offer from Iowa, and it was about as far as I could imagine. Plus, I was intrigued by the Big Ten. I had seen teams like Ohio State and Michigan on TV growing up, and it seemed like the whole thing would be fun to be a part of.

When Bill Brashier took me out onto the field at Kinnick Stadium for the first time, I looked around and saw a stadium that held 72,000 people, my first thought was, *Wow, my entire home town is just a tiny sliver of this stadium!* The warmth of the people in the program and of the players during my visit stood out, too. Matt Sherman hosted me during my recruiting visit and did a great job of selling the university. Iowa was my first recruiting visit. I had four others scheduled, but I canceled them when I got home and committed to Iowa right away.

When I think of the people who were responsible for the successes I enjoyed in school, I think it all starts with my parents. It was hard for them to let me go after all that had happened in our family, but no matter what, they always taught me to follow my dreams, work hard, and be classy in everything that I do. Being the son of a teacher and coach, they taught me that while football was a great means to get to college, my education was the most important piece of the puzzle because football won't always be there.

I have to absolutely give Coach Fry his due credit. He was the epitome of class. He cared for every one of his players and their families. He taught us how to be successful, both on and off the field, and also to respect not only the game of football, but the game of life. He always had a way of bringing humor into so many of our interactions. His involvement in all of our lives made it a big honor and a privilege to be a Hawkeye. He is a coaching legend, but his influence goes far beyond the game of football. I will forever be indebted to Coach Fry for his amazing influence on my life.

Playing football at Iowa afforded me the opportunity to get to know so many great teammates. My teammates filled a huge void in my life left by the death of my brother. He was my only sibling, but in essence, I feel like I picked up a team full of brothers whom I could count on to be there for me through thick and thin, and these brothers still perform that role for me, even today. Without my teammates and this great Hawkeye family, my life would have never been as blessed and as fulfilling as it has become. Even today, more than a dozen years after my playing days, I look to my Iowa teammates for things that I can't look to my brother for anymore.

In particular, Vernon Rollins was and still is one of my best friends. We got some press back in the day because, on the surface, we were polar opposites and should have never gotten along. He was from the big city in Hackensack, New Jersey, and I was from small town, dry county, Eastland, Texas. He is black and I am white. Yet, football brought us together and made us the best of friends. He was the best linebacker I had ever seen. I idolized the way he played and tried to emulate him on the field. We became so tight that we helped each other in all aspects of life. One of my worst memories as a Hawkeye was watching him get hurt the first play of the second half against Iowa State in 1997. After the game, when we found out his season was over,

As a three-year starter at linebacker, Matt Hughes ranks eighth in career tackles at Iowa with 354. *Photo courtesy of Bob Rasmus*

we just cried together for the longest time. We had plenty of good times, but you remember some of the bad times just as vividly.

On the field, there were many individual games that stand out. I was fortunate enough to be named Chevrolet Player of the Game against Ohio State in both 1997 and 1998. I earned Big Ten Defensive Player of the Week in 1996, following the Indiana game, and was proud to be named an all-conference player during my career. But probably my greatest moment was being named one of four cocaptains prior to my senior season. This was voted on by my teammates, and to have earned the respect of the players within the locker room meant more to me than any external accolade imaginable.

A couple team moments that were special to me included beating Penn State in 1996. It was a really wet and rainy day at Happy Valley, and our team played our hearts out and came out on top 21–20. Dominating Texas Tech in the 1996 Alamo Bowl was especially sweet to me because I was playing against so many teammates from my high school all-star game. Then, of course, I had a huge crowd of family and friends from Texas in attendance.

Off the field, I feel like I was able to follow my parents' advice and I got a great education at Iowa. I worked hard in the classroom, maintained good grades, managed to earn Academic All–Big Ten honors all four years, and also made the Dean's List. Another great off-the-field memory was having the opportunity to touch the lives of kids throughout the state by speaking on behalf of Athletes in Action. Jim Goodrich, who still is director of Athletes in Action, gave me the chance to speak at elementary schools, father/son banquets, and other social gatherings to help serve as a positive role model for kids who follow Iowa football, which seemed to be most kids in the state!

Playing football at Iowa has taught me that if you want something bad enough, all you need to do is work hard, and good things are bound to happen. There are so many lifelong lessons that are learned because of the sport of football. Hard work, dedication, and winning and losing with class and character are just a few of the lessons that were seasoned and developed while playing football at Iowa. I was fortunate to have my dad as my high school coach. He is the one who first introduced me to so many of these principles that were then hammered home after playing for the great coaches at Iowa like Coach Fry, Bill Brasier, and Bret Bielema (who was my linebackers coach for the three years that I started at Iowa).

Even though I came from Texas, Iowa is home to me and my family. This is where I grew to be a man. The people who I have met here and developed friendships with are the ones I wouldn't trade for anything in the world. Iowa is a great place for my wife, Brandi, and I to raise our four children. We have great school systems and plenty of activities for our family to participate in, which of course includes Hawkeye sports! Since I graduated from Iowa, my parents have retired and moved up to Coralville. I consider my children to be extremely blessed to have both sets of grandparents living here in the state of Iowa with us.

I have taken a lead role in organizing the Iowa Hawkeye Football Club, which is comprised of more than 350 members who all are former Hawkeye football players. Our motto is, "Always a Hawk." To me, this really sums up what it means to be a Hawkeye. What this means is we are family and will do anything for our brothers. This applies not only to guys who walked with us, but guys who have worn the black and gold before or after us. We have a common thread and recognize that all of us have played some role in helping to build the outstanding reputation of the program that exists throughout the state and the country. We have an annual reunion, and it is funny how the stories year after year are so similar, and only the characters seem to change. I'm proud to be a Hawkeye and wouldn't trade my experiences, my friendships, or my school for anything in the world.

Matt Hughes hails from the small town of Eastland, Texas, but ever since his playing days in the mid-1990s, he has called Iowa home. As a three-year starter at linebacker, Hughes ranks eighth in career tackles at Iowa with 354. He was selected as one of four cocaptains his senior year in 1998, while also earning honorable mention All–Big Ten that season. Hughes was an academic standout, as well, earning Academic All–Big Ten honors for four straight years. He currently resides in North Liberty and is actively involved in a number of local businesses.

MATT BOWEN

SAFETY

1996–1999

I STILL SEE MAGICAL BEAUTY when I cross the Mississippi River into the state of Iowa, with its slow rolling hills, open land, and changing seasons. I felt that as an incoming freshman back in 1995—a 180-pound option quarterback. A kid, really, from the Chicago area who fell in love with the Black and Gold.

That was 15 years ago. Now, as a 33-year-old husband and father of three little boys, I still have those same thoughts when I cross that I-80 bridge on the drive from the city.

I am home—again.

It is hard to focus on just one aspect when we talk about being a Hawkeye—because it stays with you. It is bigger than wins and losses, or championship rings and touchdowns. Yes, we ultimately get judged as football teams by that final record, and we all have goals or aspirations to win trophies. I was no different when I set foot on campus back in '95. Visions of holding those roses in Kinnick Stadium on a late November afternoon ran through my mind, with oily gray skies, early winter wind, and fans rushing the field. That is the dream of every kid who heads off to play college football in the Big Ten Conference. Win that title and head out to Pasadena and the Rose Bowl.

I didn't make it to Pasadena as a player. We made three bowl games under Hayden Fry and experienced a season of change under Kirk Ferentz in 1999. My senior year will be forgotten when we talk about number of wins,

Matt Bowen was Iowa's team captain and MVP in 1999. *Photo courtesy of Bob Rasmus*

but it was a new beginning of Iowa football. Our 1999 team helped lay the foundation for future success. The passion and the excitement of wearing that uniform were always there on that team. We were not the most talented in the Big Ten, but we played hard—and we hit. We did things the right way and followed what Kirk said. We really believed that we were setting a standard and playing like the great teams before us—and soon to be after us.

I often get asked about my senior year and the tough times on the field. Yet, I always smile.

Why?

I smile because it goes a lot deeper than road trips to Columbus or games against the Cyclones. Instead, it is about friendships and lessons that are taught during your stay on campus and the life you live after. That's what being a Hawkeye means to me. There is a special bond that is created on those fields in practice and on game days. You learn to play for each other, but it doesn't stop after the fourth quarter or after meetings or after that last time you sit in that Kinnick locker room dressed in full gear with tears in your eyes. It doesn't stop when you're wanting to keep that jersey on for one more week or even one more series.

In fact, it never stops, and it stays with you. Those friendships are unbreakable and speak to the culture of the Iowa football player. Raised on great coaching from Hayden and Kirk, my teammates and I were built—and tested—on work ethic and dedication to a program. It isn't a quick ticket to the National Football League that we were after. Instead, it is a program that is formed with players who have to work hard, have to prepare better, and have to use the skills learned to compete. Coached tough, yet coached to play the game the right way. We aren't Ohio State, Miami, LSU, or other teams loaded with five-star recruits and overwhelming talent. At Iowa, we had to outwork those teams in practice, in the weight room, and in the classroom.

And you grow up in Iowa City because of football. We all came onto campus as kids, really. I remember eating lunch the day before fall camp in 1995 with my parents downtown, questioning if I was ready. That's probably normal for a kid going off to school to compete with Big Ten–caliber athletes. Part of me wanted to jump back in the car and head home.

However, I had to be dragged off of that campus when I left. Sure, there were ups and downs, games that should have ended differently and records that should have been better. But once you become a Hawkeye, I believe that you welcome those days when adversity does show its face, because you want the challenge.

We are all adults now—my teammates and I—with families, jobs, and other commitments. But life only gets tougher as you get older—new challenges and new obstacles to overcome. For me, there have been times when

I needed them—someone to lean on—both coaches and players. It comes from those fall afternoons when the shadows start to creep over the press box at Kinnick; the feel of a Big Ten Saturday and the swarm when we ran out of that tunnel onto the field. It starts there—but in reality it just keeps going.

I love my teammates and coaches, and after playing seven years in the National Football League, I can attest that we are different at Iowa. We treat the game with pride and we treat each other with respect and with honor as the calendar turns from year to year.

Do I miss it? Sure, I miss the bus ride past the fans, the smell of the locker room on game day, and the rush of playing on that field in Iowa City. I always miss the games and that competitive fire we all had. I would give up a pro career to go back for another week preparing to play at Kinnick. But I miss the names more and the time we spent together on campus and on that practice field. It goes too fast, but when you are a Hawkeye, it doesn't end. So if you asked me what it means to play for the University of Iowa, I would point my finger at the guys whom I shared the huddle with on Saturday afternoons. That is the reason I come back and the reason I feel at home when I cross the Mississippi River time after time.

I am so proud still to talk about the Hawks. Watching the players now, and the success they have under Kirk, just makes me appreciate more what it is that has been created in Iowa City. A place we can all come home to and a place that always welcomes us. The door never really closes, and it is open for all of us to come back home once again.

Matt Bowen was Iowa's team captain and MVP in 1999. He led Iowa in tackles twice and recorded 222 career tackles as a strong safety from 1996 to 1999. Bowen played seven seasons in the NFL and currently resides in Chicago, Illinois.

LeVAR WOODS

Defensive Line/Linebacker

1996–2000

I grew up in a small town in northwest Iowa and graduated from West Lyon High School. We were a small school that competed in Class 2A, but we had a really strong tradition of excellence in football, dating back to the early 1990s. Football was really everything when I grew up. There were 32 senior boys in my class, and 27 of them were out for football. I grew up near the border with South Dakota and Minnesota, and as a youngster, truth be told, was a big Huskers fan. They were coming off back-to-back national titles, so that was the first program I gravitated toward.

However, my first scholarship offer was from Iowa State. I had actually reached a point were I was pretty comfortable with going to Iowa State. It was two hours closer to home, a good school, and at least I would get to play Nebraska every year. I was going to commit to Iowa State, but something just didn't feel right. It was during my official recruiting visit to Iowa State when Iowa tight ends coach Mark Hendrickson called me and said that Iowa would like to offer me a scholarship. So I came home from Ames feeling confused and not sure about what to do. A few days later, Iowa State sent defensive coordinator Larry Coyer to our house to try to get me to commit (he is now the D-coordinator with the Indianapolis Colts). My mother and my sister both loved Coyer. But, still something just didn't feel right. Eventually, my mother stepped up and said I was never going to be sure until I at least went to Iowa for a visit, and it only took me a week after that visit to finally commit to Iowa.

The very first time I came through the tunnel at Kinnick in uniform as part of the swarm is a vivid memory. It happened to be against Iowa State, and it hit me that I was living my childhood dream of playing college football. It was a very overwhelming moment for me. Although I got a little ribbing from the older guys for it, I actually remember tearing up a little on the sideline.

I remember coming off the disappointing loss to close the 1998 season at Minnesota my sophomore year and hearing the news about Coach Fry retiring and being shocked. While it might have been more clear to just about everyone else, it just never dawned on me he would ever retire. But for me, the coaching change really happened at the perfect time, because my first few years, I wasn't playing a whole lot, but I was on the cusp of earning significant playing time.

Then Coach Ferentz came in. Certainly I noticed a different personality with Coach Ferentz compared to Coach Fry. I remember the first few team meetings after Coach Ferentz was hired. Coach Fry would always come in making jokes and having everyone in stitches laughing. Coach Ferentz was the total opposite. I remember being just a little nervous because you weren't sure just how serious he was. My first impressions of Coach Ferentz were that he was a very polished man, he knew what he wanted, and he was very clear in getting across his vision of what he expected of us. He let us know off the bat that it wasn't going to be easy. There were going to be changes and it might be uncomfortable for some. Another big change was in the schedule. We went from more of a collegiate schedule under Coach Fry to a schedule that was more similar to the NFL under Coach Ferentz.

I think both are outstanding coaches. Hayden is already in the Hall of Fame, and Coach Ferentz is well on his way. They have both done a great job of carrying on the rich tradition of Iowa football. They have both done it their own way, with different styles. Hayden would find a weakness in the opponent and then exploit it like it was nobody's business. Some people have said that he ran up the score and things like that, but with him, it was just attack, attack, attack, until the game ended. And with Coach Ferentz—the great thing about him is he believes in his way, and he does a great job of developing players, both on and off the field. He believes in excellence on the field, in the classroom, in the community, at home, and at everything that you do.

One play I will probably forever be remembered for was a field-goal block against Northern Illinois in 1999 that was returned for a touchdown. This

LeVar Woods was co–Most Valuable Player and team captain as a senior in 2000 and earned second-team All–Big Ten honors after recording 97 tackles. *Photo courtesy of Bob Rasmus*

game is memorable for the program, too, because it was Coach Ferentz's first win as head coach. I go back and look at the play now, and the first thing I notice is how screwed up my technique was. The cool thing about it is that one of my best friends, Matt Bowen, made the block. Matt made the real play, and it just so happened that the ball hit me in the hands. I really was just standing there. The play was critical because I remember the game being a lot closer than the final score of 24–0 might have indicated. This play is something Matt and I talk about a lot to this day.

Coming out of Iowa, I was an undrafted free agent and had to do everything possible just to make an NFL team. Looking back, I credit so much of what I learned at Iowa under Coach Ferentz with allowing me to make it to the next level. Coming out of Iowa, I already knew things like the schedule, what to expect in practice, the pace of practice, how to practice, whether you were in full pads, shells, or shoulder pads only. Those kinds of things may not seem like a big deal, but they end up being a big deal once you move up. I think there were plenty of guys with more talent than me who were more heralded, higher draft picks, who didn't know how to do those things, and it made it more difficult for them. For me, it was a pretty quick transition from Iowa to the NFL.

Something else Matt Bowen and I reminisce often about is our experience in the NFL with teammates from other colleges. Sitting around in the locker room, the talk always gets back to everyone's alma mater. Saturdays in the NFL are hilarious because of all the friendly wagering on the college games. Of course, I would always bet on the Hawks, no matter what. But then you get to talking about your college experience, and it is amazing how many guys in the NFL hated their college coach or hated their college experience. Of course, you talk to the Iowa guys, and it is the complete opposite. Everyone is dying to get back, they love the city, love the fans, love the coach.

Early in my NFL career, I remember my locker was between a guy from Maryland and Florida State and across from guys who went to Nebraska and Texas. I came in from two-a-day practices one day, and there was a box sitting in the bottom of my locker. Inside it was a handwritten note from Coach Ferentz with a Hawkeye T-shirt and hat. The note wished me luck in the upcoming season and thanked me for all I had done for the program. And after the Alamo Bowl win in 2001, Coach Ferentz sent guys on the 1999 and 2000 teams an Alamo Bowl watch. Although we didn't have the success we wanted during Coach's first two years, he recognized that guys on those teams set the foundation. Those are the types of things that separate both Coach Ferentz and the University of Iowa from the rest.

After I graduated, I had the opportunity to play on four NFL teams and traveled all over the country. Everywhere I went, I found the Hawkeye fans to be unreal. Everywhere you go, it's "Go Hawks." There is such a connection between the Iowa people and the Hawkeye program. I tell people all the time, I have played in every NFL stadium in the country (minus the few new ones added the last couple years), and there is nothing like playing in Kinnick Stadium.

I remember there were times in the NFL when I should have been channeling all my energy toward beating the Seattle Seahawks the day before a big game, and I was glued to the TV watching the Hawks play Northwestern. People around me who aren't Hawkeyes probably get tired of hearing me talk about how great it is to be a Hawkeye. Sometimes, you take some flack for that. People wonder, how can it be that great in Iowa? In a lot of ways, being a Hawkeye is something that can't be fully explained unless you come experience it for yourself. Only then will you begin to truly understand what it means to be a Hawkeye.

Being a Hawkeye is being a part of something special. It means that you represent an entire family. You represent a state, a town, an entire alumni base. It isn't something that you just do. It's not a place that you just go. You just don't play football at Iowa. You, as a Hawkeye, represent this much larger group. You work your tail off just for the opportunity to run out of the tunnel in that swarm…and you know the guy to the left or right of you has done the same thing. No matter where you come from, you come to Iowa to be a part of something special, to be part of something much bigger than you will ever be. It was here before us, we have it here now, and it will be here long after we are all gone, too.

LeVar Woods lettered as a member of the Iowa Football team from 1998 to 2000 and was a two-year starter at outside linebacker. Woods signed a free agent contract with the Arizona Cardinals in 2001 and spent the first four years of his NFL career with Arizona. He would go on to a seven-year NFL career that also included stops in Tennessee, Chicago, and Detroit. Woods currently serves as an administrative assistant with the Iowa football program.

ANTHONY HERRON

DEFENSIVE END

1997–2000

I WAS BORN IN YOUR AVERAGE South Chicago neighborhood, which meant it was too dangerous for the adults in my family to let us kids leave the house to play. We got up in the morning, put on our green-and-yellow plaid uniforms, and waited for Mr. Gilley's bus to pick us up at the door and take us to Catholic school. Upon getting dropped off at home, it was time to hang out indoors with the grown-ups, other than our occasional trips onto the porch to play games. This didn't make for the most eventful childhood as I watched the world in action from the other side of a window, but that was certainly for the best. Once my siblings and I started going to school in the suburbs, it literally broadened our horizons as there were bigger neighborhoods, wider streets, and yards to play in. I experienced a different type of isolation here, though, as I went from having restricted access in my comfortable environment to having freedom to roam on what felt like another planet with people and places that were foreign to me. This feeling lasted for a bit but faded as I began to meet other kids, while joining teams and playing sports.

Most of the youth football leagues in our area had weight limits per age group that I always exceeded. They worried that a kid my size would hurt other players my age but that older kids would hurt me, so I was stuck in limbo. This meant that I had to focus on other sports and activities. The first organized sport I played was soccer. I really wasn't excited about the idea, but basketball season hadn't started yet, I didn't care much for baseball, and there was no way I was leaving the park district that day without a team. To my surprise, soccer was much tougher than I anticipated. The coach had us running laps nonstop, and the ball just didn't seem to like staying in between my feet while I ran. I eventually found a home as the goalkeeper, and while I ached to score a goal (which I finally did in my last game), that time on the soccer field was the first sign that much of my future would be spent playing defense.

While I dreamt about lining up next to Samurai Mike Singletary or lead blocking for Sweetness [Walter Payton], there was no doubt that the Bulls were on the rise in the early '90s, and they had my heart. Basketball has always been huge in the Chicago area anyway, so once Jordan turned into the best player on the planet and he had the team on the cusp of a championship, I had every intention of being the next Charles Oakley. Then once we figured out that my blurry vision was hurting my game, my folks bought me a pair of prescription goggles, and my new nickname was Horace [Grant]. Unfortunately for my hoops career, the physical part of the game came far more naturally to me than the finesse parts. If you needed a screen, I'd set it. If you needed a rebound, I'd get it. If you needed a shot blocked, I'd either block the shot or foul that shooter really hard. This became my role, and I liked it. The thing I didn't realize at the time was that all these activities helped to shape the football player that I later became. My endurance and coordination developed early by playing soccer. My quickness and aggressive nature developed while playing basketball. I even believe that being a first-chair trombone in both the symphonic and jazz bands set me up for football by having to diagnose sheet music on the go and reacting to it as the conductor directed traffic. I'm certainly not suggesting that every Hawkeye football player wore goggles and played in the brass section on his way to Kinnick Stadium, but I know that every one of us can look back and point to a variety of contributing factors that aided us along the way.

When I enrolled at Bolingbrook High School, they were known as one of the most talented football teams in the state of Illinois that had never won a championship. This was a stigma that would not change in my time there and still hasn't to this day. What also hasn't changed is the amount of highly respected Division I talent that comes out of there every year. Even though I'd never played on a football team before I got to BHS, I was well-versed in their winning tradition and high expectations. My career started pretty slowly. I was always young for my grade, so as a 13-year-old freshman, it took me some time to pick the game up. Then, as a sophomore, I stopped growing taller and started filling out, so by the time I was a junior, I finally started coming into my own on the field. As a late bloomer, it caught my coaches off guard how well I was playing. While I still preferred basketball, it was football recruiting letters that came in. I noticed that there weren't any 6′3″ power forwards in the NBA and started realizing that my bread was more likely to be buttered on the gridiron than the hardwood.

As my senior football season came around, I was a bona fide, big-time football recruit. There were countless boxes of mail coming in from all around the country, and the phone constantly rang with coaches offering full scholarships. I remember my very first Division I offer came from Northern Illinois University, and once I hung up the phone with that coach, I went right down the hall to my parents. I told them I got an offer, and my father exhaled and said, "Well, now that you've got one, let's see what happens next." It wasn't more than two weeks later before I had at least another 10, and things just snowballed bigger and better from there.

As I waded through the recruiting waters, there were definitely certain schools and individual coaches that stood out from the rest. I was so excited to talk about that day's cloudy weather in Lincoln with Tom Osborne when he called to offer me a scholarship to Nebraska after their back-to-back national titles. It was cool anytime a Michigan coach called, because I knew about their tradition and loved their fight song. But I found myself looking forward to calls from one school I didn't know as much about. A young guy with a funny last name had just become the linebackers coach at Iowa, and he wanted me to be a part of the first group of recruits that he brought in. His name was Bret Bielema, and I can speak from experience that his national reputation as a great recruiter was well-deserved. He had a way of projecting energy without seeming jittery and love for the institution without sounding like he was selling you. The genuine admiration he had for Hayden Fry and the whole Iowa football program just bled through the phone and made me believe I'd be making a mistake if I didn't at least check this place out in person.

By the time I took my Iowa visit, I had already been to several other schools and had a great time. The main rule I set for myself was that I didn't want to commit during the campus visit, because that's when schools are presenting themselves at their most perfect, thus putting your judgment at its

Defensive end Anthony Herron was voted a team captain and named All–Big Ten as a senior in 2000. *Photo courtesy of Bob Rasmus*

most clouded. I wasn't sure if I'd take all five official visits that were allowed, but I knew I wanted to be at home with a clear head when I made my decision (too bad contestants on *The Bachelor* don't apply this same logic). I can honestly say that I had less fun on my Iowa visit than I did at a couple of other schools, but there was something about Iowa City that spoke to me. The energy on campus appealed to me with the Hawks as the biggest show in town, the players on the team seemed to be an extremely close-knit group, and I don't even know where to begin describing Coach Fry. If you're reading this book, then you probably get what I mean.

There were a modest number of recruits brought in on the weekend I visited Iowa City. Schools often bring in 12 to 15 guys on some weekends, but there couldn't have been much more than a handful of us on this trip. One guy I hit it off with immediately was a running back out of Blue Springs, Missouri, named Ladell Betts. The two of us had similar demeanors and seemed to trust each other's opinions on things right away, so we ended up staying in touch after the weekend was over. Once my parents and I got back home, I weighed my options, and it didn't take too long to figure out that I wanted to be a Hawkeye. I kept Coach B in suspense until the next time he came to my parents' house, and then I made my verbal commitment to the University of Iowa. This led to plenty of hugging and tears in the Herron living room. Next, I set in on the task of confirming that we had a big-time back in the class. I called up that Betts guy, who was apparently a highly sought after recruit in his own right, and talked to him about my choice to go to Iowa. He already viewed the Hawkeyes as his favorite but hadn't pulled the trigger on a choice yet. By the time we got off the phone, I had myself a future roommate, and Iowa football had a guy who would go on to become one of its most underappreciated running backs ever. We hadn't figured out all those details yet, though.

I enrolled at Iowa in 1997 as a 17-year-old freshman with no designs on playing my first year. My plan was to sit back and watch the team that just thumped Texas Tech in the Alamo Bowl and had plenty of talent returning. When I met the entire team for the first time, I was struck by how old some of them looked. Guys like Jon LaFleur and Epenesa Epenesa, who Coach Fry lovingly called "Repeat," were really only a few years older than me but seemed like they had to be at least 30. I barely had a few chin hairs while a lot of the older players had full beards. This left me with the first impression that I'd have to wait a while before I was able to compete at this level. But once we actually hit the field and started practicing, I realized that while there were a bunch of great players out there, none of them were superhuman.

My sophomore and junior seasons were difficult ones on the field. Nineteen ninety-eight was Coach Fry's last year, and there's still a part of me that feels he might've stuck around a little longer had we found a way to perform better for him that year. Then there was the transition to Kirk Ferentz, which was hard on many of the guys for a number of different reasons. I believe a big part of that was the feeling of loss from watching a legendary coach and much of his staff leave. The added news that Bobby Elliott was battling a very dangerous type of cancer also shook us to the core. Then there were flunk-outs, dropouts, kick-outs, and defections, which made the '98 to '99 transition that much tougher because the program was sapped of its depth. A lot of youngsters had to take major roles as essential players and leaders long before they were ready. The common thread among those of us who stayed and worked was that we believed beyond a doubt that the program would soon return to prominence. We knew it would take some work, but there haven't been many guys to successfully don the black and gold who were scared of a little work. It was impossible to ignore the slings and arrows, excuse me, the grenades that came at us almost daily, but we plowed ahead with a focus on achieving the program's new mantra to "Break the Rock." I appreciate the fact that Coach Ferentz still references his first couple years on the job as building blocks that laid the foundation for future success.

We could feel things turning during my senior year in 2000. Many of the games still didn't end in victory, but there was a consistency to our play. We got back to a point where guys made plays at crucial times that gave us a chance to win late. A 13-game skid was finally snapped when we beat Michigan State at home, but that wasn't my favorite game. As sweet as that was, my favorite games came later that season in back-to-back weeks. We won at Beaver Stadium, knocking off Penn State in double overtime to stop Joe Paterno from getting the all-time wins mark and then we beat Northwestern in my final game at Kinnick Stadium to keep them from a berth in the Rose Bowl. I cried like a baby before, during, and especially after that game.

My career at Iowa didn't have the team or individual fanfare that I anticipated, but I know now that I learned more through all the hardships and losses than I could've learned if everything was smooth sailing. The reason I turned down offers from schools like Nebraska and Michigan was because I wanted to be a part of a program where I could build something. Going to a perennial national title contender didn't appeal to me in the same way as joining a program with a winning tradition that was trying to take that next step. There's not a doubt in my mind that I was part of building the Iowa football program back up to where it should be.

When I think about what it means to me to be a Hawkeye, three things occur to me—character, tradition, and hard work. The coaching staff always works to recruit character guys, and the tradition of the program has always been about hard work. I got to experience all of the above as a member of the Iowa football team.

Anthony Herron was voted a team captain and named All–Big Ten as a senior in 2000. He then played eight seasons of professional football between the NFL and Arena Football League. Herron coached Arena Football for a few years and won an AFL championship as an assistant coach in 2008. He is currently a football commentator with both the Big Ten Network and the NFL Network.

The NEW MILLENNIUM

NATE KAEDING

KICKER

2000–2003

LOOKING BACK NOW, I can say with complete certainty that my decision to accept a scholarship to play football at the University of Iowa was the single most important (and best) decision of my life. In my case, it all happened very fast. Before I accepted Iowa's offer, the only other offer I had was from Iowa State. I spent an afternoon in Ames with Coach McCarney and came away very impressed. I left ISU that day thinking that I might actually be a Cyclone.

It wasn't long after the visit to Ames that Iowa offered a scholarship and I was able to spend some extended time with Coach Ferentz and Coach [Chris] Doyle. Their enthusiasm, coupled with my lifelong love for all things Hawkeye, made my ultimate decision very easy. It wasn't any longer than a week until I accepted. I ended up being Coach Ferentz's first ever in-state recruit.

I had several reasons for choosing Iowa. First, I grew up a Hawkeye, and being a part of that tradition was a big draw. I remember growing up in Coralville and listening to Jim Zabel on my dad's old radio outside in the yard while raking leaves or playing football with my friends. I grew up trying to shoot three-pointers like my all-time favorite, Chris Kingsbury, or run over defenders like Nick Bell. I was a disciple of the Tom Davis baseline pass and the Jess Settles multiple pump-fake lay-up. Once a scholarship was offered, and it seemed as if I would have an immediate role on the team, I simply couldn't envision playing anywhere else. I had to take my shot at being a Hawkeye.

The things that Coach Ferentz stands for was another draw for me. It was obvious from the beginning that Coach would run a program of integrity. He vowed to be committed to developing me not only as football player, but as a person. In some naïve way, as an 18-year-old kid, that fit this sort of Hollywood-like vision of what collegiate athletics is all about. A place where you go and showcase your talents on the national stage, but also where you are cared for and developed as a person. Looking back on it and talking to some of my teammates in the NFL, I realize how rare it is to be associated with a program that cares more about the development of young men than they do about wins and losses.

Having a chance to be part of building the Iowa program was another big attraction for me. The rally cry when I was being recruited was, "Come join us and help grow this program into a champion." The idea was to get in on the ground level and confront the many challenges associated with building a program up from a 1–10 season. I've always had a very prominent competitive streak and was definitely inspired to take on this challenge.

After struggling some early my freshmen year, I kind of had my breakout game at Penn State. I connected on three long field goals and another short one in overtime to help clinch the win. The long kick to win the Alamo Bowl in 2001 is another one of my favorites. We came a long way from 1–10 in 1999 to that bowl win in 2001. The next year was just a great year for both the team and myself. The streak of 20 consecutive field goals made during that year is one of my greatest personal memories from the 2002 season. Then, in the last Big Ten game of my senior year in 2003, I remember we were at Wisconsin on a cold, rainy day. We lined up for a 50-yard field goal at the end of the first half, and Barry Alvarez called two timeouts to ice me. Thankfully, it didn't work, I made it, and we went on to win 27–21.

I did my best to serve as a leader on the team. That had its share of challenges because I was the kicker. First, I tried to lead through actions, not words. The kicker isn't the rah-rah guy. I thought I should be seen, not heard. You get respected by how you prepare and by how you play, it's as simple as that. I took great pride in overriding any or all of the negative kicker stereotypes. I spent extra time in the weight room and the practice field. I never once even thought about making an excuse or blaming someone else for one of my mistakes. I never did any speaking up in front of the team or give any big pep talks like some of our other great leaders like Robert Gallery or

With 373 points, Nate Kaeding is the Hawkeyes' all-time leading scorer. He won the Lou Groza Award in 2002 and has played seven seasons with the San Diego Chargers. *Photo courtesy of Bob Rasmus*

Dallas Clark. That's not my role as a kicker. My job was to bust my ass during the week and kick the ball between the uprights on Saturday. I think guys respected that approach.

Growing up a Hawkeye fan, it was neat to experience the loyal support of the Hawkeye fan base as a member of the program. Win or lose, Iowa fans are not fickle. In today's era of message boards and talk radio, it's easy for an athlete to become jaded and cynical of fans because of the rants of a few anonymous crazies. I always got an outpouring of support (miss or make) from the true Hawk Fans who constitute at least 98 percent of the fan base. I also felt that when we lost, the fans were hurting with you, rather than hurting *at* you. I think that kind of loyalty and support is rare in big-time athletics today.

There is no doubt that I am where I am today because of my experiences as a Hawkeye at the University of Iowa. I think the NFL is more about having the right set of intangible skills than it is talent. Talent will get you in the door, but in order to have a prolonged career, you better be a self-starter, hard working, diligent, and most of all, tough. You play so much more football in the NFL that you are bound to make more mistakes and fall under intense scrutiny at times. You have to be tough to withstand the many ups and downs of professional athletics. These intangible skills are the hallmark of Coach Ferentz's program.

If you really want to know what it means to be a Hawkeye, then all you need to do is get to know Coach Reese Morgan. He's the embodiment of that. Coach Morgan was my high school coach all four years at West High, and his first year at Iowa as offensive line coach was my freshman year. He is the single most important person in my life in terms of my development, outside of my parents. Coach Morgan is my inspiration for choosing the field of education in school, and I hope to one day have the same impact on young people's lives that he had on mine. It was a godsend to be able to spend eight of my most formative years around Coach Morgan.

Some of my fondest memories as a Hawkeye aren't the big bowl game wins, the All-America honors, or the school records. It's the couple of quiet seconds Coach Morgan and I would share in the midst of a jubilant locker room after a big win. We would shake hands and congratulate each other on the success of the day. My reward was in knowing that I made him proud. That, more than anything, captures what being a Hawkeye is all about.

A native of Coralville, Iowa, Nate Kaeding was the starting place-kicker all four years during his career. He is Iowa's all-time leading scorer, with 373 points; shares the Big Ten Conference record with 367 career kick scoring points; and is Iowa's career leader in PATs, with 166. Kaeding was 67 of 83 in field-goal attempts and 166 of 169 in PAT attempts during his Iowa career, and also scored one rushing touchdown from field-goal formation. He also holds the Iowa record for consecutive field goals made (22) and PATs made (60). Following his senior season in 2003, Kaeding was named consensus first-team All-America and first-team All–Big Ten. Kaeding was a Lou Groza Award finalist in 2003, after winning the award as the nation's best kicker in 2002. Kaeding also performed in the classroom, earning Academic All–Big Ten honors for three consecutive seasons from 2001 to 2003 and twice earning Academic All-America honors. Kaeding was selected in the third round of the 2004 NFL Draft by the San Diego Chargers (No. 65 overall). The 2010 NFL season was Kaeding's seventh with the Chargers.

SEAN CONSIDINE

Defensive Back

2000–2004

I was fortunate to play in high school in Byron, Illinois, under a legendary Hall of Fame coach, Everett Stine. He had a great program that was all about family and had a lot of traditions that he brought to the program. I played linebacker and running back in high school. We had quite a bit of success on the field, too. My senior year, we went undefeated and won the state championship.

Coming from a small town like Byron and playing the positions I played in high school, I really wasn't drawing very much interest from many bigger Division I colleges. The most interest came from Northern Illinois. The coach there at the time, Joe Novak, was actually the secondary coach for my dad, Rick Considine, who started for three years at Northern. They were recruiting me pretty heavily, and it seemed like a natural fit at Northern Illinois. However, while they had intended on offering me a scholarship, at the last second, that fell through and they asked me to walk on. At that point, I kind of went into a scramble to test the waters at some bigger schools like Iowa, Purdue, and Illinois to see if I could at least have the opportunity to walk on at those schools.

Out of all those schools, Iowa was the one that showed the most interest. Most important, Iowa offered me the chance to go to training camp, which was something they could only offer to 105 kids. I also had some opportunities that involved scholarships at smaller places like Augustana and Winona

One of Iowa's top special teams players, Sean Considine blocked a total of five kicks as a Hawkeye. *Photo courtesy of Bob Rasmus*

State, but after sitting down with my dad, I decided that if I was going to play football in college, I might as well try to walk on at a school like Iowa and see if things worked out. At the very least, I was going to get a great education. I wanted to go into the business school at Iowa. So football wasn't the only thing Iowa had to offer.

Coming into the Iowa program as a walk-on provided me with plenty of challenges. It was an uphill climb at times, but those challenges also were instrumental in making me into the football player and person I am today. When you start off behind so many others, you really need to find ways to set yourself apart. It instilled a work ethic in me, as I approached things with a chip on my shoulder, because I felt I was overlooked by the bigger programs coming out of high school.

So I came to Iowa and tried to really focus hard to make things work out. The year before I arrived, they went 1–10, so at that time, Coach Ferentz was looking for anybody and everybody who was willing to buy in to what they were doing. It didn't matter if you were a walk-on or a five-star recruit, they wanted guys who wanted to work and help build the program from the foundation, and that's exactly what I was there for.

Fortunately, at Iowa they had a great strength and conditioning program, which is the bedrock foundation of the program, right alongside the leadership of Coach Ferentz. I think Coach Chris Doyle is the best strength and conditioning coach in the country, hands down. I bought into what Coach Doyle was doing and spent a lot of time and extra effort in that weight room to improve my strength and improve my speed and agility. I was very fortunate to have the type of coaching and resources at Iowa that allowed me to vastly improve in those areas. I think this was the key ingredient in my rise from walk-on to scholarship player, and ultimately to starter.

Maybe just as important to my development was having the opportunity to play under Coach Phil Parker as my DB coach. He really respects hard workers like me. He knew I was a student of the game, a smart football player. I think Coach Parker is the best coach in the country at developing players in the secondary. He has a great knowledge of the game of football and has proven over the last 10-plus years at Iowa that he is able to take guys like me, who have a lot of development ahead of them, and turn them into great players.

I also really enjoyed playing for Norm Parker because he actually reminded me a lot of my high school coach. Norm is an old-school, the-way-things-used-to-be type of coach. I have a lot of respect for coaches like this because I was around it so much in high school. Coach Parker is a guy who had done things the same way for years. He was very consistent as to what he expected out of his defense and what he expected out of his players. Year in, year out, his defenses are always tough, and I think it comes directly from him because of the consistency.

I redshirted my first year, got playing time on special teams my second year in the program, and had risen to second-string safety, behind Derek Pagel. After my redshirt freshman year, I sat down and had a heart-to-heart discussion with Coach Parker about where I stood. I explained that it was important to me and my family that I be put on scholarship, and if that wasn't going to happen at Iowa, I might need to explore options at other schools. Phil really calmed my nerves and encouraged me to be patient. He couldn't make any promises, but explained that every year, something unforeseen happens, where scholarships tend to open up unexpectedly. Sure enough, during training camp two-a-days my redshirt sophomore year, a scholarship opened up. Coach Ferentz called me in and said they were putting me on scholarship. That was a big moment in my career.

We had some really successful years during my time in the program. We won some big New Year's Day bowl games in thrilling fashion. But, I'll tell you, one of the greatest times I had at Iowa was that Alamo Bowl win. I was just a redshirt freshmen on that team, but that was one of the most fulfilling wins I have ever been a part of—we had come so far. It wasn't a great season, compared to what Iowa is doing nowadays, but we had come from 1–10, then 3–9, then we find ourselves in a bowl game playing Texas Tech. That was a long season, but we finished strong in November that year and went into that Alamo Bowl and got a hard-fought win. I think guys got a taste of winning on a big stage, and that really catapulted the program going forward. That win made us realize all the hard work that went into the win, but we also realized that there was a lot of hard work yet to do in order to get us to where we really wanted to be, Big Ten champions.

My last game in an Iowa uniform was against LSU in the Capital One Bowl on New Year's Day 2005. I don't think you could script a better ending—it is certainly something I will never forget. I remember being at the bottom of that pile when we all jumped in the end zone to celebrate Warren [Holloway]'s touchdown on the last play of the game.

One of the great things about Iowa is having the opportunity to come together, play, and bond with so many great teammates from all across the country. Heck, I lived with the punter, Dave Bradley, for four straight years. He is from San Diego, California, and I'm from Byron, Illinois. We have become best friends for life through our football experience. It is a great opportunity for a small-town Midwest boy like myself to get to know some guys from California, Florida, Texas, and places like that.

One of the things being a Hawkeye is to me is being a part of a family. The experience that best exemplifies this was having the opportunity to get to spend time with and know Coach Norm Parker's son, Jeffrey. He worked down in the equipment room. Jeffrey had Down syndrome and passed away during my senior year. He was a huge part of the Iowa program, and everybody loved Jeff. Coach Ferentz allowed a couple of us to fly out to Jeff's funeral in Michigan. Even if it was a tragedy that brought us together, spending time with Coach Parker's family was a neat opportunity. It was enlightening for me to see how Coach Ferentz personally dealt with this tragic loss with Norm and his family. It allowed me to see that Coach Ferentz is so much more than just a football coach.

The whole team was around Jeff every day. Everybody knew the type of special person he was. While, of course, we would have rather not had to face this situation, being forced to deal with Jeff's passing ended up being a great bonding experience for our team. Everyone has great respect for Coach Parker, so this situation also allowed the team to rally around Norm and help him through the loss of his son. Looking back now, the whole experience gave me so much insight into how things are done around the Iowa program. A lot of it is just so simple: people in the program treat people well, plain and simple.

One of the better measuring sticks for a college is how well it prepares you for whatever you end up doing after college. I don't think I could have been any more prepared for the NFL coming out of college. Coach Ferentz runs a program that is very similar to any of the currently successful NFL programs. The practice tempo, all the things you need to be successful in the NFL, you are taught at Iowa. Of course Coach Ferentz's coming from an NFL background helps tremendously. I had a smooth, easy transition into the NFL because of the way things are done at Iowa.

Being a Hawkeye is something that certainly doesn't end upon graduation. I try to get back to Iowa City as often as I can to work out, see the coaches, and get to talk with the current players. Coach Doyle is always willing to open up the weight room to anyone who wants to come back and work out during the off-season and I have taken advantage of that. It is getting tougher now that I'm married with a child, but I still try to come in whenever I can.

I also keep in touch with Phil Parker quite a bit. I consider Phil a really close friend, and it has been interesting to see our relationship evolve from that player-coach interaction to friendship as time has passed. We probably talk weekly. I still follow the players in the Iowa secondary and love to hear about how guys like Tyler Sash and Brett Greenwood are doing. Phil has been my eyes and ears into that program since I have been gone.

If there is any one thing that characterizes what it means to be a Hawkeye to me, it would be the word *work*. There has been so much work, from so many people, that has gone into making the program what it is today. Coach Ferentz has done a great job of setting the foundation and the template for success. He is very consistent with his expectations for the program, the players, the coaches, everyone. His loyalty to his players and coaches is a great tribute to him and is the reason why you see such a low turnover rate with the assistant and position coaches, which is very rare at that level.

The success that so many of Coach Ferentz's players have had over the years beyond Iowa, whether it is the NFL or some other profession, can be traced directly to all the hard work they put in while they were at Iowa. The system that has worked so well for Iowa (and for me) is to bring in young men that, first and foremost, are willing to work hard. They might not be the most sought-after recruits in the country coming into Iowa (or maybe hardly recruited at all, like me), but you leave as one of the better players in the country because you bought into what they were preaching and you were willing to work.

Sean Considine joined the Iowa program in 2000 as a walk-on and redshirted his first year. He initially made a name for himself on special teams, seeing action in all 12 games in 2001. Considine would end his Iowa career as one of the top special teams players in Iowa history, blocking a total of five kicks during his career. He started at free safety his junior and senior seasons, earning honorable mention All–Big Ten recognition his senior season. Considine earned Academic All–Big Ten honors all four years. He was drafted by the Philadelphia Eagles in the fourth round of the 2005 NFL Draft (102nd overall). Considine spent four seasons in Philadelphia and signed a two-year contract with Jacksonville in 2009.

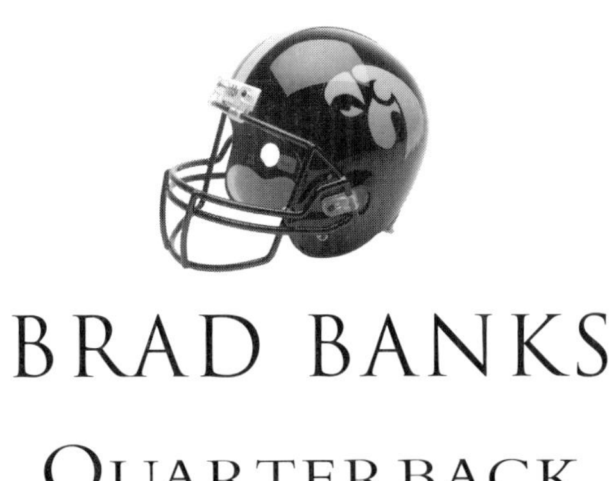

BRAD BANKS

QUARTERBACK

2001–2002

UNLIKE SO MANY OF MY TEAMMATES who were from the state of Iowa, going to high school in Belle Glade, Florida, I may not necessarily have dreamed of being a Hawkeye during my younger years. It's funny how so many different circumstances came together perfectly for me, with the ultimate result leading me down a road that probably wasn't very well traveled from Florida to Mississippi and finally to Iowa City. Now, having had a chance to look back on things, I couldn't have been happier with the way things turned out.

I was fortunate to have some success from a team standpoint in high school as we got to the state high school championship my senior year. I decided to enroll at Central Florida after high school, but transferred after my first year there for academic reasons. I ended up at Hinds Junior College in Mississippi for two years. It was at Hinds where things started to come together for me.

One of my coaches at Hinds by the name of Tony Hughes happened to be buddies with the Iowa defensive line coach at the time, Ron Aiken. Coach Aiken came down to Hinds for a recruiting visit, but the funny thing is, he wasn't even visiting Hinds specifically to see me. He actually was down recruiting a defensive lineman and caught me on some of the film. So Coach Aiken asked Coach Hughes, "What's the deal with Brad? Would he have any interest in coming to Iowa?" Coach Hughes told Coach Aiken that I would be willing to go to basically any Division I program in the country that would provide me an opportunity to play. Then Coach Aiken approached me and asked if Iowa would have a shot at me. As long as I was given a chance to play, I said, I would certainly be willing to come to Iowa.

Although I must admit I didn't know too much about the University of Iowa and Iowa City because I was from Florida and then spent two years in Mississippi, I did know a little bit about the program. I could remember seeing regular highlights on *Sportscenter* featuring Tavian Banks and Tim Dwight and a very explosive offense from the 1996 or 1997 timeframe. I thought the program looked really good back then. Back in those days, Iowa was still having regular success, but of course, they did fall on a few lean years immediately after that as the transition occurred from Coach Fry to Coach Ferentz. That didn't matter to me. I was presented with an opportunity to play football at a Big Ten school with a proud and rich tradition, and the recent lack of success that Iowa had had didn't factor into my decision-making process at all. I ended up enrolling at Iowa in January 2001.

The team we had my first year in the program in 2001 might not have had a spectacular record (we finished 7–5), but I thought we had a really solid team that year. I think if you asked anyone else around the league about our 2001 team, you will find that nobody wanted to play us. We lost an awful lot of close games that year. During the off-season, I thought about the mistakes we made, the things that we should have done, and the opportunities we had that we missed and thought that if we could just fix a few little things, then we were going to be a difficult team to beat. That 2001 year definitely set up our memorable 2002 season, but I always felt that 2001 could have been a special year also, if we could have gotten over the hump a little sooner and won a few of those close games.

Looking back on it now, one of the first things I remember about 2002 is how focused I was on my schoolwork. Balancing school with football can be tough, and it was important to me to be successful at both. I think I really fed off of having to focus on two very different things that year. My focus on my school work made my football focus that much sharper, and vice versa.

One particularly vivid memory I have of that 2002 year was the game against Purdue. It was a see-saw game with many twists and turns of momentum. It was late in the fourth quarter when Purdue had retaken the lead that they had enjoyed for most of the first half. We had one last chance with just a few minutes left to play. On our last drive, we started deep in our own territory, but we came out of the gate with a quarterback draw that went for big

Brad Banks placed second in balloting for the Heisman Trophy, was winner of the Davey O'Brien Award as the nation's best quarterback, and was named Associated Press College Football Player of the Year in 2002. *Photo courtesy of Bob Rasmus*

yardage that quickly got us into Purdue territory. That first play kind of struck that drive alive. Of course, we capped that drive with a clutch fourth down touchdown pass to Dallas Clark. The crazy thing about that play is that while we practiced it often, we had never run it in a game up to that point. Coach O'Keefe liked to keep a few special plays in his hip pocket and only pull them out of the bag at special times. I think this time ended up being the perfect time for that play call. I think the key to our execution was holding on to the ball as long as possible and drawing as many defenders to me before lobbing it up for Dallas.

That Purdue game was so important because it came on the heels of a disappointing loss to Iowa State the game or two before. The terrible feelings from that loss were still fresh in everyone's minds, and I think we used that as motivation on that last drive against Purdue. That Purdue game was the key to our season. If we didn't pull that one out at the very end, then I think we would have had a totally different 2002 season.

Finishing that 2002 year by going to New York City as a Heisman Trophy finalist was an awesome experience for me. The Heisman Committee does a really nice job of laying things out for the finalists. You get to meet many of the former winners. It was really something sweet. Just to be there spoke so much about my sort of nontraditional path from Belle Glade through Hinds and finally to Iowa.

There were so many reasons for our success, but to me, it all started with everyone playing together as a team. There were no egos. There was a lot of camaraderie...from guys who were walk-ons right up to the starters. Any time you have a team like that, I think it goes beyond football. The coaches did an excellent job of preparing us—week in and week out. Not only the Xs and Os guys on the coaching staff, but the strength and conditioning staff was absolutely fantastic. The atmosphere around the complex was something that was just really sweet. You would have to be in it to know it.

I think that is probably one of the strongest characteristics about the Iowa program: it is about family, first and foremost. I absolutely love coming back to Iowa City to visit with old friends, coaches, teammates, support staff, and everyone. When I'm back in Iowa City, sometimes it feels like I never left. I try to get back to Iowa City as often as possible. It still feels like a home to me!

Being from Florida, I still keep in touch with quite a few guys who went to Florida and Florida State. Many of these guys now have little or no connection to their schools. They don't keep in touch, don't go back to campus. Coming from Iowa, this is something that I have a very hard time comprehending. Sure, those schools may have produced some decent football teams down through the years, but other than that, what do you really have if you don't even feel connected enough with the program to want to stay in touch or come back and visit? When you play football at Iowa, you are forever part of a special family. Once a Hawkeye, always a Hawkeye!

In closing, I wanted to provide one final example that perfectly exemplifies what I think it means to be a Hawkeye. I happened to be up in Iowa this past summer doing a football camp with LeVar Woods in Okoboji. Matt Kroul also participated in the camp and happened to be traveling back to Iowa City after the camp. I ended up hitching a ride with Matt back to Iowa City. Although we had never met before, we talked during that long car ride like we had known each other for years. It seemed to me that he and I shared practices, locker rooms, and games as teammates, even though we actually played several years apart. And I later found out from Coach Doyle that Matt felt exactly the same way!

In short, we got along so well because it was clear that we were cut from the same cloth. That speaks to the type of people Coach Ferentz and his staff consistently bring into the football program—high-character guys who really care about football, of course, but more generally exhibit the work ethic and dedication needed to continue to keep the program at such a high level. I am so proud to be associated with this program and to have played a small role in its great history.

After transferring to Iowa from Hinds Junior College, Brad Banks was a two-year letterman, from 2001 to 2002. He started all 13 games at quarterback his senior season in 2002 and led the Hawkeyes to a perfect 8–0 Big Ten record. Banks placed second in balloting for the Heisman Trophy, was winner of the Davey O'Brien Award as the nation's best quarterback, and was named Associated Press College Football Player of the Year in 2002. He was a Walter Camp Foundation first-team All-American and won the *Chicago Tribune* Silver Football award as Big Ten MVP. Banks signed a free agent contract with the Washington Redskins after college and spent parts of six seasons in the Canadian Football League with Ottawa, Winnipeg, and Montreal. In 2011 Banks played for the Iowa Barnstormers of the Arena Football league.

WARREN HOLLOWAY

Wide Receiver

2001–2004

My journey through the University of Iowa and the Hawkeye football program began following my junior year in high school in Homewood, Illinois. I was coming off a pretty successful junior year in high school, and I remember working out after school one day and being approached by Coach Carl Jackson. That eventually led to an unofficial campus visit in September 1999.

Of course, 1999 was Coach Ferentz's first year as head coach and is probably remembered more for the lack of success on the field than anything else. Well, I just happened to time my unofficial campus visit to coincide with what would end up being Iowa's one and only victory that year: a 24–0 triumph over Northern Illinois. The highlight of the game itself was LeVar Woods' long return of a blocked field goal for a touchdown. Both my dad and I were really impressed that such a big guy had the speed to return the ball some 70 yards!

I had never been to a pro or major college game before that one, and the electricity and enthusiasm the fans brought to the stadium and the game that day had a lasting impression on me. I remember hearing that trumpet song they play all the time at Kinnick in my sleep that night. I think you know the tune I'm talking about: da-na-na-na-na-na-na-na-na…GO HAWKS!

During my official visit in December, I got to spend some quality time with the coaching staff. The temperament of Coach Ferentz was something that stood out for me. I found him to be very approachable and down to earth. The temperament of the head coach was something that was critically important to me because the head coach sets the tone for the entire program. Coach Ferentz and his staff really made me feel at ease.

After playing for Coach Ferentz for five years, it turned out that my first impressions of him were dead on. This is the way he is. People have often asked me, what he is like behind the scenes? Everybody sees how he handles things publicly with the media and whatnot. People wonder if that is just a corporate front or something. Well, I can honestly say that is the way he is with us, too. The most intense I have ever seen him get in terms of verbal emotion is with the officials. He rarely directed that type of verbal emotion at his players. If he wasn't satisfied with your performance, he wouldn't rant and rave. Instead, he gave you this dry sarcasm, where you knew you were in trouble but he didn't really have to say anything. As a player, when you saw him take this approach with you, it was clear that it was in your best interest to continue to try hard. That is his unique way of motivating players. He really wasn't negative and demeaning at all. He tried to always keep it positive.

He was absolutely the same guy when we were winning as he was when we were losing. That type of consistent, level-headed behavior made for a stable atmosphere for the players. It was something that I genuinely appreciated. I think this steady demeanor has been a major reason for the success the program has had during his time as head coach.

Then there were the players I saw during my recruiting visit. My December visit fell a few weeks after the conclusion of Iowa's 1999 season. During my visit, I had the opportunity to see a few of the players' off-season workouts. The thing that struck me was that the intensity of those workouts was off the charts. You would have thought that they were preparing for another game the following week. But the next game wasn't until the following September. The players were in the weight room pushing themselves because they wanted to improve. It was the off-season, and the coaches weren't necessarily there cracking the whip. It was clear to me that the players were determined to do whatever it took to assure that the dismal 1–10 season they had just experienced would never be repeated. The mentality of the players coming off such a tough season was easy for me to relate to because my senior year in high school, we didn't see a lot of success, either. We went 2–7. It was very easy to see myself as a player for Iowa down the road.

The combination of the dedicated, professional coaching staff and committed, hardworking players was about all I needed. I committed to Iowa before I left campus on that official visit back in December 1999.

Once I stepped on campus, I felt like I fit in nicely with the culture of Iowa football. Working hard before practice, after practice, or during the off-season was something that I found myself doing quite often while at Iowa. Being a wide receiver, I of course needed someone to throw me balls, and I feel like I owe a great amount of gratitude to all the quarterbacks I played with at Iowa. Even if a guy maybe didn't see much game time, behind the scenes, the quarterbacks I played with were critically important to my development. Everyone knows guys like Brad Banks, Drew Tate, and Nathan Chandler because they were the starters during my time on the team. However, others like Jason Manson, Dave Raih, Matt Bohnet, and Mark Phillips were just as important to me.

I happened to enter the program at a time when we had some young guys who would end up being significant impact players in the defensive secondary, guys like Benny Sapp, Bob Sanders, and Sean Considine. It just so happened that the coaching staff wanted to get them ready for live game action during training camp. As a result, I quickly found that in practice, defensive pass interference was basically nonexistent. I remember running routes in practice and being completely creamed. I'd get up and wonder what was going on. Eventually, the receivers figured out that that was just going to be the way practices were going to go. However, in the long run, I think that it ultimately benefited us, as we were forced to develop techniques to help create separation and get ourselves open.

One of the catchphrases from school that is etched in my mind came from Coach Norm Parker: "Players do what they want to do, and men do what they have to do." When deciding how to manage my time—both with school, football, track, whatever—I did my best to try to take the emotion out of the equation. Let's face it, if we only did things that we felt like doing, very little would get done. There are many times when you must get something done, even though you might not feel like doing it. Balancing football, track, and school gave me plenty of opportunities to test this creed!

While I would have loved to have had a bit more playing time on offense in all those games leading up to the Capital One Bowl, it just wasn't meant to be. I had a few issues with my hamstring my junior year that kept me out

Warren Holloway worked hard to make every practice count so he could be ready when called. His work paid off in the last game of his career, the 2005 Capital One Bowl, where he caught his only touchdown pass as a Hawkeye in the final play of the game to beat LSU 30–25 . *Photo courtesy of Bob Rasmus*

the first half of that year. That injury was particularly frustrating because we had a rash of injuries at the wide receiver position, and I felt like that was really a golden opportunity for me to break into the offensive rotation and show what I could do.

However, I am comfortable with the way my Iowa football career went today because I can honestly say that I did everything I could do to be ready for the game situations on offense. Plus, I was able to contribute on a regular basis on special teams. I remember my dad always saying, "You are a football player first," and you do whatever it takes to help the team win. To try to stay ready to contribute on the offensive side of the ball, I honestly treated the practices as if they were the games. I tried to make every practice play count. Thus, when the time came for me to contribute on offense in the bright lights of the big game, I was ready to accept the challenge.

Which brings me to the last play of the 2005 Capital One Bowl against LSU.

I felt like things were very calm in the huddle during that last drive. We performed this drill every Thursday in practice, so we weren't nervous. If anything, there was more excitement than nerves, because now we had an opportunity to see if our hard work in practice was going to pay off in a real game, and a New Year's Day bowl game, no less!

I will say that coming out of the huddle on that last play, we were not aware that the clock was running. We were thinking that it would have stopped following the false-start penalty on the play before. But, it didn't and was still running. Oddly, the main reason we got in and out of the huddle as fast as we did on that last play really wasn't related to the clock running. Instead, we were trying to take advantage of a defense we sensed wasn't quite ready. It just so happened that helped us out relative to the clock, also.

On the snap, the DB nearest to me on the line of scrimmage didn't get a good jam on me at the line of scrimmage, which gave me a free release down the field. Not only that, but the DB on me at the line of scrimmage didn't follow me downfield. That left the safety to cover both me and Scott Chandler, who was running a route over the middle to my left. The safety drifted toward Scott, which left me open. When Drew first threw the ball, because of the way it hung, I initially thought it was going to Ed Hinkel, who was split wide to my right. Then, it seemed to drift over my head and it became apparent to me that I had the best shot to catch it.

I wasn't 100 percent sure that there wasn't another safety on the weak side who was ready to knock my head off after I caught it, but it being the last play of the game—and of my college career—that certainly didn't discourage me at all. Worst case, I figured we might still be able to get a field goal if I could at least hold onto the ball. Then, as I came down with the ball, Ed got a little shove on his defender, the only LSU guy who had a chance at me. From that point on, it was nothing but green into the end zone!

The play itself was amazing enough, given the circumstances of the game. But, for me to end my college career like that, scoring my only college touchdown, was a complete fairy tale ending, absolutely unheard of. I must admit that it was a bit awkward for me, who had been more or less a role player up to that point, to be thrust under the bright lights.

The fame and notoriety was definitely something new to me. I think the best example of how that one single play changed my life is the time I was at the video store just looking for a movie. I happened to strike up a conversation with a pretty girl in the store when right in the middle of the conversation, a guy politely interrupted us and asked me to sign his old, worn out Nerf football for him. He wasn't a kid. He was an older guy who probably had kids. Of course, this impressed my new young lady friend and subsequently made attaining her phone number a heck of a lot easier!

I don't think that the idea of what it means to be a Hawkeye is actually that difficult to sum up for me. When I was a senior, I was quoted as saying, "Giving 100 percent doesn't make you special, it just makes you part of the team." This was simply an honest observation I made at the time, but looking back, I think it really perfectly sums up the Iowa culture.

In high school, I was the hardest working guy on my team and one of the more talented, too. At Iowa, I truly was just another member of the team, because most everybody on the team had that high work ethic, and of course everyone had talent. For me, this culture was a bit of a reality check. When I arrived as a freshman, I remember coming to the realization that even if I tried my absolute hardest and consistently gave that 100 percent, I couldn't really try any harder, and that was only enough to keep up with the rest of the team! Honestly, that was a little unexpected when I walked through the door.

Future players looking at Iowa who strive for similar success are going to have to carry on this type of tradition. They should not expect to stand out because they are giving 100 percent and working hard. Plus, they should expect nothing less of their teammates. I think it is this mind-set and culture that led us to the results that we had during my time at Iowa and it is going to be a similar mind-set and culture that will allow future teams to thrive.

Warren Holloway is from Homewood, Illinois, and is a graduate of Homewood-Flossmoor High School. He lettered at Iowa from 2002 to 2004. Holloway's only touchdown of his Iowa career came on the final play of his last game his senior year on a 56-yard touchdown catch against LSU in the Capital One Bowl on New Year's Day. He graduated from Iowa with a degree in economics and currently resides in the Chicago area.

CHAD GREENWAY

Linebacker

2001–2005

I grew up on a farm in Mt. Vernon, South Dakota. I really enjoyed growing up on the farm and all the work associated with that. Working hard was certainly something I was used to growing up.

We played nine-man football, which, to us, was just normal. That was just how we played in our division, and to be honest, that is all we thought about. We were certainly proud and excited to be a part of that. There were a lot of very talented players involved and a lot of players who went on to play in college.

I was the starting quarterback and starting free safety in high school. I started at safety for four years and played quarterback starting in seventh grade. I was sort of recruited more as an athlete than anything else.

As far as Iowa goes, Jon LaFleur, a former player whose family is from southeastern South Dakota, right in the corner near Iowa and Nebraska, saw me play in my state championship game. Jon called Coach Ferentz and asked whether he was looking at me. After that, Iowa sent me some information, and eventually Coach Reese Morgan came out to Mount Vernon to see me in person. From there on, it really just sort of blossomed.

Iowa ended up being the only Division I school to offer me a scholarship. Nebraska asked me to walk on. I did take a visit down there. And that was it. Other than Iowa and Nebraska, I was looking at South Dakota and South Dakota State, along with North Dakota. So the choice for me was obvious.

For someone coming from where I came from to even be offered a Division I scholarship was pretty much unheard of. Of course, there was pressure and expectations that came with that, and I was obviously very excited.

I remember my first drill at Iowa was as a quarterback. It didn't last long. They moved me to safety almost right away—they just wanted to see what I was going to be better at, offense or defense. I was at safety for most of training camp my freshman year and then the first part of the season. Then, within the first month, the coaches came to me and asked what I thought about playing linebacker. I remember the first time I went in as linebacker, not really knowing what was going on, but you just listen to what the coaches are telling you, read your keys, and just play. Once I got there, I felt pretty comfortable.

I certainly owe a lot to Coach Morgan. He was the lead recruiter. He allowed me to believe that I was going to be a player at Iowa. It was a little hard for me to justify coming from the nine-man to the regular 11-man game at a Big Ten school, no less. Coach Morgan helped convince me that I was going to be okay and be able to not only make it, but be a valuable part of the team.

Coach Ferentz was certainly very instrumental in my career at Iowa. He is a great leader, someone everyone looks up to and wants to be like. Coach Chris Doyle and James Dobson (who has since moved on to Nebraska) had a huge effect on me, too. Because when I did move from the mold of a safety and quarterback to linebacker, there was a lot of work to be done. I had to gain a lot of weight. I had never really worked too much in a weight room before—I had just worked on the farm. They basically taught me everything I know regarding strength and conditioning.

It was a great thrill to be part of Coach Norm Parker's defense. Like the team in general, we didn't have as many of those five-star or blue-chip recruits as some of our rivals, but I think we held our own on the football field. One of the things Norm always said was that there are football players everywhere. You don't necessarily need to come from a bigger city, you can come from anywhere...even South Dakota.

I think the best thing about Norm was he kept things simple. Also, his defenses were based on fundamentals. He had some simple rules, and if you stuck to them, no matter how great an athlete you might be or how great an athlete you were matched up against, if you followed the rules, it generally served you very well—they gave you something to fall back on. Sometimes

Chad Greenway made first-team All–Big Ten his junior year and was co-MVP and permanent team captain his senior year. He was a first-round draft pick of Minnesota and still plays for the Vikings. *Photo courtesy of Bob Rasmus*

you don't necessarily have to have the best athletes, you just need to play together. He wasn't going to overwhelm you mentally, he let you just go out there and play. He never accepted complacency once you became a good player. He always wanted you to take it to the next level. He has a knack for finding tough guys who will just go out there and play hard.

Coach Parker had so many catchphrases that we had T-shirts made up to document them. In fact, I looked in my closet the other day, and sure enough, I still have it. Here is a sampling of the quotes, followed by a loose translation:

> "A million dollars, waiting on a dime." That would be said if someone was late for a meeting or the last one to something that the group was doing, like a linebacker drill or something.
>
> "Run like a scalded-ass dog." If you're in man coverage and you're getting beat, then you need to run as fast as you can to catch the guy you are covering.
>
> "There ain't a bull never been rode or a cowboy never been thrown." Said if you get beat on a play or whatever—it does happen to everybody at some point—even the best of them!
>
> "Rob Peter to pay Paul." Certainly a classic, but he used that one a lot.

"The three fastest ways to die: natural gas, electricity, and cover 2."

"Common sense is not that common."

"Don't talk to me...talk to the judge." If someone was in trouble or late or something, he would want you to go talk to Ferentz.

"Dancing bears." If you had two big guys standing up going against each other and nobody was really winning the battle.

"Elephants on parade." If the offense runs a bootleg or something, and the entire O-line turns and runs in one direction.

"Run it again." He said this a lot. Like if we screwed something up in practice, this was the common response. It wasn't necessarily the saying itself, but it was the way he said it, in a way that only Norm could.

The linebackers had this shirt made up my senior year. The sayings are all on the back of the T-shirts, with a big picture of Norm on the front.

I played with so many great teammates. My freshmen roommate was C.J. Barkema from Muscatine, Iowa. That freshman year, C.J. was a huge influence as far as becoming acquainted with everything at Iowa. As far as football goes, Abdul Hodge was probably the most influential on me, because the competitiveness and knowledge of football he had completely rubbed off on me, really from the very beginning. He was such a heady player and oftentimes had to one up everyone when it came to being mentally prepared. He was always someone who was basically right there beside me for my whole career and was obviously a very good player.

Then, as far as guys that were older, I looked up to Bob Sanders. I think he changed the mentality of the whole Iowa program. I think Bob really displayed what everyone was trying to get to, in terms of how to play defense. Especially as a Hawkeye. To fly around and just hit anybody who moved and to just be so physical with guys. I think he was one of the first guys to do that. When you were in the huddle with Bob, you always wanted to raise your level of play, because you knew that Bob was always going to be playing at a whole new level. That was big.

With him being a tight end, I got to go against Dallas Clark quite a bit in practice. He was very influential in terms of how he carried himself, how he handled his business.

I grew up in a pretty tight-knit family. And now, even though I have moved on from the Iowa football program, I still feel like not only myself, but my wife, my daughters, and even my parents are still warmly welcomed as a part of the Iowa football family. Our family just loves coming back to Iowa City. We actually still have a home in North Liberty. When we are back, we are welcomed with open arms by people like Coach Ferentz and Coach Doyle. It is almost like I never left the program. My parents won't be treated or talked to like parents of a player, they will be treated and talked to like family members. They will sit down with the coaches and have conversations about not only football, but just life in general. Things like, How is the farm doing? and stuff like that. I think that most everyone in the program truly cares about me and my family. It wasn't just they used me for four years to get wins, it's much more than that. It's a family, and as long as Coach Ferentz is there, it always will be.

Summing up what it means to be a Hawkeye is definitely something that I found difficult to pull together. Probably the first thing that comes to my mind is that it means being a tireless worker. You never quit. Also, a Hawkeye wants to be the best and get as much out of his ability as possible. Although we certainly have had talented guys come through the program, I think your typical Hawkeye isn't necessarily the most talented. It means putting the team before yourself. Toughness is another key attribute. Hawkeyes are as tough as anybody. They are going to give it to their opponent each and every snap. Then, at the end of the day, they will give their opponent due respect and credit. A Hawkeye will also be sure to give his teammates plenty of credit because individuals are nothing without the team.

These attributes all originated with Coach Ferentz and the coaching staff. And the coaching staff goes out of its way to bring in players with these attributes. Together it is the people—the players and the coaches—who make the program what it is.

Chad Greenway was a four-year letterman at Iowa. He started at linebacker all 13 games during his sophomore year in 2003, while earning second-team All–Big Ten honors. Greenway earned a spot on various All-America teams his junior year, along with first-team All–Big Ten recognition. Greenway was co-MVP and permanent team captain his senior year, while being named to additional All-America squads and first-team All–Big Ten. He was drafted in the first round of the NFL Draft by the Minnesota Vikings (No. 17 overall). The 2011 NFL season will be his sixth year with the Vikings.

BRIAN FERENTZ

Offensive Lineman

2001–2005

It was getting very late in the spring of my senior year, and my only firm Division I-A football scholarship offer was from Northern Illinois. No disrespect to that program, but that was not where I wanted to end up. I had spent nearly all of my football life working toward one goal: to play football at the University of Iowa. Then one night, I will never forget it: my father came into my room and said, "We are going to go ahead and give you a scholarship, so do you want to come play for us?"

Sure, I was prepared to go to Northern Illinois, but at the same time, I thought that I deserved a Division 1-A scholarship, so had Iowa not come through for me, I would have been off to DeKalb, Illinois. I am forever thankful to those at Iowa involved in getting me the scholarship because, at the time, in the spring of 2001, my father only had two seasons under his belt as head coach. With four wins to his credit, it wasn't exactly the greatest PR move for the head coach on the hot seat to bring in an undersized local offensive lineman who just happened to be his son. Coming out of high school, I was generously listed at maybe 6′3½″ and a paltry 220 pounds, which certainly was considered small by Division I-A college football standards.

One of my early special personal memories on the field at Iowa was my first start against Miami, Ohio, back in 2003. That same year, as shameful as it seems now, our win over Iowa State early in the year was a nice feather in

Brian Ferentz grew up with the sole goal of playing for Iowa and was recruited by his father, head coach Kirk Ferentz. He worked hard to earn his teammates' respect and distinguish himself as his own person, and became a permanent team captain his senior year in 2005. *Photo courtesy of Bob Rasmus*

our cap. While the pendulum lately has swung back in our direction in this heated in-state rivalry, remember that back in 2003, we actually had lost five straight to Iowa State, so that particular win was a big one.

Then I tore my knee up for the second time in two years midway through the 2003 season and missed the second half of that year. After the season, the knee just wasn't responding the way I wanted it to, so I had another elective surgery early in 2004, but unfortunately developed an infection that led to more surgeries and also missed out on the first four games of the 2004 season. Because of my knee troubles, there were some serious doubts as to whether I would ever play football again. So, needless to say, my first game back against Michigan State is vivid in my memory.

But the clear highlight of that year was the Capital One Bowl miracle win over LSU. On that last play of the game, coming out of the huddle, it was clear to all of us that we had mismanaged the clock terribly. Of course, we didn't feel great about that as the last snap went off. While it pains me to say it, one of the things that ran through my mind as I got down in my stance on that last play and noticed the clock running was, *How are we going to explain this to the media after the game?* Perhaps a sad commentary on what the college game has become, but I must admit that did run through my head. Then, the next thing I remember is running down the field to celebrate.

My last game at Kinnick as a senior was against Minnesota...another team we don't necessarily have the greatest relationship with. What I remember about the Minnesota rivalry was that every year was going to be the year that they really took it to us. Many of those Minnesota teams had some real talent on both sides of the ball. Yet, every year, we found a way to get it done. I think we had won something like four or five in a row coming into that game. I'll never forget it, we were ahead 38–7 at the half, and the only reason they were on the board at all was an interception return for a TD late in the half. Then, with just over a minute to go, immediately following the interception, we responded by marching right back down the field and put up a field goal to make it 38–7, pretty much demoralizing them and salting the game away right there.

At the coin toss to start the second half, I remember the Minnesota captains not even being able to look us in the eye—certainly a very proud moment for me. That was the game that Ed Hinkel scored four touchdowns, which certainly was a fitting end to his great career at Iowa. His last touchdown is one of my all-time favorite moments at Iowa. It was midway through the second half, and the coaches were rotating some of the backup players in by that time, but a good number of the seniors came back in for one more series and managed to get another score. It was a very fitting way for us to end our careers, to say the least. It was almost scripted and certainly something I will never forget.

Probably the greatest experience for me as an Iowa football player was the opportunity to get to play for my father. While there were a few negatives attached to this from my perspective, the overwhelming majority of the experiences playing for my father were positive. My first year, there were those outside the program who said I was the worst on the offensive line, I was this, I was that. Even though I fully expected it going in and knew it came with the territory, and even if some of the criticism was justified, it was still hurtful at times. Plus, it was extra tough because a good portion of it came my way primarily because of my last name.

Another challenge I found myself having to face because I was the coach's son was earning respect and credibility with my teammates. It was very important to me that my teammates knew I belonged and was more than willing to do the work necessary to help the team win, that I wasn't there just because I was the coach's son, that I fit right into the team's culture, which I firmly believe can be summed up as a culture of work. I was really put in a position where I was forced to work because of my knee injuries. Looking back on it, facing that adversity, battling the way I did to get back on the field was something else that gave me instant credibility with my teammates.

I am proud to say that, eventually, I believe that my teammates didn't look at me as the coach's son. I was my own person. There was Coach Ferentz and then there was Brian, and they were two different people. I believe establishing that separation was critically important in my situation. I think this is an issue that my younger brother, James, is also going to have to face as his young career develops at Iowa.

In fact, that separation is so important to me that looking back on it, and I am absolutely dead serious about this, I would never have played for my father had he not been the head coach at Iowa. Playing football at Iowa was what I wanted to do, and it just happened to be a bonus that my father was the head coach. I joke around now that on the day I signed my letter of intent, it was like only realizing half of my dream. Because I actually had always wanted to play football for Hayden Fry at Iowa, not Kirk Ferentz. Of course, now I would never trade those experiences playing for my dad for anything.

Overall, I felt tremendously fortunate to have simply been able to spend so much time together with my father during my time in the program. I count it as one of the most valuable experiences I have ever had. Those five years together were very special, especially because we weren't able to share a lot of moments together before then, since when I was playing high school football, my dad was frequently working.

In the years since I have graduated, it has become even more apparent to me that the Iowa football program is something very, very special indeed. You have teammates who you care about, you have a program that you care about, you have a tradition that you care about. While at Iowa, I always had the feeling that I was playing for things that were much bigger than myself—the team, the program, what the program stood for .

Then you leave to go to the NFL, and few of those things that mattered in college matter anymore. It is basically just "studs for hire." Your loyalty is to your paycheck and not much more than that. Coming out of the Iowa program, that was a difficult lesson for me to learn because of the special experiences I had in college.

Our fans always supported us, not only at home but also on the road. Some of my most special memories at Iowa were celebrating with fans, in places like Minnesota, Wisconsin, Michigan, and Penn State. The Penn State game in 2004, in particular, was something I will never forget. My grandfather had passed away that week. We had the funeral on Friday and drove up to State College for the game the next day. In probably the ugliest game in the history of the Big Ten, we won 6–4. The last snap of the game, we happened to be in the end of Beaver Stadium opposite the student section, where there was this one sliver of black and gold in the corner in the sea of white and blue. I have vivid memories of jumping up into the stands to celebrate with our great fans as the game ended. That was one of the few times during my time at Iowa that I think I let my emotions get the best of me.

As I embark upon my new professional career as a coach, I realize today that the Iowa football program has made me the person I am today. The guys like Reese Morgan and Chris Doyle have made such a difference in my life and in the lives of the other young people they coach at Iowa. Guys like this have inspired me to do the same with the people I coach.

I realize that it is cliché to say this, but the types of skills you learn in the Iowa football program transcend football and sports, in general. The coaches and support staff in the football program are just as valuable as the faculty and staff within any academic department on campus. The lessons I learned and skills I attained during my time in the program will serve me for the rest of my life.

Brian Ferentz is a graduate of City High School in Iowa City. Ferentz played offensive guard and center at Iowa from 2001 to 2005. He was a permanent team captain in his senior year in 2005, when he earned honorable mention All–Big Ten recognition by the media. Ferentz spent 2006 and a portion of 2007 in the NFL with Atlanta and New Orleans. He is currently an offensive assistant coach with the New England Patriots.

ED HINKEL

Wide Receiver

2001–2005

The road from Erie, Pennsylvania, to Iowa City, Iowa, had already been paved for me. A guy by the name of Bob Sanders came from Erie to Iowa City the year before me and did pretty well for himself, even in his first year in the program. I certainly noticed that when I was making my decision on where to go late in my high school days.

Even with the above connection, it wasn't necessarily a slam dunk that I would come to Iowa. Yes, I was very impressed with Coach Ferentz and his staff during the recruiting process. There was just something about his demeanor that impressed me. It seemed like he had this aura of confidence about him and the program he represented, but he was very low-key about it. Unlike so many other coaches who play the recruiting game, Coach Ferentz didn't need to do a lot of talking to convince me to come to Iowa. That was something that really resonated with me. I'm more of a lead-by-example guy rather than the rah-rah guy, so I was sold on Coach Ferentz almost right from the very beginning.

Of course, living in Pennsylvania, I tended to gravitate a little toward Penn State. I visited State College my junior year, but I didn't hear from them until at least halfway through my senior year. By then, it was too little, too late. Plus, one of the most important things to me was going someplace where I would be able to play on a regular basis. I didn't necessarily want to go to a glamorous traditional power and be buried on the depth chart. I wasn't sure that this wasn't going to happen to me if I went to Penn State.

I also visited Syracuse. It was a traditional eastern football power, obviously much closer to home than Iowa. Upon returning from my recruiting visit to Syracuse, I called one of my good friends from school, John Patrick Moore, who was the grandson of one of our high school coaches, Joe Moore. Of course, this is the same Joe Moore who was Kirk Ferentz's high school coach and mentor, back in the day, in Pittsburgh. I told John Patrick I was going to commit to Syracuse. Well, John Patrick took this news right to his grandfather, who promptly called me to inform me in no uncertain terms that I would be absolutely crazy if I didn't go to Iowa. Coach Moore always had a way with words! I guess that was about all I needed. So, with that bit of sage advice, I was off to Iowa, and of course have not for one minute ever regretted that fateful decision.

In addition to the connection with Bob Sanders, I also spent some time together during a few different summers with Brian Ferentz when he would come out to Erie to visit Coach Moore. Both Brian and I entered Iowa at the same time. It was really nice to see at least a few friendly faces upon my arrival in Iowa City, especially because I was traveling such a long distance to go to school.

I started out at Iowa as a defensive back. Matt Stockdale was an older guy on the team in the defensive secondary and helped show me the ropes a little bit. But, as often seems to happen in the Iowa program, coaches experiment with guys at different positions. The experiment with me at DB lasted just a short time before they tried me at wide receiver. I also give a lot of credit to Tim Dodge, who was one of the elder statesmen in the receiving corps when I starting playing that position.

As he does with almost everyone, Coach Chris Doyle quickly took me under his wing and provided invaluable guidance, mentorship, and training with regard to strength and conditioning. Once you enter the program as players, I found that we tended to spend more time with Coach Doyle than any of the other coaches, because so many of the coaches were out recruiting during the off-season. Conversely, the off-season is when we would spend huge amounts of time with Coach Doyle building up our strength and conditioning.

By far the closest bonds I have woven with my teammates have been with guys in my graduating class. We were a pretty tight-knit group. We were a

Wide receiver Ed Hinkel's 15 career touchdown receptions are third best in Iowa history. *Photo courtesy of Bob Rasmus*

group that was fortunate enough to have an awful lot of success during the period from 2002 through our senior year of 2005. Two Big Ten titles, four trips to bowl games (all to the state of Florida), so many memories. It was a real honor to play side by side with guys like Chad Greenway, Abdul Hodge, Brian Ferentz, Marcus Schnoor, and Jovon Johnson.

While the team's success was certainly the most memorable part of my Iowa experience, I had a few individual moments at Iowa that I certainly will always remember. The first one came in my freshman year in a very memorable game that opened the Big Ten season that year at Penn State in 2002. I was able to haul in a long touchdown pass from Brad Banks in the very back of the end zone at full extension that put us up really big in the second quarter.

It just happened to be right in the corner where they stuck all of the visiting team's crowd at Beaver Stadium. As a result, the picture I have of the catch includes a few of the 150 or so of my friends and family in the background who were there to support me and the Hawkeyes. As it turned out, we would need every single point that day, as Penn State came roaring back in the second half, forcing us to win it in overtime. That memorable game put us squarely on our way to our perfect 8–0 Big Ten record that year.

Being a native of Pennsylvania, it didn't take much to get me up for those games against Penn State. In fact, I am proud to say that I personally never lost to Penn State as a Hawkeye, with wins in 2002, 2003, and a very ugly but memorable 6–4 triumph in 2004.

The 2004 game was memorable to me as much for the events that happened before the game as the game itself. That was the week that Coach Ferentz lost his father, and I remember that the funeral was the day before the game. As one of the leaders on the team at the time, I clearly remember that it was very important to us as a team to go out and win that one for Coach Ferentz. Although as an offense, we certainly didn't light the world on fire that day, the defense came up absolutely huge, and we mustered just enough offense to get the W that memorable day.

I was also lucky enough to be on the field for the last play of the Capital One Bowl against LSU on New Year's Day in 2005. I was running down the right side of the field together with Warren Holloway and was being trailed by an LSU cornerback. I actually ended up within a few yards of Warren as the ball was being thrown and thought for a second that Drew was passing to me. However, I quickly realized that Warren had the better play on the ball, as no one was really on him. So I quickly backed off and let Warren grab it, but I was able to get a little shove in on the defender who was near Warren as he caught the ball. I wasn't sure the game was over on that play until a few seconds after the play, when I looked up and saw the clock read 0:00.

Then, during my senior year, after I broke my arm against Purdue about halfway through the season, I managed to come back for the last two regular season games at Wisconsin and our home finale against Minnesota. In my first game back, we beat Wisconsin handily in what was Coach Barry Alvarez's last game at Camp Randall Stadium. Then, the next week, we came out and blew Minnesota right out of the water. That game was memorable for me, as I was able to haul in four touchdown passes from Drew Tate. What a way to finish my senior year! It's certainly something I will never forget.

Having had the opportunity to spend five great years in the program, I feel very fortunate that I stumbled upon a system that was a perfect match for me in terms of the qualities I brought to the table. I felt very comfortable in the program, as a result. In general, the Iowa guys may not necessarily be the biggest, fastest, strongest, or the so-called five-star recruits, but boy, they were going to bring a gritty toughness and we would work hard as a team, both on the field and off.

The emphasis on these key qualities begins at the top of the program with Coach Ferentz and filters right down through all of the rest of the staff—a coaching staff that amazingly has remained largely intact over the 12-year tenure of Coach Ferentz. He always instilled in me the key value that it was so important to do things the right way. If you did that, then most everything would take care of itself. And guess what? By and large, he was correct! I had experiences both on and off the football field at Iowa that will last me a lifetime.

Our big game on Senior Day in 2005 against Minnesota was the climax of my time playing in front of the home crowd at Kinnick Stadium. It's funny that, now having had a chance to informally poll many of my peers at various college all-star games, the NFL Combine, and in talking with various NFL guys over the years, the consensus from the rest of the Big Ten is that Kinnick is their least favorite stadium in the entire Big Ten. I think this really is quite a tribute when you consider the much larger and probably more famous venues like the Big House at Michigan, the Big Horseshoe in Columbus, and Beaver Stadium in State College. The fact that the fans are literally right on top of you at Kinnick has a direct impact on the game. As a result of the fan's proximity to the players, I can tell you that the visiting players truly notice the presence of the fans.

The impact Iowa football has had on my life continues to this day. The great people who I have met because of football and the lessons I learned from the coaching staff have allowed me to excel in my current career working with the sale of medical products. I introduce myself to someone new during the course of my job, and almost immediately I can see them light up when they realize that I'm the same Ed Hinkel who played wide receiver on some of those great Iowa teams of the early 2000s.

One thing is for sure, once you are a Hawkeye, you are a Hawkeye for life! To get that type of reaction from people I meet every day is very humbling. It was certainly an honor to represent the University of Iowa on the football field for those four years, and I am truly honored the people of Iowa have such fond memories of me and my time on the football field.

Ed Hinkel was a four-year starter at wide receiver. He ended his career with 135 receptions, which is ninth all-time at Iowa, and 1,588 yards, which is 14th all-time. Hinkel earned honorable mention All–Big Ten honors his junior and senior year and was Iowa's co-MVP his senior year in 2005. He currently lives in the Iowa City area.

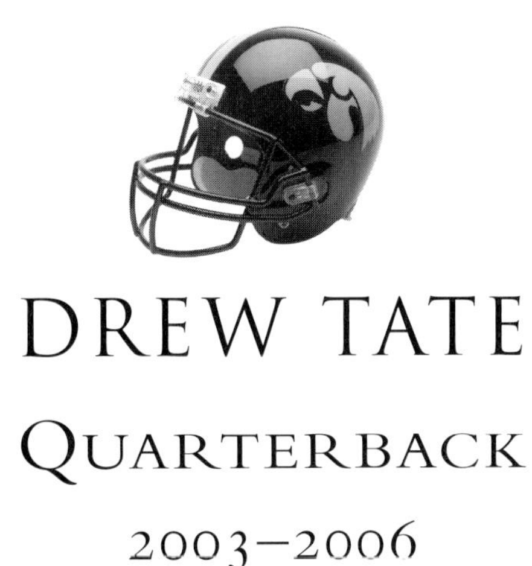

DREW TATE

QUARTERBACK

2003–2006

I PLAYED MY HIGH SCHOOL FOOTBALL down in the Houston, Texas, area. Playing with all the guys I grew up with, that was a special time in my life. It was the absolute best. Plus, I got to play for my dad, which made it even cooler. We had some fun times, as we employed the spread offense at a time in the early 2000s when it was still kind of up-and-coming and many of the defenses we faced didn't have a real good feel for how to defend it. We had our share of success as a result, and it also allowed me to put up some impressive numbers that caught the eye of a few colleges.

When it came time to pick a college, I ended up committing to Texas A&M the summer before my junior year in high school. But, then head coach R.C. Slocum got fired about two months before signing day. They ended up bringing in Dennis Franchione, who had been at Alabama and TCU before coming to Texas A&M. Because Coach Slocum was the one who recruited me, things just didn't feel right for me with the new staff. It just didn't mesh very well. So I decided to consider other options. Because of the timing of A&M's coaching change, I basically had just a couple of months to find another school.

My dad is actually from Iowa, and he happened to know Carl Jackson really well. Carl Jackson was the Iowa running backs coach who recruited in the Texas area. He went up to Iowa with Hayden Fry from Texas. Carl could see what was going on at Texas A&M and told my dad that if I was interested in looking at other options, Iowa would be interested in talking. It was interesting because all of this started in late October or November of my senior year, so it was really late in the game.

My first trip to Iowa City was actually for the spring game the year before I got there in 2003. They were just coming off that big run the year before when they played USC in the Orange Bowl. My dad and I flew into Chicago and drove over. I remember seeing signs for Minnesota on the way there and thinking, *Oh dude, that shit is up by Canada! Far away!*

Once I got to Iowa City, it seemed like a special place. People are just passionate about the football team. At the time, that was all I cared about. I was just a kid. I thought it was awesome. The atmosphere. The town. It was just the perfect college town.

There were a few other schools down in Texas that I looked at. I also ended up canceling a visit to Iowa State because I just didn't feel like Ames and Iowa State measured up to the Iowa City and Iowa.

Having the opportunity to play quarterback, I certainly took it upon myself to be one of the leaders on the team. I think that the quarterback position naturally lends itself to being a leader. It was a great honor to lead teams like the teams we had because the culture at Iowa put such a high emphasis on hard work. You work hard, you keep your mouth shut, you do what you are told. However, my leadership style was a little unorthodox at times compared to the way others on the team might have done things. While I admittedly might have been the first one to maybe bite your ass and say something if something was wrong, I also was the first one to offer congratulations for something done really well. It is possible that my style might have rubbed some the wrong way, but it was never my intention to hurt anyone. I think that was just my competitive nature expressing itself with my teammates.

I would say that my best friend at school was Anton Narinskiy. This name might not ring a bell with a lot of people. He was born in St. Petersburg, Russia, and moved to Ohio when he was in the second grade. He is one of the smartest people I have ever met. He made the President's List, which is higher than the damn Dean's List! He is just a sharp, sharp, dude. He lived with me, Ed Hinkel, and C.J. Barkema in the summer of 2004. Anton and I are still good buddies.

I lived with Ed and C.J. for two years. Both of them are great guys. Ed Hinkel is just a super guy. He works hard. Just a blue-collar guy. It was cool to be around him and see his approach to things and how it rubbed off on me and the whole team. C.J. Barkema is another great guy. I have never met anyone who has not liked C.J.

I also lived for a time with Sam Brownlee, who everyone knows as our running back from the 2004 year (when we had, like, five guys get hurt at running back that year) and Bryan Ryther and Mike Elgin. These are all Iowa guys and all great examples of what it means to be a Hawkeye.

I think so often the team accomplishment of just getting to a bowl game is taken for granted these days. Since leaving Iowa, I have had the chance to meet so many guys up here while playing pro ball in Canada who are all good players in their own right, but never had the team success that we enjoyed while I was at Iowa. Every one of my four years at Iowa was special to me because we got to go to a bowl game every year. I think sometimes the Iowa fans don't realize how lucky they are to have a great team and program like Iowa and a coach like Coach Ferentz.

Probably my most memorable moment during my Iowa career came in the Capital One Bowl on New Year's Day in 2005. It was a back-and-forth game. LSU had won the national championship the year before and they were damn good. They were stacked. On LSU's final kickoff, I remember thinking if we could just get a good return, then we should be able to drive into field goal range. Maybe two first downs would do it. Plus, we had timeouts, so we felt comfortable and confident. Kyle Schlicher, our kicker, was having a good year. Plus, we had moved the ball on them with some success during the game.

We went out and did end up getting a good return. We went out and threw a couple passes and picked up some yards. Then I threw a quick slant to Warren Holloway, and we all thought it was a first down, but he ended up being just short. So we needed to spike the ball to stop the clock. But there was a flag on the play, and that stopped the clock. We were thinking that the clock would not start up again until the ball was snapped. But as we were calling the play in the huddle, the ref told us that the clock was running. So, shit, it was like everyone just go, go, go.

As soon as I threw it, I thought I had overthrown Warren. As the ball was in the air, I looked downfield because Warren was the inside receiver. Hinkel was on the outside, and they were both running vertical routes. The guy on Warren went down to the flat, but was supposed to be on man coverage. That left Warren open. So, as I threw it, I thought the corner on Ed Hinkel was going to fall into it and maybe pick it off. He was running with Ed at the

Drew Tate had a prolific high school football career in Baytown, Texas. He was a four-year varsity starter and holds Texas career records for completions, attempts, passing yards, and touchdown passes. *Photo courtesy of Bob Rasmus*

same level, about eight yards apart from Warren, but fortunately, he never got there. Then Ed threw the block at the very end to push the corner away, so Warren could just walk in, basically. It was just meant to be.

I don't think the play would have happened if Warren Holloway was not on our team. I swear. That guy is unbelievable. I don't know how Iowa does it, but they continue to find guys like that, and it is just awesome! Warren is a great dude, and I don't think that play changed him one bit. And I know it changed a few people. It changed me for a couple years, but that was mostly because I was so young. Warren had been there for five years and, damn, he had never scored a touchdown before that play! It was just meant to be for him.

When I think about some of the reasons why Iowa has been successful over the years, a major factor is consistency with the coaching staff. Turnover with coaches is something that is so common in college football these days. Position coaches want to be coordinators, and coordinators want to be head coaches. I learned that early on with my Texas A&M experience. But things at Iowa are truly different. Now, I'm not saying that the assistants at Iowa don't feel that way, too, but there was not one coaching change in my four years. The offensive line coach, Joe Philbin, went to the Packers the year before I got there. Then, the year I left, Coach Aiken went down to the Arizona Cardinals. That is about the only turnover I have seen, and neither change occurred during my four years.

If you think about that and really look at the Iowa blueprint, that is a recipe for success. Consistency is the key. You've got the same coaches coaching the exact same way, repeatedly, year after year. Then the kids, I mean, shit, Iowa is like a factory. Kids come in, the coaches get them going, they develop players, then they send them off. There is a formula for success in college football, and I think it really does start with how everything is done at Iowa. Coach Ferentz is a very smart man. He runs a tight ship, but more important, he does it the right way.

Even though I wasn't from Iowa, the people in the program and the Iowa fans went out of their way to make me feel at home. I think the Iowa fans are the best. It was a second-to-none experience. I felt very blessed to be in that situation. It was a cool thing to experience. There are so many good people I met during my time at Iowa. Friends that I am going to have for the rest of my life.

Being a Hawkeye means doing the right thing every time. Paying attention to all the details that go into producing a successful program. Mediocrity is something that simply does not exist in the Iowa culture. Nothing is done half-assed. You finish everything. When I think of the prototypical

Iowa football player, I think of a guy who is extremely hardworking, unselfish, respectful, and loyal to the program.

Drew Tate was a three-year starter at quarterback at Iowa from 2004 to 2006 and is the fourth-winningest quarterback in Iowa history. Tate led Iowa to the Big Ten title as a sophomore in 2004 while earning first-team All–Big Ten honors. Tate has gone on to a professional football career in the Canadian Football League. He spent two seasons with the Saskatchewan Roughriders, and the 2011 season will be his third year with the Calgary Stampeders.

MITCH KING

Defensive Tackle

2004–2008

While I may not have come from one of the more decorated high school football programs in the state of Iowa, I really loved my time growing up in Burlington, Iowa. Following my older brother, Vince, through the program was a lot of fun, hearing people compare us and stuff like that. I played running back and linebacker in high school.

I certainly have to give a lot of credit to my high school coach, Ron Glasgow, who was tremendously helpful in getting me noticed by Division I colleges like Iowa State and Iowa. By early in my junior year, I had a scholarship offer from Iowa State. Then, a couple weeks later, I got the offer from Iowa. Coach Ferentz, the Iowa staff, and the way they went about things is what tipped the scales in favor of Iowa. Their professionalism really stood out. Also, it didn't hurt that they were consistently winning during that period in 2002–2004 when I was being recruited.

I came to Iowa as a linebacker, and another big draw for me was that I would get an opportunity to learn the position from tremendous players like Chad Greenway and Abdul Hodge. They were juniors when I redshirted my first year. But, as fate would have it, because of injuries and a few other things, I ended up moving to D-line. I remember the switch happened in spring ball my freshmen year. After practice one day, I made a joke to Coach Norm Parker about getting a ride from practice in his golf cart. His response was, "Nobody rides in my golf cart besides me." Then it wasn't more than

After moving from linebacker to the defensive line his freshman year, Mitch King saw success early in his Iowa career, earning first-team Freshmen All-America honors from rivals.com, Scout.com, collegefootballnews.com, and the Football Writers Association of America. *Photo courtesy of Bob Rasmus*

three or four days after that, Coach Parker told me to sit down in his cart, and we took off for a ride. So I thought either I was in big trouble or he was going to give me some really good news.

Coach Parker said that because of some injuries and things, they wanted to try me out at D-line for a couple days. I don't know whose idea this was, but Coach Parker first approached me with this because he was my linebackers coach at the time. To be honest, I was hurt by it at first because I thought I was playing well at linebacker. I don't think the coaches intended the move to be a demotion or anything, but that was the way I took it. But with time, I ended up loving it. Plus, there were those who were saying that I couldn't excel at the new position, so that served as extra motivation for me. My brother also played D-line, so it was nice to follow in his footsteps again. The position change also allowed me to see quite a bit of playing time my redshirt freshmen year in 2005 because we weren't as deep on the D-line as we were at linebacker.

Looking back, it probably wasn't until my senior year in 2008 that I started to really appreciate what it truly means to be a Hawkeye. We had a pretty good year my freshmen year in 2005, still got to a bowl game in 2006, but missed out in 2007. We had a few off-the-field things happen with a couple kids during 2006 and 2007 that didn't reflect well on our program. All these things combined to make the success we saw during the second half of my senior year in 2008 all the sweeter. Closing out my Iowa career at the Outback Bowl in Tampa against South Carolina was the perfect ending. We put a pretty good whupping on them, and I remember that by the second quarter, a few of the Carolina fans started to file out. Our fans always travel really well, and that game was no exception. It was really cool to see how the fans rallied around us, especially given the things we had gone through as a team earlier that season and the prior couple of years. Boy, those Iowa fans stick with us through thick and thin!

There were so many people at Iowa who helped me along in my career. Coach Ron Aiken was the D-line coach for the first half of my career. Coach Aiken was the consummate professional. Every day was a day to improve as far as Coach Aiken was concerned. I really needed coaching like this early in my career, especially with the change to D-line. He helped me with all my fundamentals like footwork, handwork, and the basic techniques.

Coach Chris Doyle was an invaluable resource for me at Iowa. He helped me get bigger, stronger, and faster than I ever thought I could be to meet the demands of my new position. This really helped me out on the field. That aspect of my career really took off under the guidance of Coach Doyle.

Then, Coach Rick Kaczenski was my position coach my last two years. I wouldn't say that Coach K didn't help me with my techniques and fundamentals, but his primary contribution for me was that he really sparked another level of motivation and competition across our D-line as a whole.

Of course, Coach Norm Parker orchestrated the whole defense. I tell everybody, whether it's high school, college, or my limited professional experience, I think Coach Parker is one of the most knowledgeable football coaches I have ever been around. He is going to forget more about football than a lot of people will ever know. His brilliance was that he made the game so simple, and I think that helped tremendously. Coach Parker also instilled a real sense of discipline with us. Everybody had a certain assignment on every play. I felt that if I didn't complete my assignment on every play, then I was letting down the entire team. And I think just about all of the defense felt the same way. One thing I have learned through the years is that you can't do someone else's job out there. When you do that, you're not doing yours well and you probably are doing theirs half-assed, too. So you might be playing two positions, but you're not playing either one well.

Some of the teammates I was closest with weren't necessarily the big-name guys. Wes Aeschliman was an offensive lineman who is one of my best friends. He didn't play a lot, but he worked his butt off every day at practice and gave his all. You have to respect a guy like that. Anton Narinskiy was behind Matt [Kroul] and me at defensive tackle. The same goes for Anton. He came in together with Matt and me and kind of got stuck behind us, so got a little bit of a raw deal. But, he definitely worked hard in practice. I really admired Anton for so many things. The first year I started in 2005, I played in front of Hodge and Greenway. Just knowing that if you messed up, they had the ball was such a great relief. I also got to play with Drew Tate for a couple years. He was one of the more electrifying players I have played with.

Then, I can't leave out Matt Kroul. He was alongside me from day one. Matt is a different personality and has a different style of play, but I always say that is just another example of opposites attracting. He was my freshman roommate, and we bonded right away. Of course everybody works hard at Iowa, but I don't think there is another guy I have been around who works as hard as Matt.

I still feel connected enough with the Iowa program to come back as often as I can. This past summer, I trained back in Iowa City. I lifted, ran, and trained with the team and Coach Doyle. I had lunch and dinner with Coach K a couple times and got to catch up with other coaches around the complex. I always feel welcome whenever I come back.

I have been fortunate enough to spend a few years in the NFL now with both Tennessee and Indianapolis. Seeing the different personalities, work ethic, and character of guys in the locker rooms, you can tell that personality or that work ethic was instilled in college. Obviously, many of these guys are incredible talents, they are professionals in the NFL. But some of these guys just would have never made it at Iowa.

So many of the good things in my life I attribute to being a Hawkeye. Looking back on it, I'm so glad I went to Iowa because if I didn't go there, I probably would not be where I am now because the work ethic at some other places is nowhere near what it is at Iowa. Perhaps the greatest attribute of our system is that we need guys to want to work hard, not for themselves, but for the team. Not wanting to let your teammates and coaches down was such huge motivation for me.

The pride instilled in me that has come from playing for the Iowa program is something I will always have close to my heart, right up to my deathbed. That I played for the Iowa program. This is what I did. It won't matter how long I played in the NFL, how well I did, or how many Super Bowl rings I get (if I ever win one). The years in my life I will remember the most fondly will be the time spent at the University of Iowa. Playing for the fans, playing for Coach Parker, playing for Coach Ferentz, and playing with the guys I played with. Those years will be the best I will ever have as a football player and as a guy.

Mitch King is from Burlington, Iowa, and was a four-year starter at Iowa from 2005 to 2008. King earned first-team All–Big Ten his junior year and was the Big Ten Conference Defensive Lineman of the Year his senior year, along with a first-team All-America selection by ESPN.com. He signed a free agent contract with the Tennessee Titans in 2009 before joining the Indianapolis Colts in 2010.

MATT KROUL

Defensive Tackle

2004–2008

I attended high school only 30 minutes away from Iowa City, in Mt. Vernon. I grew up on a farm in a pretty close family, so it was important to me that I go to college relatively close to home, so it would be easy for my family to come and see me play. I was able to gather quite a bit of information about Iowa at Junior Day the summer after my sophomore year. Then, sitting down together with my family after Junior Day, I really didn't see a better fit or a better opportunity out there, so I felt very comfortable committing to Iowa. It ended up being a pretty easy decision for me. Looking back, I guess I avoided the whole recruiting process. But, doing it the way I did, I don't feel at all like I missed out on anything. I just decided to go with Iowa and didn't think twice about it. I have not regretted it one bit.

I came into the program in 2004 and redshirted that first year. But just being in the program that year afforded me the opportunity to learn the ropes from a tremendous defensive unit. Our entire D-line that year of Derreck Robinson, Tyler Luebke, Matt Roth, and Jonathan Babineaux were a rock solid group. Of course, a linebacking corps led by Abdul Hodge and Chad Greenway wasn't too bad, either. Then, after they graduated, it was left to the younger guys like Mitch [King] and me to step in on the D-line. I joke around now that my first year in 2005, there really wasn't anyone else left to play, so they had to throw me in there!

Once I cracked the starting lineup early in my redshirt freshmen year, I was fortunate enough to stay there until I graduated. It was a great ride that lasted 50 games. To me, being a Hawkeye meant coming in and doing your job, day after day after day. That included my classwork, practice, film study, and, of course, the games. The biggest challenge in college was time management. Also, I thought it was very important to take care of my body. Coach Chris Doyle was a huge influence in this area. I tried to always get enough rest. Plus, Coach Doyle emphasized that what you put in your body is critically important to what you get out, so nutrition was a key part of my formula. Basically, I just tried to do the right thing all the time. Now, I might have caught a little grief from the guys as a result, but I just shrugged that off and tried to stick with it day by day.

Coach Ron Aiken was the D-line coach my freshmen and sophomore years. You hate to say he was a tough coach to play for, but the reason some might think that is because he would take an awful lot out of you. But it was all done to make you the best you could be, and I certainly recognize and sincerely appreciate that now. He showed me all the proper techniques a D-lineman needed to employ. This was critical to me because I didn't play D-line in high school. Having a coach like this who was so well versed in the techniques and finer points of the game really helped me establish the base for my entire career.

Of course, Coach Ferentz was always there for me my whole career. You could talk to him about anything. Not that needing to feel secure was a critical thing for me, but I found that this always gave me a nice secure feeling—just knowing he was there if you needed him. We had our conversations, and I would go out and do my thing. With Coach Ferentz, as long as you were on the straight and narrow, you would always be good to go.

It was also special playing for Coach Norm Parker. I remember he would always have a story for us during our team meeting on Fridays before games. The guy has been through a lot in his life, so he has an awful lot to offer in the way of his vast experiences. Some stories were funny. Some made you think about things in different ways. He had a special gift to get you to see things from a different perspective. The net result was that guys certainly played hard for him.

Being a Hawkeye is also about being a part of an extended family. I had the opportunity to go back home and spend some time in the complex last week during our bye week. Some places, you go back and nobody knows

Matt Kroul set an Iowa record by starting 50 consecutive games, every game during his career, a streak that led the Big Ten Conference and was third in the nation at the end of Kroul's senior year in 2008. *Photo courtesy of Bob Rasmus*

who you are. Here, you better have at least an hour freed up, because you have to talk to every coach and every assistant and secretary. They all remember your name and know exactly who you are. You are not forgotten once you walk out that door. It really does feel like a family to me. No matter whether you were an All-American or a role player, you are going to be remembered for the person you were.

It's funny because some guys here on the Jets and others around the league joke with me about going back to college. They figure that I'm two years out now, and nobody would know who I am, so why bother going back? It's not like that at Iowa and, hopefully, it never stops being the way it is now.

I realized how good I had it at Iowa shortly after the beginning of my pro career. It was my very first NFL minicamp, and I remember answering a question in a meeting, and the first thing Coach said was, "Ah, an Iowa guy!" It was meant as a compliment because of the way things are done at Iowa. They expect you to know the answers. They expect you to work hard. They expect you to be on time and do what you are supposed to do. These are all things that are expected at Iowa, too. That is how the program is run at Iowa. My experiences at Iowa were excellent preparation for my professional career in the NFL.

So when I think of the prototypical Iowa football player, the first thing that comes to my mind is guys who seem to always have that chip on their shoulder—guys who always have something to prove. We have a great tradition of walk-ons making tremendous contributions. I think of guys like Dallas Clark, Sean Considine, and Brett Greenwood. They are disciplined, hardworking, and just come to play each and every day—and that is both on the playing field and in the classroom. It takes a well-rounded person to really be successful in the program.

I personally got so much out of being a Hawkeye, it is difficult to succinctly sum it up. I think the essence of being a Hawkeye is being a hard worker. That is the most common thread. If you stick with it for four or five years of hard work and follow the guidance from the coaches, you do what you are told and buy into the system, by the end of those four or five years, lo and behold, you will find that you have achieved things you never thought were possible. And this could be from a personal standpoint, but more important, from a team standpoint. I know for sure that the Iowa system really worked for me, and I'm sure I'm not the only one to have experienced the same growth and development at Iowa.

The other key ingredient that goes into being a Hawkeye that you hear and see an awful lot around the complex is the word *respect*. You respect the game, the program, the people around you, yourself, your teammates, your coaches, and your opponent. I always believed that respect isn't something that is just handed to you, it is something that must be earned. There is no greater compliment than to be respected, no matter what it is you do. Being a Hawkeye afforded me the opportunity to go out and earn that respect. And that is something for which I will be forever grateful.

Matt Kroul was a model of consistency during his Iowa career. He set an Iowa record by starting 50 consecutive games, every game during his career, a streak that led the Big Ten Conference and was third in the nation at the end of Kroul's senior year in 2008. He was named second-team All–Big Ten by league media and honorable mention All–Big Ten by league coaches his senior year. Kroul also excelled off the field, earning Academic All–Big Ten honors all four years during his career. After graduating with a degree in health promotion, Kroul signed with the NFL's New York Jets as an undrafted free agent in May 2009, and the 2010 season was his second with the Jets.

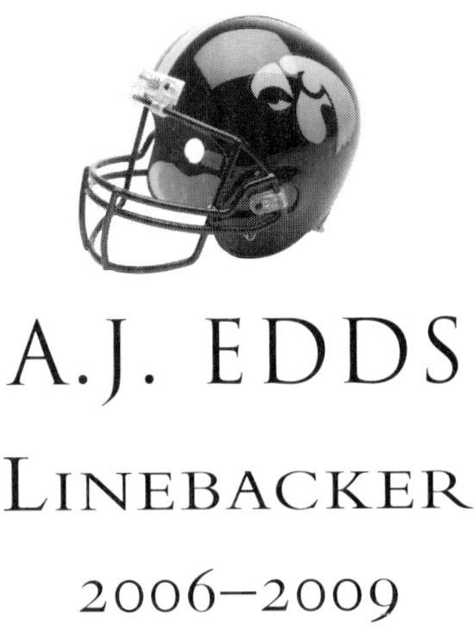

A.J. EDDS

Linebacker

2006–2009

I moved to a new high school in Greenwood, Indiana, right before my freshman year. I played mostly linebacker, although I kind of got my break into playing varsity football as a long snapper. I played some fullback, tight end, and a little bit of tail back. I basically was able to make a name for myself at linebacker.

Once that initial communication occurred with Iowa, the ball started rolling pretty quickly. Eric Johnson is the one who recruited me, and he really did a great job. After my first trip to Iowa City and meeting the coaching staff and getting my first glimpse of what the program was all about, it was pretty clear in my mind that the University of Iowa was the place I needed to be. That was the place that would give me the best opportunity to be successful.

I think what sold me the most was Coach Ferentz individually, but the whole coaching staff collectively. One thing I was looking for was a head coach who was going to be there for my whole time. I did not want to get caught up in a changing-of-the-guard situation with the coaching staff because you never know what you are going to get if that happens. So, stability was very critical to me. And it is funny that now, looking back, I think Iowa is the only place out of all the schools that recruited me where the head coach is still there.

A.J. Edds was a permanent team captain his senior year, was named second-team All–Big Ten by league coaches, and was selected to participate in the Senior Bowl. *Photo courtesy of Bob Rasmus*

I really appreciated the honesty exhibited by Coach Ferentz and his coaching staff during the recruiting process. Some of the other programs tell you what they think you need to hear to get you to commit. Honestly, my thoughts coming out of high school, knowing the skills I had at the time, was if a program was telling me that I would immediately start for them as a linebacker in the Big Ten right out of high school, that probably wasn't the most solid team, anyway!

So I came into the program and started as a tight end, but moved to linebacker early in my first camp. I was originally going to redshirt my first year, but ended up getting game experience on special teams my first year. Then, Mike Humpal went down with a knee injury, and I got my first start at linebacker in the fourth or fifth game of the year against Purdue my freshmen year. I had a pretty decent game, and I think that gave the coaching staff some confidence in me and that led to more playing time both on special teams and on defense.

As far as my maturation and my career is concerned, I owe an awful lot of credit to Coach Chris Doyle. When I came in, I wouldn't say I was skinny (I was 6′4″ and maybe 220 pounds), but I didn't have the body of a Big Ten linebacker or tight end. Then, when it became clear that I was going to get playing time my freshmen year, Coach Doyle gave me an honest assessment of how he saw things going for me in terms of building up my body and eventually designed a program for me that added strength and explosiveness gradually over my entire career. I was gaining good weight most of my time at Iowa, which looking back on it, was really the way to go.

Then there is Coach Norm Parker. You talk about putting out a lot of good players. And not only at Iowa, but everywhere he has been. He has had some tremendous defenses and is one of the most highly respected guys around the nation. It is something that you appreciate more and more the further removed you become from the situation. It is kind of like having really good parents as a kid. At the time, you don't really think much of it, but the older you get, the more mature you become, and you appreciate that stuff more. That is what it was like playing for Coach Parker. He can jump your ass, but at the same time, can keep things light and jovial. He knows there is a time and place for everything. It seems he always had the right mix of seriousness and levity. You never knew exactly what you were going to get from Norm, but no matter what, it was enjoyable, that's for sure.

People ask me all the time what my best memory was at Iowa, and no doubt that occurred my junior year in 2008 at Kinnick on a cold, damp, early November night against No. 3 and previously unbeaten Penn State. That was the game that really got us over the hump, as far as that season was concerned.

The Penn State game was really the fork in the road where we had to decide: were we really going to persevere and push through this thing and get Iowa football back to where it ought to be or were we going to show up and hope things worked out? Especially given all the close losses we had in the weeks leading up to that game. You talk about a resilient group. I think our team really showed what they were made of that night!

Being down there on the sideline, seeing that kick go through the uprights, just looking at the expressions on my teammates' and coaches' faces in the locker room after the game was really special. There is nothing that you can do that I have come across in life that gives you the feeling of working as hard as you do with a bunch of guys. You talk about a melting pot, a football team, you've got guys from all walks of life. You put in the time you do and put in the effort you do. For it to all come together down to the wire in a close game like it did that night is very difficult to put into words. There really is nothing that measures up against it. I know that not a whole lot of people get to experience that type of feeling and pure joy. It is a special feeling and something that really sticks with you, I can tell you that.

Our coaching staff is tremendous. You hear from a lot of past players that we have the best coaching staff in the nation. Going to the NFL Combine and having damn near every defensive coach and head coach I talk to relay to me, "Hey, you know Coach Ferentz and his staff, Coach Parker and his staff: one of the best, if not the best in all the nation." That's when it kind of really hits home. Because while you are in school, the Iowa way is all you really know. You appreciate it and accept it as being normal. But once you get to experience things on the next level, you find that some of the stuff that we do at Iowa doesn't happen at many other places. The coaches care and they appreciate guys. You could come to most of the coaches with almost anything. In fact, Coach [Darrell] Wilson would be so perceptive that he would often pick up on something even before I had the chance to talk to him about it.

The last piece of our puzzle is guys buying into our system. There really is going to be only a handful of guys who get serious playing time as freshmen and sophomores. The process leads to more playing time as juniors and seniors. The sooner they buy into that, the better. It's not like we have a ton of guys leaving after their junior year and we can just reload with the next recruiting class, like maybe a Florida or Ohio State.

When it comes to the fans, the story to me that best exemplifies the type of fans we have came from that Penn State game in 2008. The following week, we were in the film room watching the play early in the game where Daryll Clark put the ball on the ground near the goal line and our D-line went after it. At that moment, of course, the fans in the stands started going crazy. At that point, the film started jumping up and down so much, you couldn't tell what the heck was going on. It was impossible for the camera to stay focused on the play because of all the jumping in the stands. One thing is for sure, the success of Iowa football is so important to the fans.

Being a Hawkeye is truly being a part of something that is so much bigger than yourself. Really, you are a piece to the puzzle. That goes all the way from the top to the bottom. No one person makes our program what it is without the help of all the others. It's also being a part of a bigger family. You put in your four or five years, and it is something you can carry with you for the rest of your life.

Its funny that Coach Doyle called me on his own the other day just to check in to see how my rehab is going with my knee and how everything is going for me down here in Miami. I know personally that this does not happen at so many other programs. A lot of it can be attributed to Coach Ferentz's tenure and what he stands for and what he wants his players to leave the program with.

I think that being a Hawkeye is also about understanding that you don't get to where you want to be overnight. You have to put your time in and work hard. I think this applies not only to football, but to anything in life. Anything worthwhile does not happen quickly. You need to put the time in and develop yourself. You can't hope for that overnight fix. To me, the Hawkeyes who are really successful are the ones who embrace the grind. You need to enjoy the difficulty and hardships related to the work needed to attain those common goals, knowing that down the road, it is going to be worthwhile and something that sticks with you forever.

A.J. Edds was a four-year letterman at Iowa from 2006 to 2009 and started all four years. He was a permanent team captain his senior year, was named second-team All–Big Ten by league coaches, and was selected to participate in the Senior Bowl. Edds earned Academic All–Big Ten honors for three straight years. He was selected in the fourth round of the 2010 NFL Draft by the Miami Dolphins.

BRYAN BULAGA

Offensive Line

2007–2009

My first exposure to what the Iowa football program was all about occurred on a Junior Day back in high school. It was at that point that I had the opportunity to first visit the campus and also talk in depth with the coaching staff. In particular, conversations with Coach Morgan and Coach Erb had a lasting impression on me. In fact, the discussions have influenced me to this day!

You see, I happened to be a tight end and defensive lineman my junior year in high school, and it was Coach Morgan (who coaches the offensive line) who told me the first time we met that I was going to be an offensive lineman. Given that I have been fortunate enough to be playing as a professional in the NFL as an offensive lineman, it seems that Coach Morgan was really on to something! I certainly owe an awful lot to Coach Morgan and the Iowa staff for taking such an active interest in me and my future, literally right from the day we met.

Who knows where I would be today if it weren't for Coach Morgan. At that point, I was being recruited by the likes of Notre Dame, Wisconsin, Oklahoma, and Nebraska, and many of these schools were looking to plug me into the same positions I played in high school, because that was what they were used to seeing on tape. It was Iowa that thought outside the box a little and took an up-front and honest approach with me during not only that first official recruiting visit, but really throughout the entire recruiting process. This was something that really resonated with me and was absolutely a good match with my values and goals.

On top of all the positives I saw with the coaching staff, I just fell in love with the campus from the moment I set foot in Iowa City way back in my junior year of high school. That combination of an honest, savvy, knowledgeable coaching staff combined with the beautiful physical surroundings around campus in Iowa City was perfect for me. I really fell in love with everything Iowa had to offer very early on.

Coming in as a freshman in 2007, I almost immediately felt like I was a part of the Iowa football family. It has become common practice in the program that during the summer, the older guys will allow the incoming freshmen to live with them. In most cases, they stay with no rent and really no questions asked. Once they step on campus, they become part of the Iowa family, and that is just the way people are treated in the program. This was something I absolutely benefited from my freshman year. That is just one less thing to worry about, and it puts your mind at ease to focus on things like school and football. Then a few years later, when I was one of the older guys on the team, I was happy to reciprocate to the younger guys coming in.

It was such a credit to our coaching staff that I was able to come in as a true freshman in 2007 and learn the new position on the offensive line, eventually managing to work my way into the starting lineup. Being able to play alongside Seth Olsen on the offensive line for two years really helped me develop as a player. Seth and I actually roomed together at camp, so we became very close, both on and off the field. Coach Morgan was a tremendous help to me, not only during the recruiting process as I mentioned above, but also during my time in the program. Dan Clark was a graduate assistant coach during my time in the program who also worked with me a lot, in particular with so many of the fundamentals and techniques that are so critical on the offensive line.

And, of course, Coach Ferentz played a significant role in me getting to where I am today. Since his specialty is coaching the offensive linemen, I was fortunate to get so much quality instruction from Coach Ferentz himself during all those practices. There is no doubt that he sets the tone for the entire program. The way he approaches practice, film study, and emphasizes the strength and conditioning side of things all have played a vital role in preparing me for my professional career. There is no doubt that the Iowa football program provides the best opportunity to get players ready for the next level.

Bryan Bulaga earned second-team All–Big Ten honors by league coaches his sophomore year and was Big Ten Offensive Lineman of the Year while being named first-team All-America by the *Sporting News* his junior season. *Photo courtesy of Bob Rasmus*

Although we didn't come close to attaining our team goals my freshman year, as we missed a bowl game with a costly loss to close the season at home to Western Michigan, I really think the team learned from that bitter experience. I personally knew I never wanted to feel that way ever again at Iowa.

It seemed that we were a little snake-bitten as a team during the middle portion of the season my sophomore year in 2008 when we dropped four really close ballgames to Pittsburgh, Northwestern, Michigan State, and Illinois. Then came the game against undefeated Penn State on that cold, dark, windy, damp day at Kinnick. That was just a great feeling to be part of a tremendous team victory. Winning the way we did on the last drive and last kick by Daniel Murray was a huge thrill for me. We were able to ride that momentum all the way to a convincing bowl win in Tampa against South Carolina that year.

Another personal treat for me wearing the black and gold was having the opportunity to block for Shonn Greene during that 2008 season. There is nothing more gratifying as an offensive lineman than to see a running back have the kind of success and recognition Shonn earned in 2008. We could all tell that he was eventually destined for greatness. It didn't take much of a hole for Shonn to exploit, that's for sure. I think it is a tribute to our entire program that we were able to persevere through all those close 2008 losses. Shonn played as big a role as anybody on the team in helping us fight through adversity.

I think that the way we finished the 2008 season so strong certainly was used as a springboard to our memorable 2009 campaign. It seemed like every game that year had everyone on the edge of their seats. We rode an exciting wave all the way to a 9–0 record before dropping two close contests to Northwestern and Ohio State.

However, for me personally, I faced my most challenging situation during that memorable year. I missed several games early in the year with a thyroid condition. It was kind of a freak thing, but was something that I simply could not play through. It just took some time to get the whole thing sorted out. Then, once I came back, it was frustrating for me because I knew I wasn't at full strength. It took a few weeks for me to get my energy level back to normal, but I felt like I was able to battle through the condition and, in the long run, feel like I am a much better person and player having faced this difficult challenge.

Consistent with the way in which Coach Ferentz runs the entire program, the fact that I was facing a thyroid condition was kept in-house for a period of time. It seemed like there were a lot of rumors going around about my situation at the time. But my specific condition was not made public until after it had been diagnosed by the doctors with confidence and after I was on the proper medication and on my way back to playing. It is a tremendous comfort for me, as a player, to know that the program put my best interests and welfare above everything else in this situation. That is so typical of the culture in the Iowa football program.

Following our historic Orange Bowl win over Georgia Tech in January 2010, I found myself with a decision to make regarding my last year of college eligibility. Taking a hard look at my situation, in spite of all the positives Iowa had provided me during my three years in the program and the great potential memories to be made during my senior year, the opportunity to be a high pick in the NFL Draft was simply too much of an opportunity to turn down. The other guys who were on the draft board with me, the way things fell, and the grade I got back from the NFL, it all just combined to make it seem like the right time for me to take that plunge and become a professional in the sport I love and am so passionate about. All in all, I couldn't be happier about the way it all turned out. I have no second thoughts about the decision whatsoever.

However, I will say that going back to finish off my degree is certainly something I intend to do at some point in the future. After my football career is long over, I have a feeling that the communications degree from Iowa will serve me very well.

Having had the opportunity to look back on my college career, I can say with great confidence that I would have picked Iowa 100 times out of 100. It has been a tremendous honor for me to be a small part of the Iowa football family. It is a really special place. It is special because of the players and coaches who possess very similar qualities and who all come together every year to chase a common goal of winning a Big Ten championship. Your typical Iowa football player is above all else a hardworking, blue-collar type of guy. This is the kind of guy Iowa recruits, and that is the kind of product you see on the field.

Guys have come and gone through the program over the years, and their character, work ethic, and accomplishments have created such a rich tradition. The other thing that makes Iowa so special to me is that Iowa football is so much bigger than any individual. It would have been a tremendous experience to be part of the team for my senior year, but I can say with great confidence that Iowa football is still going to be just fine, even without me.

Bryan Bulaga is from Crystal Lake, Illinois, and was a three-year starter on the offensive line at Iowa. He earned second-team All–Big Ten honors by league coaches his sophomore year and was Big Ten Offensive Lineman of the Year while being named first-team All-America by the *Sporting News* his junior season. Bulaga decided to move on to the NFL Draft following his junior season at Iowa and was drafted in the first round of the 2010 NFL Draft by the Green Bay Packers (23rd overall). Bulaga was a starting offensive lineman on the Packers' 2011 Super Bowl championship team.

RICKY STANZI

Quarterback

2006–2010

Up until my senior year in high school, my scholarship offers were limited to MAC schools closer to home, in Ohio. At that point, I was leaning toward Miami, Ohio. It wasn't until after my senior season when the Iowa opportunity started to take shape. Coach Ken O'Keefe, offensive coordinator and quarterbacks coach at Iowa, was my recruiter. He visited school a few times and saw my tape. Iowa offered me a scholarship, and I took a visit there and at Miami, Ohio.

Although Miami had plenty to offer and I'm sure I could have been happy there, the Big Ten versus MAC choice wasn't much of a contest. Growing up being exposed to Ohio State and the Big Ten, I had always wanted to play in the Big Ten. Iowa gave me the opportunity, and I just couldn't pass it up.

Once I stepped on campus, it became clear to me the things I was told by the Iowa coaching staff during recruiting was the truth, which I think speaks to the integrity of the people and the program. I immediately took to the team-first concept that was preached from day one by Coach Ferentz and the rest of the coaching staff. I found that the coaches did a tremendous job of keeping you involved in the team—keeping you on board and learning at every moment. Every time we had a drill, a practice, a scrimmage, a game, it served as an opportunity for you to improve.

The team-first atmosphere helped me tremendously through some of the adversity related to playing quarterback at Iowa. Like everyone else on

After starting as quarterback for three years, from 2008 through 2010, Ricky Stanzi was selected by the Kansas City Chiefs in the fifth round of the 2011 NFL draft.
Photo courtesy of Bob Rasmus

the team, I felt the pressure to succeed, yet I had a role to fulfill and I needed to focus on doing it to the best of my abilities. If I accomplished that, it gave our team the best chance to win. At the end of the day, I was just a part of the team, and it was important having great teammates to help me through the tough situations that came up while playing quarterback.

My greatest memories at Iowa came with the feeling in the locker room after winning a game. While some wins obviously meant more than others because of the importance of certain games—the Penn State win in '08, the Michigan State win last year [2010], the bowl games—every win was special in its own way. That is really the best memory that you can derive from sports in general, and football in particular. It is what everyone on the team trains for and works toward. Coach Ferentz and the staff did a great job of keeping our minds focused on one game at a time and not letting our emotions get out of hand after a big win or disappointing loss.

If you were to piece together the prototypical Iowa football player, setting aside the obvious physical tools that are important, I think it comes down to character—a player's mental makeup. Guys who want to work hard and be a part of the team will thrive here. They aren't out to set themselves apart from the team in any way. They are more concerned with the team than themselves. They never want to let a teammate down.

I have mentioned it numerous times throughout, but when I think about the essence of being a Hawkeye, it very simply is being a part of the team. It is so important to what the Iowa DNA is all about. It is about being there for the guy next to you, holding yourself accountable to the team, putting in the time and work needed, whether it is during the season or in the off-season, so that when we hit the field, we can work together. Football is unquestionably a team game, and the Iowa way is about recognizing that what we do as individuals affects the rest of the team and even the rest of the Hawkeye family. For this reason, it is something that needs to be taken very seriously each time you put on the black and gold, from the time you enter the building as a freshman until the day you leave the program. I think it is this selfless approach that will continue to make past, present, and future players so proud to be Hawkeyes!

Ricky Stanzi was a three-year starter at quarterback from 2008 to 2010. Stanzi posted a 26–9 career record as starting QB, which ranks second all time at Iowa in career victories. Stanzi is the only Iowa quarterback, and just the third Big Ten quarterback, to start and win three bowl games. He was named a permanent team captain for his junior and senior seasons. He led Iowa to a school record 9–0 start during the 2009 campaign and followed that with one of the best statistical seasons in Iowa history in 2010, posting a school record 157.6 QB rating, 3,004 yards, 25 TD passes, and just six interceptions. He was selected by the Kansas City Chiefs in the fifth round of the 2011 NFL Draft.

HONORARY MENTION

These men did not play football for Iowa, but through their actions and deeds, they proved that they know what it means to be a Hawkeye.

JERRY BURNS

HEAD COACH

1961–1965

I'M FROM THE DETROIT, MICHIGAN, AREA. I attended the University of Michigan and was a second-string quarterback and a defensive back on the 1949 and 1950 teams. My biggest thrill playing at Michigan was when I played the last two minutes of the 1951 Rose Bowl and we beat California 14–6.

I always knew I was going to get into coaching. My first coaching job was at the University of Hawaii with Archie Kodros, who was the captain of the 1938 Michigan team. I coached with him for a year and a half. He was on Evashevski's original staff at the University of Iowa, and Kodros was the guy who convinced Evy that he should take a look at me. Although I didn't know a great deal about Iowa, I went out and interviewed with Evy, and Evy signed me for the 1954 season.

Evy was a very excellent coach, there's no question about that. He had great command of the players—handling them in recruiting, handling them on the field in practice, and handling them during the game. He controlled his players and his coaching staff. I very much enjoyed coaching for and with Evy, and I respect him to every extent. I think his player control was the outstanding thing that I remember about Forest Evashevski.

I was the backfield coach on Iowa's 1957 Rose Bowl team. We had some very fine football players on that team. I was more associated with the offense than the defense, and the one guy who really propelled that team, certainly from an offensive standpoint, was Kenny Ploen, who was an excellent player.

In his five seasons as the head coach of the Hawkeyes, Jerry Burns coached six All-Americans and led Iowa to victories over Notre Dame, Michigan, and Ohio State.

Photo courtesy Getty Images

In those days, a lot of players went up to Canada to play. Ploen went up to Canada to play for Bud Grant and the Winnipeg Blue Bombers. For about 10 or 11 years he was all-pro in the Canadian League.

I became offensive coordinator in 1957. I won't say it was the best Iowa team of all-time, but I think the 1958 team was the best Iowa team that I was associated with. Randy Duncan was the quarterback, and we had a couple of halfbacks, Willie Fleming and Bob Jeter, who were outstanding. It was a very good team offensively and defensively. The '58 team, from an offensive standpoint, was the best team that I was around when I was coaching at Iowa.

At that time in the Big Ten, they had a rule that you couldn't be a head football coach and an athletics director. Because of the rule, Evy became solely athletics director after the 1960 season. Since I had worked with Evy, he gave me the head coaching job.

I was only 34 when I was named head coach. I think when you're at that age, you really haven't gotten the total experience, perhaps in recruiting, perhaps in your relationships with players on and off the field. I was pretty young, but the opportunity came, and I accepted it.

It was very difficult. In my very first game, we played California, and we lost Larry Ferguson, a halfback who was All-America in the previous season. And then in the second game, we lost our quarterback, Wilburn Hollis, who was an outstanding player and All–Big Ten the previous season. We had some other injuries along the line, too, but those two guys were All-Americans from an offensive standpoint, and their losses were critical.

One game that was not played is still fresh in my mind. I think of my five years as the head coach, the 1963 team was our very best. We were winding up the end of the season against Notre Dame in Iowa City, and on the Friday before the game, President Kennedy was assassinated. I look back at that particular weekend and the conversations between the Iowa and Notre Dame people on whether or not to play the game. Iowa wanted to play it the following week, but Notre Dame couldn't play it then because they were playing Syracuse. They wanted to play it two weeks later, but Iowa didn't want to play it then because it would interfere with Thanksgiving vacations for the players and the students in Iowa City. So the game was never played, but my concern and everybody's concern at that time was the loss of President Kennedy.

One of the players I remember from that 1963 team was Paul Krause. I recruited him out of Flint Bendle High School, and he was a great athlete. He was an all-state football and basketball player in high school in Michigan. Perhaps his greatest ability was as a great baseball player. Actually, after his sophomore year, I thought he was going to go into baseball full-time. He had an opportunity to play for the New York Mets. But after his junior year, he dislocated his right shoulder when he intercepted a pass against Ohio State. After that, he was out of baseball and concentrated on football. He was a great player for us at Iowa and a great player for us with the Vikings. I was the one who presented him at the Pro Football Hall of Fame in Canton, Ohio.

There were some academic changes at Iowa during that time, and there also were some changes in the scholarships you could award in the Big Ten, where players had to pay so much depending on their family's incomes. Recruiting became quite difficult. The last two years were very difficult to recruit and continue at the level of play at Iowa that people expected. Evy let me go and brought in Ray Nagel from Utah, and he had a tough time, too. I have no ill feelings toward Iowa and no ill feelings toward Forest Evashevski. He treated me fine, and the people of Iowa treated me fine. I look back at my coaching career and believe that one of the finest times for myself and for my family was when we lived in Iowa City.

I had several opportunities when I left Iowa. I could have gone to the Washington Redskins, and I had the chance to go to the Pittsburgh Steelers. But the Green Bay Packers were the world champions at that time, and Vince Lombardi offered me a job. Murray Warmath was the coach at the University of Minnesota, and we were very close friends. Warmath recommended me to Vince Lombardi, and Lombardi signed me to go to Green Bay as the defensive backfield coach.

After two years there, I was the offensive coordinator for Bud Grant and the Minnesota Vikings for about 17 years. I first got to know Bud when he signed Kenny Ploen up with the Winnipeg Blue Bombers. Bud asked me to come up there in 1957 and put in the wing-T offense that we were running at that time at Iowa. I did that and was what they called an advisory coach for four years with Bud in Winnipeg. Bud is a very good, close friend of mine. I enjoyed working for him, and after he retired from coaching, I was named head coach of the Vikings in 1986. Bud Grant was a top coach and is in the Pro Football Hall of Fame. I rank him, Forest Evashevski, and Vince Lombardi all on the same level as great coaches.

I know Hayden Fry and Kirk Ferentz both very well. Hayden did a great job, and Ferentz is currently doing a great job. They're both excellent coaches.

One thing that Iowa has is one of the finest athletic facilities anyplace, and a guy who I think you can thank for that is Bump Elliott, who was the athletics director. He did a great job in fixing and building the athletic facilities for football, basketball, baseball, track, golf, and anything else you want.

Everything about my memories of coaching football at Iowa is great. The fans of Iowa football are tremendous. Iowa City is a great town, and the University of Iowa is an excellent university. Four of my five children were born in Iowa City, and it is a very fine place to live. There are wonderful people there, and the University of Iowa was a great place to coach.

Jerry Burns was an assistant coach for Forest Evashevski from 1954 to 1960. In his five seasons as the head coach of the Hawkeyes, Burns coached six All-Americans and led Iowa to victories over Notre Dame, Michigan, and Ohio State. He was an assistant coach on the Green Bay Packers teams that won Super Bowls I and II, and he later went to four more Super Bowls as the offensive coordinator of the Minnesota Vikings.

GEORGE WINE

Sports Information Director

1968–1993

I became a Hawkeye on November 7, 1942, while listening to a radio report of Iowa's 6–0 victory over Wisconsin. The Badgers were ranked No. 1 in the country at the time, and it was a stunning upset. I don't remember who called the play-by-play (it was not Jim Zabel or Bob Brooks, both now my good friends), but I do recall my heart pounding through my chest in the fourth quarter as the Hawkeyes successfully hung on to their narrow lead.

I was an impressionable 11-year-old kid, and I was hooked.

Later, as a teenager, I watched the Hawkeyes play a lot of games while I sat in the north end zone's Knothole Section, where admission was 50¢. Some of my favorite players were Earl Banks, Jack Dittmer, and Emlen "the Gremlin" Tunnell.

I became a student at the UI, beginning when Leonard Raffensperger was the coach and finishing (with time out for military duty) when Forest Evashevski was in his early years. I covered games for the *Daily Iowan* and earned some money by "spotting" for visiting radio stations. I graduated just before Evy's teams began to win Big Ten championships.

I went off to work as sports information director at the University of Northern Iowa, then the University of Memphis. When the UI gave me the chance to succeed Eric Wilson, who had been the school's SID for 44 years,

I welcomed the opportunity. I was coming home to work for my alma mater and to publicize teams closest to my heart.

So my association with the Hawkeyes has had four phases—first as a youngster, then as a student, then as an employee, and finally as a retiree who has stayed close to the university and the Hawkeyes. During that nearly 70 years, I have been privileged to develop friendships with many of the players, coaches, and others associated with Iowa football. Here are three of them.

I met Aubrey Devine when he returned to campus in 1973 to be honored as Iowa's newest member of the College Football Hall of Fame. Two things struck me about the man who had starred for the Hawkeyes 52 years earlier. At 5′9″ and 170 pounds, he was smaller than I expected, but he had enormous hands. When he greeted me with a handshake, my hand disappeared in his. His grip was firm but gentle. Big, soft hands are often the mark of a great athlete, and Aubrey Devine, in my opinion, ranks No. 1 as Iowa's all-time football player.

Devine was a consensus All-American on Iowa's unbeaten Big Ten championship team of 1921. He was an exceptional runner, passer, and kicker—the best triple-threat player of his day. His amazing versatility also made him a great defensive back, and he often played 60 minutes.

In consecutive games against Minnesota and Indiana he scored an astounding 57 points, a Big Ten record that still stands. One of his best all-around games was against Iowa State, when he intercepted three passes, scored a touchdown, passed for another, and kicked two extra points in a 14–10 Hawkeye victory.

But his personal favorite was drop-kicking a field goal that ended Notre Dame's 20-game winning streak and gave Iowa a 10–7 victory. "I kicked the ball from the 38-yard line," he recalled, "and when I looked up, it was headed for the middle of the goal posts. I'll never forget that moment."

Ozzie Simmons is the reason Floyd of Rosedale is the traveling trophy that goes to the winner of Iowa's annual game with Minnesota. Simmons was a sensational running back in the mid-1930s. He was only the second prominent African American to play for the Hawkeyes. The first was tackle Duke Slater in the early 1920s.

After Simmons put on a dazzling performance in his first Big Ten game at Northwestern, the *Chicago Tribune* called him "a slithery, rubbery, oozy flyer. Most of it seems to come natural to this Ebony Eel."

A native Iowan and a graduate of the University of Iowa, George Wine served as the University of Iowa Sports Information Director for a quarter century.

In the games that followed, Simmons experienced physical and verbal racial abuse. Recalled Simmons: "Players on the other team often hollered, 'Come on, nigger. We're gonna get you!" Then, as if to apologize for their behavior, he said, "That's just the way it was in those days."

Late hits and piling on knocked Simmons out of the 1934 Minnesota game three times. When the Gophers played at Iowa the following season, Hawkeye fans were still fuming. Iowa Governor Clyde Herring said, "If the officials stand for rough tactics like Minnesota used on Simmons last year, I'm sure the crowd won't." In essence, he suggested a public mugging, and Gopher Coach Bernie Bierman asked for police protection.

Fortunately Minnesota Governor Floyd Olson had an idea. He sent a telegram to Herring saying nice things about the Hawkeyes, then suggested a friendly wager, with "a prize hog going to the winner of the game." Herring took the bet, Minnesota won a well-played and incident-free 13–6 game, and Olson won a prize hog named Floyd of Rosedale. Minnesota had Charles Brioschi sculpt Floyd's image, which is the bronze statue of a pig that the two schools play for today.

Simmons was a kind and considerate man who never showed any bitterness about racism. He wanted to play professional football, but the NFL had an unwritten rule that prohibited players of color. He became an elementary school teacher in Chicago, where he died in 2001 at 87 years old. The next time you see Iowa and Minnesota play for Floyd of Rosedale, pause a moment to remember a great Hawkeye and a wonderful human being.

I never met Nile Kinnick; never even saw him play. But I did enjoy a friendly relationship with his father, Nile Sr. We exchanged a fair amount of correspondence, and his letters were always typed neatly on his personal stationery. After a while, I began searching for a strikeover or an erasure, but I never found one. In person, he was always neatly dressed, with his tie straight and coordinated to the colors of his shirt and suit.

When World War II ended, there was a push to name Iowa Stadium in honor of Nile Kinnick Jr., who lost his life as a Navy pilot in 1943. But Mr. Kinnick rejected the idea, pointing out that many Hawkeyes had died in serving their country during the war, and it would be inappropriate to name the stadium after his son.

Some 25 years later Gus Schrader, the influential sports editor of the *Cedar Rapids Gazette*, started another campaign for Kinnick's name to be placed on the stadium. He mobilized strong support among Iowa contributors and boosters. Momentum grew, and Mr. Kinnick softened his position.

In 1972 the UI Board in Control of Athletics voted to rename its football stadium in honor of the school's only Heisman Trophy winner and legendary leader of the 1939 Ironmen. The Hawkeyes' opener that season was with Oregon State, and a pregame ceremony on September 23 made it official: Iowa Stadium became Kinnick Stadium. Mr. Kinnick took part in the ceremony and seemed genuinely pleased.

I value the friendship I had with Aubrey Devine, Ozzie Simmons, and Nile Kinnick Sr. All three have been gone a long time, but each one left a large legacy that is indelibly written into Hawkeye football history. They are three reasons I believe it's great to be a Hawkeye.

George Wine served as the University of Iowa Sports Information Director for a quarter century. He is a native Iowan and a graduate of the University of Iowa. He is a member of the Varsity Club's Hall of Fame, the President's Club, and the Kinnick Society. He is past president of the College Sports Information Directors and a member of its Hall of Fame. He has authored two books on Hawkeye sports, including Hayden Fry's autobiography. Wine currently resides in Coralville, Iowa.

JOHN STREIF

Assistant Athletic Trainer and Travel Coordinator

1972–Present

It was 1966, Ray Nagel's first year as the football coach. I had no real plans or direction, and I really had no hints of even going into college. Jack Wiland was a student-teacher and student-coach at my high school who had played baseball at Iowa and later was a scout for years for the Montreal Expos. He just threw me in the car one day and said, "I think you'd like to be a manager down at Iowa." Without his guidance and leadership, I don't know that I'd even be in the position that I am today. I came down and interviewed, and lo and behold, they gave me their head manager's position as an incoming freshman. We all live for moments like that, where things can change our lives overnight. Without the coaches at that high school thinking I would fit in here and opening the door for me, it probably never would have happened, so I feel so honored.

I started school at the University of Iowa and worked as a manager. In the off-season, Iowa's head athletic trainer at the time, Tom Spalj, needed help in the athletic training room. He asked me if I'd come in and help him out. I went in the athletic training room and went to work, and I haven't left there since. I tell people I'm doing the same things today that I did as a student back in the '60s. I think the foundation of my work all comes from my family and the things I learned back in that small little community on teamwork and work ethic and leadership. I feel very fortunate to have had the background I have and the way I was brought up.

It's amazing how things progress. During my years as a student, I had a chance to work in Detroit with the Lions because their athletic trainer, Kent Falb, was an Iowa graduate. I did some summer internships with them, so my pro team has always been the Detroit Lions, even though they've never won! But because of my relationships over the years, I've been a big fan of theirs. I had a great opportunity there, and it helped me grow tremendously.

I graduated from Iowa in 1970 and had a chance to work at the United States Military Academy as an athletic trainer. I put my number at the head of the list and got drafted, and I went to Fort Leonard Wood for basic training. That was another valuable growing experience for me, learning about our country. When my first orders came, they were not for West Point, and I was kind of shaking in my boots. But I was sent home on leave for two weeks before my next assignment. I got a call in the middle of the night that they got my orders changed and I was to be at West Point the next morning to go on a trip with the team. I got on my feet and grabbed my medical bag and went on the trip. That's the way it all started.

To be honest, I loved the regimentation, organization, and leadership at West Point. It was such a great, positive experience. It was hard for a farm boy from the Midwest going east and getting used to their terminology and everything, but once I did, I loved it. That was back in the days when Bobby Knight was coaching at West Point. The relationships I had with the hockey, lacrosse, football, and basketball coaches there are relationships that will last forever and are a very important part of my life also.

I ended up getting out early because the Vietnam War was ending, and I came back to Iowa to try to get in physical therapy school. At that time, Tom Spalj, Iowa's head trainer who mentored me so much, passed away at a young age. When Tom died, I felt they should have a physical therapist/athletic trainer, because that's what Tom was. Iowa brought Ed Crowley back as the head athletic trainer; Ed had been an assistant under Tom and then went to Purdue as an assistant under Pinky Newell. Ed and I had worked briefly together at West Point, and Ed hired me after Tom's death. Lo and behold, I'm still here. It's been kind of an amazing story and an amazing run. Not many people have an opportunity to be at their alma mater and do what I've done over the years, and I feel so honored by it.

I've been coordinating travel for the team since 1980. It's something I've kind of taken on over time. Buzz Graham was our business manager under Bump Elliott and Evashevski for many years. In the '60s, we'd go on the road, and I would assist him and do a lot of that work even as a student. When he retired under Bump Elliott's leadership, Bump just came to me and said, "John, would you take over the travel work for the team?" I was happy to do that because I wanted to do anything I could do to make it easier for the coaches and the players. If you saw my desk, you'd realize how crazy it was, and everybody would wonder how in the world I keep it straight, but somehow it always comes off and works.

I take great pride in my job and have been fortunate to witness so many great moments for Iowa athletics. All the bowls are great, and all the Rose Bowls were great. There was nothing more first class than the 2010 Orange Bowl, and of course, winning helps. The way we were treated down in Miami was beyond anything we've ever experienced or probably will ever experience again. Still, I'd certainly like to try the Rose Bowl once more now that it's a BCS bowl and see how it's changed, because even the Orange Bowl had changed significantly from 2003 to when we were down there in 2010. There have been some great days and some great times.

It's more than just wins and losses. There are some young people who went through this program who have been walk-ons or have never stepped foot on the courts or on the fields who have gained as much as the guy who has taken us to the bowl games. A lot of those people you never get to see or hear from, but they're rewarding people. A university is about learning and growing, and I'm still learning and growing every day. It's a really rewarding job because you get to watch these young people come in and learn and grow during the four or five years they're here. And it isn't always from positive things; sometimes it's negative things. Every university has drug and alcohol problems. Every young person has girlfriend problems or problems at home or academic problems or problems with the coaches. Those are sometimes difficult or negative things but very valuable things in helping young people get through this stage in their lives. Our jobs as athletic trainers are somewhat like a counselor's job, where you get to share with them during this learning and growing experience.

We've been fortunate at Iowa to have some of the greatest leadership you could ever have. Forest Evashevski was the athletics director when I started here as a student. He'd call me into the office many times, and here I was a

John Streif joined the training staff at Iowa in 1972 and has been Iowa's travel coordinator since 1980.

young Iowa farm boy sitting there across from Evy. He was such an imposing figure and so into the football program and the whole Iowa athletic scene. When I returned in 1972, Bump Elliott was the athletics director. There are very, very few leaders like Bump Elliott. He'd know everybody's role, because he'd worked at every level before he got to be an athletics director. There was probably nobody with that experience. He hired you, gave you the resources to get the job done, and then watched you learn and grow through it. He's probably the greatest leader I've ever worked with. To me, what it all comes down to is leadership, from the president on down.

I think the littlest things in the world are what make us successful at Iowa. Coach Ferentz is not only a stickler for that on the field, but he keeps it in front of our young people off the field. He demands detail on the field, but he also demands detail in the classroom and in their everyday life. It's the simple things that are going to make us successful in the classroom and on the field, and I think those are the things that Kirk Ferentz emphasizes over and over with his young people. To me, that's the foundation of what Iowa's all about. Like I've told Hayden Fry and Kirk Ferentz and all the coaches I've worked with, unless we at Iowa can do the little things and do things right, we have no chance to be successful. But if our leadership provides us those resources to do that—and we've been fortunate that they have—then we can be successful. We're going to always have the same geographical area and the same population base. Certainly, that puts us at odds with some of the bigger metropolitan areas and the bigger schools, but when we have resources and fan support like we do and leadership like we've had, it allows the University of Iowa to have success. We've been able to have that over the years, and we feel so fortunate about that.

I get asked about 10 times a day when I'm going to retire. I tell them: No. 1, I'm too young; No. 2, I don't make enough money to retire; and No. 3, I lie awake worrying about what I'm going to do when they do retire me! I guess I'm married to the job, which you're not supposed to do! But I made it happen just because it's been enjoyable, positive, and right for me. You wouldn't do it if you didn't enjoy it, and there are so many rewards to it. When a call from a former athlete comes in just to say hello or to greet me or to remember old times, that's what I live for and what keeps me in this job.

There's nothing to quite equal being a Hawkeye. What it means to be a Hawkeye is every day living and being supported in such a great community by such great coaches, staff, and athletes. Athletics is the truest thing you can have to teamwork, in the end. I am so fortunate to be doing what I do in the setting I do, and in my book, there's nothing greater than being a Hawkeye.

John Streif attended Maquoketa Valley High School in Delhi, Iowa. He joined the training staff at Iowa in 1972 and has been Iowa's travel coordinator since 1980. Recently, the training room at the University of Iowa was named in his honor at the request of Ronnie Lester, an All-America basketball player who helped lead the Hawkeyes to the Final Four in 1980. Streif said, "I could do without the recognition, but I'm appreciative and honored and humbled, and most importantly, it's so emotional for me because it came from Ronnie Lester. He's a special person."

BILL BRASHIER

Defensive Coordinator

1979–1995

Hayden Fry and I go back a long way. We were born in the same small Texas town of Eastland. In fact, the same doctor even delivered us. We were together through third grade, and then Hayden went to Odessa and I stayed in Eastland. Our paths crossed again years later at North Texas State University.

I had played collegiately at North Texas State. After I graduated from college in 1952 and then spent a brief time in the Navy, I signed a contract to play football in Canada. When it was time to go, my college coach, Odus Mitchell, called and said, "Bill, I know you think you might want to go play pro ball, but there's a good assistant coaching job open in Sherman, Texas." It was a 4A high school, which was the highest classification at that time in Texas. I was going to be the backfield coach and the head track coach. I told the guy when he hired me, "I don't know anything about track." He said, "I'll tell you what, Bill, they've never fired a track coach in Sherman, Texas. But they've fired a lot of football coaches."

So that was my start in coaching. I then had three more coaching stops before I went back to North Texas State as an assistant coach under Rod Rust. Rod left, and then Hayden came in as the head coach. We were there together for six years before the Iowa job came up.

We knew very little about Iowa in 1978. I always knew about the great teams Forest Evashevski had, but I didn't know much else about it. When we were at North Texas State and Hayden was looking at the job, Iowa wanted him to come up there and talk. Hayden brought back a film of an Iowa game. We looked at the film, and I asked him, "Coach, what was the score of that game?" He replied, "Well, Iowa got beat by about 40 points." I said, "Did you see how many people were in the stands?" He said, "I sure did." I said, "They've had almost 20 losing seasons in a row. If they have that many people there now, can you imagine what it would be like if you won?" Hayden said, "I'll tell ya, we're going there because I think that can happen. I think it could be great." And sure enough, it was. There was no hesitation on my part to follow him.

We knew they had that great stadium, Kinnick Stadium; and they had promised Hayden if he came to Iowa they would upgrade everything, which they did. They made "the bubble," we had nice offices, and everything was going really good. Of course, now they've done even more to it, but they did everything to make it a very competitive Big Ten program. Bump Elliott was Iowa's athletics director at that time, and there never was a better athletics director anywhere than Bump Elliott.

Many of us came from North Texas with Hayden, such as Bill Snyder, Carl Jackson, Donnie Patterson, and myself, among others. We added some from the existing staff, such as Dan McCarney and Bernie Wyatt. Then Hayden added Barry Alvarez and Del Miller. It was a staff without big egos. We all worked together well and bought in on the same system we were using. It was really good harmony, and I think that's why people stayed so long. There was no backstabbing or anything like that on that staff.

Most people think of 1981 as being Hayden's breakout season. We were fortunate to have a hungry bunch of kids who were tough. That goes for the first two years we were here also, but everything just kind of came together in year three. In 1981 we beat Nebraska, UCLA, and Michigan. Back then, if you beat those three teams in the same year, you were having a special season. We were, and we ended the season playing Washington in the Rose Bowl.

We had a basic, sound, 5-2 defense without a whole lot of frills. We weren't changing alignments every play and all that kind of stuff; we just sold the kids on the fact that if they played as hard as they could, they were going to have success. They bought into everything we were trying to do. There wasn't any second-guessing about anything, and they played hard. I'll tell you, they played hard in practice. We used to have to call 'em off in practice a lot

Bill Brashier served as Hayden Fry's defensive coordinator at Iowa for 17 seasons. He and Fry grew up in the same small Texas town.

of times. Andre Tippett was probably the most decorated of those players, but every player was just as important as the next if we were going to win.

I could have left Iowa after the 1981 Rose Bowl season. North Texas opened up again and offered me the job. I thought about it, and I said, "You know, I'm 48 years old, and to be a head coach is just not that important to me anymore. I've got one of the best jobs in the United States, and I make as many decisions that depend on whether we win or lose as the head coach does." I called all the defenses. We were in the Big Ten Conference and starting to go to bowl games. All the years we were at North Texas—including once when we were 10–1—we never could go to a bowl. And so I told them I thought I had a better job here, and I've never regretted that. It was good for me and good for my family.

I enjoyed the preparation during game week almost as much as the games themselves. We had a pretty basic routine as far as what you did on Monday,

Tuesday, Wednesday, and so on. You knew your basic stuff, but you had to have ideas of what you were going to do in certain situations. You might not get it all finalized until maybe Wednesday. Thursday was essentially the last practice because Friday was just a walkthrough.

By game day, everything was in the bag. You didn't make any changes at that point. I was always in the press box during the game, communicating with the guy on the field. I'd tell him what to call, and he'd signal it. During the course of the game, your main adjustments had to come at halftime. I always thought that many coaches have a long list of offensive plays, and they think they've got to run all those plays. A lot of times what they hurt you with in the first half they wouldn't go back to in the second half. I could never understand that because I knew defensively we weren't going to make wholesale changes. That may not be true about offensive coaches, but that's kind of the way I felt about it.

By the mid-1990s, I was about ready to call it a career. Typically you think 65 years of age is when you retire, but at 65 I just wasn't sure. I decided to go one more year. I told Hayden, and everybody knew at the end of that year I was going to retire. We beat Washington that year in the Sun Bowl. I thought, *Boy, this is a great time for me to retire.* We played Washington in the Rose Bowl a couple of times, and they beat us on each occasion. I always had a lot of respect for the coaches and the program at the University of Washington, but this time we got them. We beat them handily, and I just felt it was the perfect time for me to go out.

My vantage point is still from the press box, but with a few less responsibilities. My wife and I sit up there each game, and it's a good feeling to know I don't have to make the decisions. I watch closely, but I never second-guess the coaches. I get to simply enjoy it, and there's been a lot to enjoy since I stepped down.

The university could not have found a better individual to replace Hayden Fry than they did with Kirk Ferentz. Kirk was on our staff; and I think he is not only one of the greatest coaches, but he's one of the truly great people. We were always very close, and he and I had a really good relationship. And I know Norm Parker. We talk a little bit now and then, but I never go up to the office because I remember how busy I was. Norm Parker has been through it all. I think he and I share the same principles. Our defenses aren't going to be very flamboyant, but they're going be sound. That's one thing I admire about him. Those kids know where to line up and they know that it all comes down to execution—defeat the block and get to the ball carrier.

I knew since I was a kid I wanted to be a football coach. My mother and dad never worried about what to get me for Christmas. They knew they were going to get me a new football. I came up through everything—through high school where you had to wash the uniforms, line off the football field, and all that stuff. I wouldn't trade any of those experiences for anything, because it just made me appreciate the experience I got from being at Iowa and the Big Ten. You were on the national scene playing in front of 100,000 people some games. It was just beyond anything in my wildest dreams that I'd be able to do that. I'll tell you, I coached football for nearly 50 years, and it was the best 17 years of coaching in my career. Iowa City is a great place to live, and I wouldn't want to live anywhere else after being here.

Bill Brashier served as Hayden Fry's defensive coordinator at Iowa for 17 seasons. He began his coaching career as a high school coach at Sherman and South San Antonio high schools in Texas. He got his start in college coaching as an assistant at Texas–El Paso in 1964. He spent 11 years at North Texas State, including six as Fry's defensive coordinator. He received his bachelor's and master's degrees from North Texas State, where he played football as a defensive back. He set school records for interceptions in a season and a career. Brashier currently resides in Iowa City.

CHRIS DOYLE

Head Strength and Conditioning Coach

1999–Present

From the time we approached the stadium on the bus to the time we left, the passion and dedication of the Iowa fans really struck me. The stands are right on top of you, and the fans love their Hawkeyes. As an opponent on the visiting sideline, Kinnick Stadium was a tough place to play. It was 1996, and I was an assistant coach at Wisconsin. The whole experience, that day in Kinnick Stadium, left a lasting impression. Iowa dominated the game 31–0.

Fast forward to December 1998. Kirk Ferentz was hired to replace the retired Hayden Fry at Iowa and was in the process of assembling his coaching staff. At the time, I was working at the University of Utah. Kirk always leaned on his high school coach and mentor, Joe Moore, when he was faced with important decisions. Putting a staff together was one of those times. Kirk was methodical in his approach, ensuring that he brought in the right people. Coincidently, I was fortunate enough to have worked for Coach Moore at Notre Dame. I also chose Coach Moore as my mentor. He had introduced me to Kirk eight years earlier. Coach Moore would play an integral role in me finding my way to Iowa City. Coach Moore spent quite a bit of time in Iowa City during the first five years. Coach Moore passed in July of 2003. He made a big impact on our program as we built the foundation of Iowa football under Kirk Ferentz.

It was an easy decision to come to Iowa. First, and foremost, the people who were being assembled on the coaching staff were people who were highly respected in the football world—the kind of people a young coach would want to be associated with. Kirk had an impeccable reputation, and I knew, firsthand, of his character. When the other assistant coaching positions were filled with Ken O'Keefe, Norm Parker, and Joe Philbin, it really made my decision easy. Kirk was putting a great staff together. It was a no-brainer. I would have walked to Iowa from Utah!

During one of Kirk's conversations with Coach Moore, Kirk took some notes about the importance strength and conditioning had to a successful football program and the type of person Kirk should look for to fill the role of the strength and conditioning coach. Today, I have a copy of those notes hanging on the wall in my office. They are a reminder of the standard I need to live up to at Iowa.

Our challenge in the early days was to create a winning culture. Coach Fry had established a winning tradition with the program, but with Kirk and the new staff coming in, we needed to establish that we could protect the legacy of Iowa football. Kirk serving on Hayden's staff in the 1980s certainly helped bring continuity, but we had to prove that Iowa football would compete for championships under the new staff.

We won four games in our first two years, but we stayed the course, and over time, we developed a successful culture. Today we have tangible examples of success stories. Guys who came into the program with little or no fanfare, worked hard, and reaped the rewards from all their efforts. Players like Dallas Clark, Bob Sanders, Robert Gallery, and Chad Greenway all serve as tangible examples for today's players.

Player development at Iowa is a team approach. First, it's about identifying the right players who will fit our system during recruiting. Our coaches do an outstanding job of finding guys who will fit at Iowa. Next, it's about each one of us understanding our role in the process and doing our job. Everyone is under one roof—football, sports medicine, and strength and conditioning. We all work together under Kirk's vision. We are a seamless team with excellent communication that shares a common philosophy and vision.

Commitment is an integral part of our system. In order for our system to work effectively, a mutual commitment between the players and coaches must exist. Our guys show up, bring energy, do their jobs, and don't make excuses. We ask that the players commit to Iowa football, and the coaches, in turn,

Highly respected by Iowa's athletes, Chris Doyle was an assistant strength coach at Wisconsin and director of strength and conditioning at Utah immediately before joining Kirk Ferentz's staff in 1999. *Photo courtesy of Bob Rasmus*

commit to the players. If we ask for respect, energy, enthusiasm, attention to detail, and commitment, we as coaches must be willing to give all those things back to our players.

There isn't anything remarkable about it. It's doing the ordinary things well consistently. That needs to be our edge at Iowa: holding each other accountable to the highest standards of execution. As an organization, we must trust the process. Very few of our players were privileged guys coming out of high school. They weren't born on third base. They come from modest backgrounds and really need to work to get where they are. It is a process that takes time.

Player development reaches beyond physical preparation. It's teaching athletes how to think, how to face adversity, and that there aren't any shortcuts. It's important that our athletes have a comfort level during recruiting that our system can help them attain their goals. Once they arrive in Iowa City, it's our job to make them uncomfortable for four or five years. If they are comfortable, they will not reach their ultimate potential. The mental aspect of football is inseparable from the physical. You need a certain level of mental toughness to build your physical abilities. Your improved physical abilities provide you with additional confidence, which increases your mental toughness. The mental and physical aspects feed off of one another. It's about constantly challenging people. You can't give somebody confidence. They must earn it. We challenge our players in our preparation to create a mental edge that will be carried with them onto the field.

It is important to find out what makes each player tick and how each individual derives his motivation. Developing close relationships with our athletes helps us maximize the ability of our players. Some young guys are simply trying to prove that they belong in our program. Some are trying to climb the depth chart and earn a starting role. Established starters are trying to show that they can play with the best in the Big Ten. Finally, there are the elite players who see themselves at the next level playing in the NFL. There is a next step for everybody, and it is our job to get our players to that next step, no matter where they might be on the ladder. There cannot be any sense of entitlement. It is about constant improvement.

We have an optimistic view of what each player's potential is. Of course, there is going to be a different ceiling for each player. Some will have NFL futures, and some will not, but they are all capable of having a valued role on our team. It's human nature to settle into a comfort zone, to achieve a certain level of social acceptance within the program and become content. It is our job as coaches to set the standard and not allow 18-, 19-, and 20-year-old kids to settle when they are capable of more. We need to provide a vision as to what each player is capable of, at his best.

The ideal guys who we look to bring into the program are going to have at least four major qualities: they are going to love to compete, be smart, be tough, and be willing to work. If we can get guys on the bus with these qualities, we give ourselves a chance. We certainly love to bring in four- and five-star recruits with loads of talent, but talent is only one piece of the puzzle. Talent is certainly on our list, but it is way below things like character, work ethic, and passion for the game.

The term *overachiever* is often used to describe an Iowa football player. There is no such thing as an overachiever; there are simply people who reach their potential through determined effort and persistence. Every player is different, and everyone is going to be a different kind of football player, based on his makeup. We don't pursue numbers. We pursue performance. There are so many who have maximized their physical abilities over their career. Bob Sanders comes to mind. He is an undersized guy, but every single cell in his body is football player, and he maximized his potential. Matt Kroul started 50 games in a row at Iowa. Kroul was a tireless worker who reached his ceiling at Iowa. Matt didn't miss a practice in five years. Brian Ferentz was a three-year starter. Brian had serious knee problems and wasn't the most talented athlete, but he was tough, smart, and became very strong through relentless hard work. Brian certainly got the most out of his ability.

There have also been guys who had raw talent and physical ability who simply needed direction, a position change, and time to develop. They were unselfish. They may have played a certain position in high school, but they didn't care what position they played at Iowa. They just wanted to be part of the team and wanted to help the team win. Dallas Clark was a 200-pound high school quarterback. Chad Greenway was a 200-pound high school quarterback. Robert Gallery was a 240-pound tight end. Karl Klug was a 205-pound high school tailback. All of these guys came to Iowa, worked tirelessly, and maximized their potential. They developed into tremendous players over time—and they all happen to contribute at Iowa at a different position than they played in high school.

Being the strength and conditioning coach at Iowa is the best strength and conditioning job in football, and it is due, in large part, to the culture that is in place here. It starts at the top with the leadership of Kirk Ferentz. He empowers people to do their jobs. He listens, he supports, he provides a vision, and he provides an example of the work ethic that we all strive to model ourselves after. It includes bringing in the right people. We have been very lucky to have so many high character players come to Iowa. When they get here, it's the commitment to a team-first mentality that makes it work.

When the players take the lead and provide the motivation, we know we are headed in the right direction. When they walk in the door, they give us energy. They get the coaches excited. They love football to the point where they increase our love for the game. The players with true heart and passion deserve the credit for our success over the years.

It is the relationships that are developed in football that make it a special game. This is undoubtedly the most rewarding part of the job. It is so far ahead of everything else. We enjoy seeing players come back many years after they are done playing. To see the type of husbands, fathers, and members of the community they have become is very gratifying. These are character guys who transcend football. They will forever be part of the Iowa family. That is really what it is all about.

In closing, the Iowa football program is a special place to be. It is much bigger than any single person associated with the program. We have gone through ups and downs, but in the end, I can't imagine another college football team in the country that better represents their home state than the University of Iowa. Midwest values, modest, hardworking, and a hard-nosed attitude are many of the best qualities of the people in this great state. Every day we do our best to reflect these qualities as we continue to build the Iowa football program.

Chris Doyle was a three-year starter on offensive line at Boston University from 1986 to 1988. He worked as a graduate assistant coach at Syracuse and Notre Dame before serving as offensive line coach at Holy Cross from 1992 to 1995. Doyle was an assistant strength coach at Wisconsin and director of strength and conditioning at Utah immediately before joining Kirk Ferentz's staff in 1999.

NORM PARKER

Defensive Coordinator

1999–Present

During my earlier years in coaching with Minnesota and Illinois in the 1970s and later with Michigan State in the 1980s and '90s, I had frequent encounters with the Iowa Hawkeyes. For the most part, Iowa seemed to more than hold their own against my teams over the years, especially once Hayden Fry arrived on the scene. I often wondered what their secret was. How is it that a school from the least populous state in the Big Ten was able to do it year in, year out?

Once I got to see things from the inside, I found out why those Hayden Fry Iowa teams had been so successful. It was the work ethic of the players in the program. Many of the kids on the Iowa team come from a farm background. The culture of growing up on a farm is quite simply one of work. Generally, the kids would work before school, go to school, practice, whatever, then come home and work some more before going to bed. They certainly don't plop down on the couch and play video games or something like that. Then, kids from other states who don't have that farm background are exposed to this work ethic, and soon it is rubbing off on them, too.

I think my journey to Iowa City really took shape back in the 1980s when we had an intense rivalry with Iowa while I was coaching for George Perles at Michigan State. It seemed like almost every game with Iowa would come down to the wire. One of the more memorable plays in the series was the famous Chuck Long bootleg play in 1985. Of course, back in the 1980s, Kirk

Ferentz served on Hayden Fry's staff as offensive line coach. So I think that a mutual professional respect had developed between myself and Kirk as a result of the hotly contested Iowa–Michigan State rivalry. This was especially true because my defenses were going directly up against his offenses, so I think we tended to know each other's tendencies.

My impression of Kirk and the Iowa program in general when I interviewed was that it would be a good situation for me, personally. It was an opportunity to come back to the Big Ten, and even better, it was an opportunity to become involved in a program where I thought they did things the right way. They were honest, and those associated with the program were going to be hard-working. Truly, there wasn't anything shady at all about the outfit.

I will admit that a while back, there was a time when I felt that getting the win was by far the most important and gratifying part of my job. Having now been in college coaching for over 40 years, it has given me a little bit of a different perspective. Now the most gratifying part of my job comes after a win when I get to see the looks on the players' faces—when they know they have worked hard, they have studied, and they played hard. It is so satisfying to see the expressions from the players when they realize that, *Hey, I did all of these things that were asked of me, and guess what? It all led to a victory!* Also just as special to me is the opportunity to see those proud parents outside the locker room after the game. If you could have seen the look on Pat Angerer's father's face after the Orange Bowl in 2010. He had to be the proudest father in the world because his boy had played such a great game.

It is hard for me to believe, but I have been on the coaching staff here for 12 years! I realize that is a long time to be in one place, especially for football coaches these days. Well, in my opinion, I work for the best head football coach in the country. These are the best working conditions in the country. On a day-to-day basis, it couldn't be any better. Why would I go someplace else? I have no reason whatsoever to consider taking a chance to see what things are like in some other situation.

One of the things that is a little different about our program is the fact that families generally are welcome here within the complex. It isn't uncommon at all for wives, kids, maybe even grandkids, to make appearances here in the office. Heck, some days, it can be like a nursery school around here! I can tell you that isn't something that goes on in all programs. But I think this is healthy. It also helps put some coaches at ease and allows them to do their jobs to the absolute best of their abilities.

Having coached at Illinois, East Carolina, and Michigan State, Norm Parker joined the Hawkeyes' staff as defensive coordinator in 1999. *Photo courtesy of Bob Rasmus*

Something else that makes our situation so special to me is the fact that the coaching staff is so comfortable with their positions and their jobs with Kirk. Everybody is on the same page. I think the kids sense that mutual trust between the head coach and the assistant coaching staff. It's not like a kid raised in a household where the parents are fighting with each other all the time. I think the kids in our program know that everybody gets along. As a result, the kids are completely comfortable coming over to the office talk to with any one of us about anything, because it is a good situation for everybody.

It seems that over the years, Iowa has developed a bit of a reputation for developing great players who might not necessarily come into the program as the hyped four- or five-star recruits. While all of the above things certainly are a tremendous benefit to our program, some of our success is because we don't get kids coming here for the wrong reasons. By that, I mean a kid doesn't come to Iowa because we have a nice beach or good snow skiing. A kid comes to Iowa to play football and get a good education. Everybody knows we are not the sexiest place in the world. But, while we don't necessarily have the picturesque oceans or mountains, what we do have is each other. So I like to think that what we don't have works to our advantage.

In general, I like to think that my defensive philosophy melds pretty well with the types of players we have. In my opinion, mixing apples and oranges on defense just doesn't work well. You really can't have a little bit of this and a little bit of that. It doesn't work out. I think you need to establish your brand of football, however you are going to do it, and you need to stick to it. I think the key to our defensive system is the players knowing what they are doing. When you get out there on the field at Kinnick Stadium and there are 72,000 people screaming and hollering, you better know what you are doing. There is no tricking the other guy. Our program is not about magic tricks. Our program is about hard work and trying to be fundamentally sound and outplaying our opponents.

When you look back at the last 10 to 12 years, it is gratifying to see that we have had so many guys come through here and make it to the NFL. I can think of a few things that are ingrained in our culture that have helped to get our players to the next level. First, when you come here to play football at Iowa, you are going to have to work. I mean, you are going to need to develop really solid work habits to play here. Our players are going to have to study film. They are going to need to really like football. If a player doesn't do all those things, he won't survive here.

Basically, my whole experience at Iowa has been one of the best personal and professional experiences I have ever had. Having the chance to represent good, hardworking people and doing it with a team of good kids in a clean and honest program has been incredibly rewarding. To me, this is what being a Hawkeye is all about.

Norm Parker earned his BS degree in special education in 1965 and his MA in physical education in 1967 from Eastern Michigan, where he lettered four times in football and was a member of the wrestling team for two seasons. He served as an assistant coach at Eastern Michigan and Wake Forest before joining the Minnesota staff as defensive line coach in 1972. Parker coached at Illinois and East Carolina before becoming outside linebackers coach at Michigan State in 1983. He added the duties of defensive coordinator in 1990. Beginning in 1995, Parker then spent four seasons at Vanderbilt as linebackers coach and defensive coordinator. He joined Iowa's staff in 1999 as defensive coordinator and linebackers coach.

WIN "ERV" PRASSE · HENRY "HANK" VOLLENWEIDER · GEORGE

LGENBERG · WARREN "BUD" LAWSON · JERRY REICHOW · FR

NGSTON · RAY JAUCH · CHARLIE LEE · AL MILLER · MARK MANI

ON MESKIMEN · BILL WINDAUER · DAN DICKEL · JIM JENSEN ·

RLY · CHUCK HARTLIEB · BRAD QUAST · DANAN HUGHES · MA

OODS · ANTHONY HERRON · NATE KAEDING · SEAN CONSID

RENTZ · ED HINKEL · DREW TATE · MITCH KING · MATT KROU

NE · JOHN STREIF · BILL BRASHIER · CHRIS DOYLE · NORM PA

D" FRYE · TONY GUZOWSKI · JOHN TEDORE · JACK DITTMER · J

LLIAM · KEN PLOEN · JIM GIBBONS · RANDY DUNCAN · JEFF L

L RINGER · WILBURN HOLLIS · MIKE REILLY · SILAS MCKINNIE

ZAR · CHUCK LONG · MIKE HAIGHT · LARRY STATION · QUIN

ERMAN · JARED DEVRIES · MATT HUGHES · MATT BOWEN · LEV

RAD BANKS · WARREN HOLLOWAY · CHAD GREENWAY · BRIAN

DS · BRYAN BULAGA · RICKY STANZI · JERRY BURNS · GEORGE

WIN "ERV" PRASSE · HENRY "HANK" VOLLENWEIDER · GEORGE "

LGENBERG · WARREN "BUD" LAWSON · JERRY REICHOW · FRA

NGSTON · RAY JAUCH · CHARLIE LEE · AL MILLER · MARK MAND

ON MESKIMEN · BILL WINDAUER · DAN DICKEL · JIM JENSEN · J